HMH

math expressions
Common Core

Dr. Karen C. Fuson

Watch the moose come alive in its snowy environment as you discover and solve math challenges.

Download the *Math Worlds AR* app available on Android or iOS devices.

Grade 3
Volume 1

This material is based upon work supported by the
National Science Foundation
under Grant Numbers
ESI-9816320, REC-9806020, and RED-935373.

Any opinions, findings, and conclusions, or recommendations expressed in this material
are those of the author and do not necessarily reflect the views of the National Science Foundation.

ISBN   978-0-544-91975-4

7 8 9 10 11 12   0029   25 24 23 22 21 20

4500797270   C D E F G

BIG IDEA 4 - Multiply with 1 and 0

BIG IDEA 1 - The Remaining Multiplications

BIG IDEA 2 - Problem Solving and Multiples of 10

Unit 3 · Multidigit Addition and Subtraction (continued)

Student Resources

Dear Family:

In this unit and the next, your child will be practicing basic multiplications and divisions. *Math Expressions* uses studying, practicing, and testing of the basic multiplications and divisions in class. Your child also should practice at home.

Homework Helper Your child will have math homework almost every day. He or she needs a Homework Helper. The helper may be anyone — you, an older brother or sister (or other family member), a neighbor, or a friend. Please decide who the main Homework Helper will be and ask your child to tell the teacher tomorrow. Make a specific time for homework and give your child a quiet place to work.

Study Plans Each day your child will fill out a study plan, indicating which basic multiplications and divisions he or she will study that evening. When your child has finished studying (practicing), his or her Homework Helper should sign the study plan.

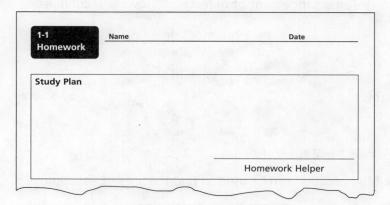

Practice Charts Each time a new number is introduced, students' homework will include a practice chart. To practice, students can cover the products with a finger or pencil. They will say the multiplications, sliding the finger or pencil down the column to see each product after saying it. Students can also start with the last problem in a column and slide up. It is important that your child studies count-bys and multiplications at least 5 minutes every night. Your child should study each division on the Mixed Up column by covering the first factor.

Keep all materials in a special place.

	In Order	Mixed Up
	$1 \times 5 = 5$	$9 \times 5 = 45$
	$2 \times 5 = 10$	$5 \times 5 = 25$
	$3 \times 5 = 15$	$2 \times 5 = 10$
	$4 \times 5 = 20$	$7 \times 5 = 35$
5s	$5 \times 5 = 25$	$4 \times 5 = 20$
	$6 \times 5 = 30$	$6 \times 5 = 30$
	$7 \times 5 = 35$	$10 \times 5 = 50$
	$8 \times 5 = 40$	$8 \times 5 = 40$
	$9 \times 5 = 45$	$1 \times 5 = 5$
	$10 \times 5 = 50$	$3 \times 5 = 15$

To help students understand the concept of multiplication, the *Math Expressions* program presents three ways to think about multiplication.

- **Repeated groups**: Multiplication can be used to find the total in repeated groups of the same size. In early lessons, students circle the group size in repeated-groups equations to help keep track of which factor is the group size and which is the number of groups.

4 groups of bananas

$$4 \times \bigcirc{3} = 3 + 3 + 3 + 3 = 12$$

- **Arrays**: Multiplication can be used to find the total number of items in an *array*—an arrangement of objects into rows and columns.

5 columns

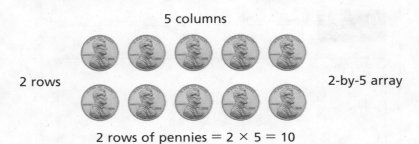

2 rows   2-by-5 array

2 rows of pennies = 2 × 5 = 10

- **Area**: Multiplication can be used to find the area of a rectangle

3 units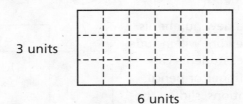

6 units

Area: 3 units × 6 units = 18 square units

Please contact me if you have any questions or comments.

Thank you.

Sincerely,
Your child's teacher

CC SS **Unit 1 addresses the following standards from the** Common Core State Standards for Mathematics: **3.OA.A.1**, **3.OA.A.2**, **3.OA.A.3**, **3.OA.A.4**, **3.OA.B.5**, **3.OA.B.6**, **3.OA.C.7**, **3.OA.D.9**, **3.MD.B.3**, **3.MD.C.5**, **3.MD.C.5.a**, **3.MD.C.5.b**, **3.MD.C.7**, **3.MD.C.7.a**, **3.MD.C.7.b**, **3.MD.C.7.c**, **3.MD.C.7.d** and all Mathematical Practices.

Estimada familia:

En esta unidad y en la que sigue, su niño practicará multiplicaciones y divisiones básicas. *Math Expressions* usa en la clase el estudio, la práctica y la evaluación de las multiplicaciones y divisiones básicas. También su niño debe practicar en casa.

Ayudante de tareas Su niño tendrá tarea de matemáticas casi a diario y necesitará un ayudante para hacer sus tareas. Ese ayudante puede ser cualquier persona: usted, un hermano o hermana mayor, otro familiar, un vecino o un amigo. Por favor decida quién será esta persona y pida a su niño que se lo diga a su maestro mañana. Designe un tiempo específico para la tarea y un lugar para trabajar sin distracciones.

Planes de estudio Todos los días su niño va a completar un plan de estudio, que indica cuáles multiplicaciones y divisiones debe estudiar esa noche. Cuando su niño haya terminado de estudiar (practicar), la persona que lo ayude debe firmar el plan de estudio.

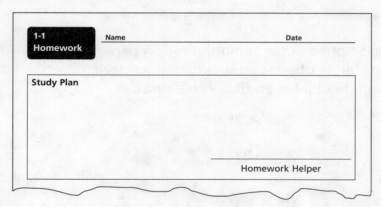

Tablas de práctica Cada vez que se presente un número nuevo, la tarea de los estudiantes incluirá una tabla de práctica. Para practicar, los estudiantes pueden cubrir los productos con un dedo o lápiz. Los niños dicen la multiplicación y deslizan el dedo o lápiz hacia abajo para revelar el producto después de decirlo. También pueden empezar con el último problema de la columna y deslizar el lápiz o el papel hacia arriba. Es importante que su niño practique el conteo y la multiplicación por lo menos 5 minutos cada noche. Su niño debe estudiar cada división en la columna de Desordenados cubriendo el primer factor.

Guarde todos los materiales.

	In Order	Mixed Up
	$1 \times 5 = 5$	$9 \times 5 = 45$
	$2 \times 5 = 10$	$5 \times 5 = 25$
	$3 \times 5 = 15$	$2 \times 5 = 10$
	$4 \times 5 = 20$	$7 \times 5 = 35$
5s	$5 \times 5 = 25$	$4 \times 5 = 20$
	$6 \times 5 = 30$	$6 \times 5 = 30$
	$7 \times 5 = 35$	$10 \times 5 = 50$
	$8 \times 5 = 40$	$8 \times 5 = 40$
	$9 \times 5 = 45$	$1 \times 5 = 5$
	$10 \times 5 = 50$	$3 \times 5 = 15$

Para ayudar a los estudiantes a comprender el concepto de la multiplicación, el programa *Math Expressions* presenta tres maneras de pensar en la multiplicación. Éstas se describen a continuación.

- **Grupos repetidos**: La multiplicación se puede usar para hallar el total con grupos del mismo tamaño que se repiten. Cuando empiezan a trabajar con ecuaciones de grupos repetidos, los estudiantes rodean con un círculo el tamaño del grupo en las ecuaciones, para recordar cuál factor representa el tamaño del grupo y cuál representa el número de grupos.

4 grupos de bananas

$$4 \times ③ = 3 + 3 + 3 + 3 = 12$$

- **Matrices**: Se puede usar la multiplicación para hallar el número total de objetos en una *matriz*, es decir, una disposición de objetos en filas y columnas.

5 columnas

2 filas   matriz de 2 por 5

2 filas de monedas de un centavo = 2 × 5 = 10

- **Área**: Se puede usar la multiplicación para hallar el área de un rectángulo.

3 unidades
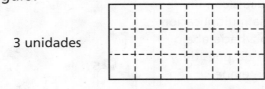

6 unidades

Área: 3 unidades × 6 unidades = 18 unidades cuadradas

Si tiene alguna duda o algún comentario, por favor comuníquese conmigo. Gracias.

Atentamente,
El maestro de su niño

© Houghton Mifflin Harcourt Publishing Company • Image Credits: ©dolphfyn/Getty Images

CC SS **En la Unidad 1 se aplican los siguientes estándares de los** Estándares estatales comunes de matemáticas: .OA.A.1, 3.OA.A.2, 3.OA.A.3, 3.OA.A.4, 3.OA.B.5, 3.OA.B.6, 3.OA.C.7, 3.OA.D.9, 3.MD.B.3, 3.MD.C.5, 3.MD.C.5.a, 3.MD.C.5.b, 3.MD.C.7, 3.MD.C.7.a, 3.MD.C.7.b, 3.MD.C.7.c, 3.MD.C.7.d, **y todos los de** Prácticas matemáticas.

area

Associative Property of Multiplication

array

column

Associative Property of Addition

Commutative Property of Addition

The property which states that changing the way in which factors are grouped does not change the product.

Example:
$(2 \times 3) \times 4 = 2 \times (3 \times 4)$
$6 \times 4 = 2 \times 12$
$24 = 24$

The total number of square units that cover a figure.

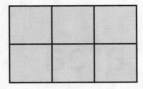

Example:
The area of the rectangle is 6 square units.

A part of a table or array that contains items arranged vertically.

An arrangement of objects, pictures, or numbers in columns and rows.

The property that states that changing the order of addends does not change the sum.

Example:
$3 + 7 = 7 + 3$
$10 = 10$

The property that states that changing the way in which addends are grouped does not change the sum.

Example:
$(2 + 3) + 1 = 2 + (3 + 1)$
$5 + 1 = 2 + 4$
$6 = 6$

Commutative Property of Multiplication

division

Distributive Property

divisor

dividend

equal groups

The mathematical operation that separates an amount into smaller equal groups to find the number of groups or the number in each group.

Example:
$12 \div 3 = 4$ is a division number sentence.

The property which states that changing the order of factors does not change the product.

Example:
$5 \times 4 = 4 \times 5$
$20 = 20$

The number that you divide by in division.

Example:
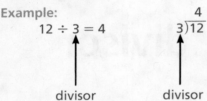

You can multiply a sum by a number, or multiply each addend by the number and add the products; the result is the same.

Example:
$3 \times (2 + 4) = (3 \times 2) + (3 \times 4)$
$3 \times 6 \quad = \quad 6 \quad + \quad 12$
$18 \quad = \quad 18$

Two or more groups with the same number of items in each group.

The number that is divided in division.

Examples:
$12 \div 3 = 4 \qquad 3\overline{)12}^{\,4}$

dividend   dividend

equation	function table
even number	Identity Property of Addition
factor	Identity Property of Multiplication

A table of ordered pairs that shows a function.

For every input number, there is only one possible output number.

Rule: add 2	
Input	Output
1	3
2	4
3	5
4	6

A mathematical sentence with an equals sign.

Examples:
$11 + 22 = 33$
$75 - 25 = 50$

If 0 is added to a number, the sum equals that number.

Example:
$3 + 0 = 3$

A whole number that is a multiple of 2. The ones digit in an even number is 0, 2, 4, 6, or 8.

The product of 1 and any number equals that number.

Example:
$10 \times 1 = 10$

Any of the numbers that are multiplied to give a product.

Example:

$4 \times 5 = 20$

factor   factor   product

(>) is greater than

odd number

(<) is less than

pictograph

multiplication

product

A whole number that is not a multiple of 2. The ones digit in an odd number is 1, 3, 5, 7, or 9.

A symbol used to compare two numbers.

Example:
6 > 5

6 *is greater than* 5.

A graph that uses pictures or symbols to represent data.

Favorite Ice Cream Flavors	
Peanut Butter Crunch	🍦🍦
Cherry Vanilla	🍦🍦🍦
Chocolate	🍦🍦🍦🍦🍦

Each 🍦 stands for 4 votes.

A symbol used to compare two numbers.

Example:
5 < 6

5 *is less than* 6.

The answer when you multiply numbers.

Example:
4 × 7 = 28

factor   factor   product

A mathematical operation that combines equal groups.

Example:

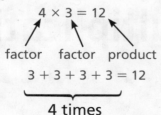

4 × 3 = 12

factor   factor   product

3 + 3 + 3 + 3 = 12

4 times

(>) is greater than

odd number

(<) is less than

pictograph

multiplication

product

A whole number that is not a multiple of 2. The ones digit in an odd number is 1, 3, 5, 7, or 9.

A symbol used to compare two numbers.

Example:

6 > 5

6 *is greater than* 5.

A graph that uses pictures or symbols to represent data.

Favorite Ice Cream Flavors	
Peanut Butter Crunch	🍦 🍦
Cherry Vanilla	🍦 🍦 🍦
Chocolate	🍦 🍦 🍦 🍦 🍦
	Each 🍦 stands for 4 votes.

A symbol used to compare two numbers.

Example:

5 < 6

5 *is less than* 6.

The answer when you multiply numbers.

Example:

4 × 7 = 28

factor   factor   product

A mathematical operation that combines equal groups.

Example:

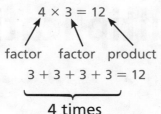

3 + 3 + 3 + 3 = 12

4 times

quotient

variable

row

Zero Property
of
Multiplication

square unit

A letter or symbol used to represent an unknown number in an algebraic expression or equation.

Example:
$2 + n$

n is a variable.

The answer when you divide numbers.

Examples:
$35 \div 7 = 5$ $7\overline{)35}$ ← quotient

quotient

If 0 is multiplied by a number, the product is 0.

Example:
$3 \times 0 = 0$

A part of a table or array that contains items arranged horizontally.

A unit of area equal to the area of a square with one-unit sides.

Name _____

PATH to FLUENCY Explore Patterns with 5s

What patterns do you see below?

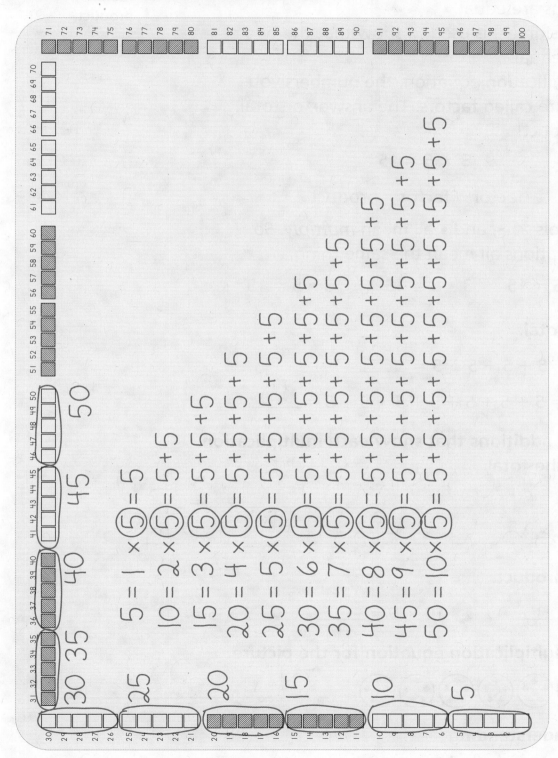

PATH to FLUENCY **Practice Multiplications with 5**

VOCABULARY
equation
multiplication
factor
product

An **equation** shows that two quantities or expressions are equal.

An equal sign (=) is used to show that the two sides are equal.

In a **multiplication** equation, the numbers you multiply are called **factors**. The answer, or total, is the **product**.

$$3 \times 5 = 15$$

factor   factor   product

The symbols ×, *, and • all mean *multiply.* So these equations all mean the same thing.

$$3 \times 5 = 15 \qquad 3 * 5 = 15 \qquad 3 \cdot 5 = 15$$

Write each total.

1. $4 \times \text{⑤} = 5 + 5 + 5 + 5 = \underline{20}$

2. $7 \cdot \text{⑤} = 5 + 5 + 5 + 5 + 5 + 5 + 5 = \underline{35}$

Write the 5s additions that show each multiplication. Then write the total.

3. $6 \times \text{⑤} = \underline{5 + 5 + 5 + 5 + 5 + 5} = \underline{30}$

4. $9 * \text{⑤} = \underline{5 + 5 + 5 + 5 + 5 + 5 + 5 + 5 + 5}$

Write each product.

5. $8 \times 5 = \underline{40}$

6. $10 \times 5 = \underline{50}$

7. $5 \times 5 = \underline{25}$

Write a 5s multiplication equation for the picture.

8.

$7 \times 5 = 35$

✓ **Check Understanding**

Describe ways to find 8 × 5.

© Houghton Mifflin Harcourt Publishing Company

Name _____

Explore Equal Shares Drawings

Here is a problem with repeated groups. Read the problem, and think about how you would solve it.

Ms. Thomas bought 4 bags of oranges. Each bag contained 5 oranges. How many oranges did she buy in all?

You could also find the answer to this problem by making an equal shares drawing.

Think:

Equal Shares Drawing

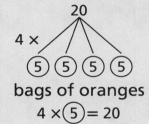

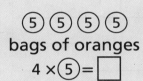

bags of oranges

4 × ⑤ = ☐

bags of oranges

4 × ⑤ = 20

Make an equal shares drawing to solve each problem.

Show your work.

9 Ms. González bought 6 boxes of pencils. There were 5 pencils in each box. How many pencils did she buy in all?

_____

10 Mr. Franken made lunch for his 9 nieces and nephews. He put 5 carrot sticks on each of their plates. How many carrot sticks did he use in all?

_____

Multiplication as Equal Groups **9**

PATH to FLUENCY **Practice with Equal Groups**

Complete each function table.

11

Number of Tricycles	Number of Wheels
1	
2	
3	
4	
5	

12

Number of Rabbits	Number of Ears
1	
2	
3	
4	
5	

13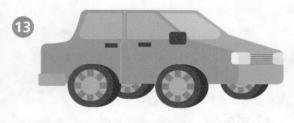

Number of Cars	Number of Wheels
1	
2	
3	
4	
5	

14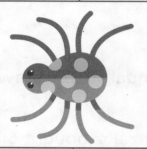

Number of Spiders	Number of Legs
1	
2	
3	
4	
5	

✓ **Check Understanding**

Draw an equal shares drawing to find the number of markers in 8 packages of markers with 5 markers in each package.

Multiplication as Equal Groups

Dear Family:

Over the next few weeks your child will bring home a Practice Chart for each new number to practice multiplications and divisions. Other practice materials will also come home:

- **Home Study Sheets:** A Home Study Sheet includes 3 or 4 practice charts on one page. Your child can use the Home Study Sheets to practice all the count-bys, multiplications, and divisions for a number or to practice just the ones he or she doesn't know for that number. The Homework Helper uses the sheet to test (or retest) your child by giving problems. The Homework Helper should check with your child to see which basic multiplications or divisions he or she is ready to be tested on. The helper should mark any missed problems lightly with a pencil.

If your child gets all the answers in a column correct, the helper should sign that column on the Home Signature Sheet. When signatures are on all the columns of the Home Signature Sheet, your child should bring the sheet to school.

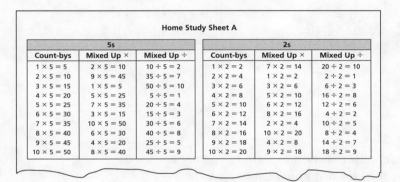

Home Study Sheet A

5s			2s		
Count-bys	**Mixed Up ×**	**Mixed Up ÷**	**Count-bys**	**Mixed Up ×**	**Mixed Up ÷**
1 × 5 = 5	2 × 5 = 10	10 ÷ 5 = 2	1 × 2 = 2	7 × 2 = 14	20 ÷ 2 = 10
2 × 5 = 10	9 × 5 = 45	35 ÷ 5 = 7	2 × 2 = 4	1 × 2 = 2	2 ÷ 2 = 1
3 × 5 = 15	1 × 5 = 5	50 ÷ 5 = 10	3 × 2 = 6	3 × 2 = 6	6 ÷ 2 = 3
4 × 5 = 20	5 × 5 = 25	5 ÷ 5 = 1	4 × 2 = 8	5 × 2 = 10	16 ÷ 2 = 8
5 × 5 = 25	7 × 5 = 35	20 ÷ 5 = 4	5 × 2 = 10	6 × 2 = 12	12 ÷ 2 = 6
6 × 5 = 30	3 × 5 = 15	15 ÷ 5 = 3	6 × 2 = 12	8 × 2 = 16	4 ÷ 2 = 2
7 × 5 = 35	10 × 5 = 50	30 ÷ 5 = 6	7 × 2 = 14	2 × 2 = 4	10 ÷ 2 = 5
8 × 5 = 40	6 × 5 = 30	40 ÷ 5 = 8	8 × 2 = 16	10 × 2 = 20	8 ÷ 2 = 4
9 × 5 = 45	4 × 5 = 20	25 ÷ 5 = 5	9 × 2 = 18	4 × 2 = 8	14 ÷ 2 = 7
10 × 5 = 50	8 × 5 = 40	45 ÷ 5 = 9	10 × 2 = 20	9 × 2 = 18	18 ÷ 2 = 9

Children practice by covering the answers with their finger or a pencil and sliding down their finger or pencil to check each answer as soon as they say it.

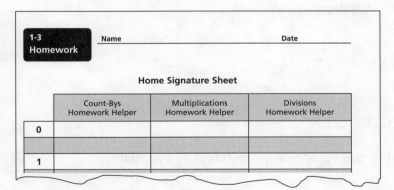

| 1-3 Homework | Name _____ | | Date _____ |

Home Signature Sheet

	Count-Bys Homework Helper	Multiplications Homework Helper	Divisions Homework Helper
0			
1			

Put all practice materials in the folder your child brought home today.

- **Home Check Sheets:** A Home Check Sheet includes columns of 20 multiplications and divisions in mixed order. These sheets can be used to test your child's fluency with basic multiplications and divisions.

- **Strategy Cards:** Your child should use the Strategy Cards to practice multiplication and division by trying to answer the problem on the front. That card is put into one of three piles: *Know Quickly, Know Slowly,* and *Do Not Know.* The *Know Slowly* and *Do Not Know* cards are practiced until they are known quickly.

Sample Multiplication Card   **Sample Division Card**

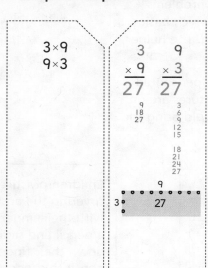   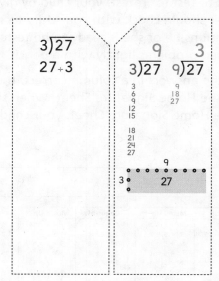

Ask your child to show you these materials and explain how they are used. Your child should practice what they do not know every day.

Please contact me if you have any questions or comments.

Thank you.

Sincerely,
Your child's teacher

Keep all materials in the Home Practice Folder. Keep the folder in a special place.

© Houghton Mifflin Harcourt Publishing Company

Unit 1 addresses the following standards from the Common Core State Standards for Mathematics: **3.OA.A.1, 3.OA.A.2, 3.OA.A.3, 3.OA.A.4, 3.OA.B.5, 3.OA.B.6, 3.OA.C.7, 3.OA.D.9, 3.MD.B.3, 3.MD.C.5, 3.MD.C.5.a, 3.MD.C.5.b, 3.MD.C.7, 3.MD.C.7.a, 3.MD.C.7.b, 3.MD.C.7.c, 3.MD.C.7.d, and all** Mathematical Practices.

Estimada familia:

Durante las próximas semanas su niño llevará a casa una tabla de práctica para cada número nuevo para practicar multiplicaciones y divisiones. Otros materiales de práctica también se llevará a casa:

- **Hojas para estudiar en casa:** Una hoja para estudiar en casa incluye 3 ó 4 tablas de práctica en una página. Su niño puede usar las hojas para practicar todos los conteos, multiplicaciones y divisiones de un número, o para practicar sólo las operaciones para ese número que no domine. El ayudante de tareas usa la hoja para hacerle una prueba (o repetir una prueba) con problemas. Esa persona debe hablar con su niño para decidir sobre qué multiplicaciones o divisiones básicas el niño puede hacer la prueba. La persona que ayude debe marcar ligeramente con un lápiz cualquier problema que conteste mal. Si su niño contesta bien todas las operaciones de una columna, la persona que ayude debe firmar esa columna de la hoja de firmas. Cuando todas las columnas de la hoja de firmas estén firmadas, su niño debe llevar la hoja a la escuela.

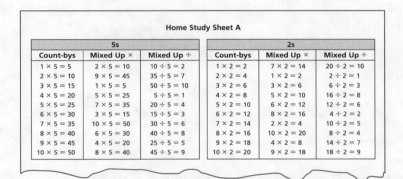

Los niños practican cubriendo las respuestas con su dedo o un lápiz y deslizan su dedo o lápiz hacia abajo para revelar cada respuesta después de decirlo.

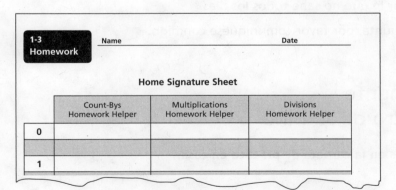

Guarde todos los materiales de práctica en la carpeta que su hijo trajo a casa hoy.

© Houghton Mifflin Harcourt Publishing Company

- **Hojas de verificación:** Una hoja de verificación consta de columnas de 20 multiplicaciones y divisiones sin orden fijo. Estas hojas se pueden usar para comprobar el dominio de su niño con las multiplicaciones y divisiones básicas.

- **Tarjetas de estrategias:** Su niño debe usar las Tarjetas de estrategias para practicar la multiplicación y división al responder el problema del frente. Esa tarjeta se pone en una de las tres pilas: *Contesta Rápidamente, Se Demora En Contestar y No Sabe*. Las tarjetas de *Se Demora En Contestar* y *No Sabe* se practican hasta que las contesten rápidamente.

Ejemplo de tarjeta de multiplicación   **Ejemplo de tarjeta de división**

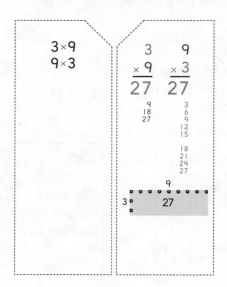
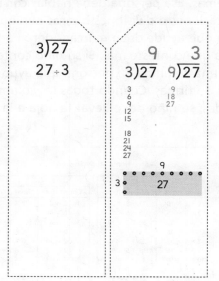

Pida a su niño a que le muestre estos materiales y a que le explique cómo se usan. Su niño debe practicar lo que no sabe todos los días.

Si tiene alguna duda o pregunta, por favor comuníquese conmigo.

Atentamente,
El maestro de su niño

Guarde todos los materiales en la carpeta de práctica en casa.

CCSS En la Unidad 1 se aplican los siguientes estándares de los Estándares estatales comunes de matemáticas: 3.OA.A.1, 3.OA.A.2, 3.OA.A.3, 3.OA.A.4, 3.OA.B.5, 3.OA.B.6, 3.OA.C.7, 3.OA.D.9, 3.MD.B.3, 3.MD.C.5, 3.MD.C.5A, 3.MD.C.5.B, 3.MD.C.7, 3.MD.C.7.A, 3.MD.C.7.B, 3.MD.C.7.C, 3.MD.C.7.D, y todos los de Prácticas matemáticas.

Name _____

Signature Sheet

	Count-Bys Partner	Multiplications Partner	Divisions Partner	Multiplications Check Sheets	Divisions Check Sheets
5s				1:	1:
2s				1:	1:
10s				2:	2:
9s				2:	2:
				3:	3:
3s				4:	4:
4s				4:	4:
1s				5:	5:
0s				5:	5:
				6:	6:
6s				7:	7:
8s				7:	7:
7s				8:	8:
				9:	9:
				10:	10:

Name _____

Dash Record Sheet

Dash Number	Accurate	Fast	Really Fast
1			
2			
3			
4			
5			
6			
7			
8			
9			
9A			
9B			
9C			
10			
10A			
10B			
10C			
11			
11A			
11B			
11C			
12			
12A			
12B			
12C			

Dash Number	Accurate	Fast	Really Fast
13			
14			
15			
16			
17			
18			
19			
19A			
19B			
19C			
19D			
20			
20A			
20B			
20C			
20D			
21			
21A			
21B			
21C			
22			
22A			
22B			
22C			

Dash Record Sheet

PATH to FLUENCY

Study Sheet A

2s

Count-bys	Mixed Up ×	Mixed Up ÷
1 × 2 = 2	7 × 2 = 14	20 ÷ 2 = 10
2 × 2 = 4	1 × 2 = 2	2 ÷ 2 = 1
3 × 2 = 6	3 × 2 = 6	6 ÷ 2 = 3
4 × 2 = 8	5 × 2 = 10	16 ÷ 2 = 8
5 × 2 = 10	6 × 2 = 12	12 ÷ 2 = 6
6 × 2 = 12	8 × 2 = 16	4 ÷ 2 = 2
7 × 2 = 14	2 × 2 = 4	10 ÷ 2 = 5
8 × 2 = 16	10 × 2 = 20	8 ÷ 2 = 4
9 × 2 = 18	4 × 2 = 8	14 ÷ 2 = 7
10 × 2 = 20	9 × 2 = 18	18 ÷ 2 = 9

9s

Count-bys	Mixed Up ×	Mixed Up ÷
1 × 9 = 9	2 × 9 = 18	81 ÷ 9 = 9
2 × 9 = 18	4 × 9 = 36	18 ÷ 9 = 2
3 × 9 = 27	7 × 9 = 63	36 ÷ 9 = 4
4 × 9 = 36	8 × 9 = 72	9 ÷ 9 = 1
5 × 9 = 45	3 × 9 = 27	54 ÷ 9 = 6
6 × 9 = 54	10 × 9 = 90	27 ÷ 9 = 3
7 × 9 = 63	1 × 9 = 9	63 ÷ 9 = 7
8 × 9 = 72	6 × 9 = 54	72 ÷ 9 = 8
9 × 9 = 81	5 × 9 = 45	90 ÷ 9 = 10
10 × 9 = 90	9 × 9 = 81	45 ÷ 9 = 5

5s

Count-bys	Mixed Up ×	Mixed Up ÷
1 × 5 = 5	2 × 5 = 10	10 ÷ 5 = 2
2 × 5 = 10	9 × 5 = 45	35 ÷ 5 = 7
3 × 5 = 15	1 × 5 = 5	50 ÷ 5 = 10
4 × 5 = 20	5 × 5 = 25	5 ÷ 5 = 1
5 × 5 = 25	7 × 5 = 35	20 ÷ 5 = 4
6 × 5 = 30	3 × 5 = 15	15 ÷ 5 = 3
7 × 5 = 35	10 × 5 = 50	30 ÷ 5 = 6
8 × 5 = 40	6 × 5 = 30	40 ÷ 5 = 8
9 × 5 = 45	4 × 5 = 20	25 ÷ 5 = 5
10 × 5 = 50	8 × 5 = 40	45 ÷ 5 = 9

10s

Count-bys	Mixed Up ×	Mixed Up ÷
1 × 10 = 10	1 × 10 = 10	80 ÷ 10 = 8
2 × 10 = 20	5 × 10 = 50	10 ÷ 10 = 1
3 × 10 = 30	2 × 10 = 20	50 ÷ 10 = 5
4 × 10 = 40	8 × 10 = 80	90 ÷ 10 = 9
5 × 10 = 50	7 × 10 = 70	40 ÷ 10 = 4
6 × 10 = 60	3 × 10 = 30	100 ÷ 10 = 10
7 × 10 = 70	4 × 10 = 40	30 ÷ 10 = 3
8 × 10 = 80	6 × 10 = 60	20 ÷ 10 = 2
9 × 10 = 90	10 × 10 = 100	70 ÷ 10 = 7
10 × 10 = 100	9 × 10 = 90	60 ÷ 10 = 6

Make a Math Drawing to Solve a Problem

Make a drawing for each problem. Label your drawing with a multiplication equation. Then write the answer to the problem.

Show your work.

14 The clarinet section of the band marched in 6 rows, with 2 clarinet players in each row. How many clarinet players were there in all?

_____

15 Mali put some crackers on a tray. She put the crackers in 3 rows, with 5 crackers per row. How many crackers did she put on the tray?

_____

16 Ms. Shahin set up some chairs in 7 rows, with 5 chairs in each row. How many chairs did she set up?

_____

17 Zak has a box of crayons. The crayons are arranged in 4 rows, with 6 crayons in each row. How many crayons are in the box?

_____

Model Commutativity

The **Commutative Property of Multiplication** states that you can switch the order of the factors without changing the product.

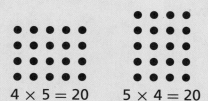

Arrays: $4 \times 5 = 5 \times 4$

$4 \times 5 = 20$ $5 \times 4 = 20$

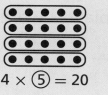

Groups: $4 \times ⑤ = 5 \times ④$

$4 \times ⑤ = 20$ $5 \times ④ = 20$

Solve Problems Using the Commutative Property

Make a math drawing for each problem. Write a multiplication equation and the answer to the problem.

18 Katie put stickers on her folder in 6 rows of 2. How many stickers did she place?

19 Marco put stickers on his folder in 2 rows of 6. How many stickers did he place?

20 Juan packed glass jars in 3 boxes, with 7 jars per box. How many jars did Juan pack?

21 Ty packed glass jars in 7 boxes, with 3 jars per box. How many jars did Ty pack?

✓ Check Understanding

Draw arrays to show why 2×5 equals 5×2.

Multiplication and Arrays

Name _____

Explore Division

Write an equation and solve the problem.

1 Marc bought some bags of limes. There were 5 limes in each bag. He bought 15 limes altogether. How many bags did he buy?

_____

2 There were 10 photographs on a wall. The photographs were in rows, with 5 photographs in each row. How many rows were there?

_____

The problems above can be represented by multiplication equations or by **division** equations.

	Multiplication			**Division**		
Problem 1	☐ number of groups (factor)	× ⑤ group size (factor)	= **15** total (product)	**15** total (product)	÷ ⑤ group size (factor)	= ☐ number of groups (factor)
Problem 2	☐ number of rows (factor)	× **5** number in each row (factor)	= **10** total (product)	**10** total (product)	÷ **5** number in each row (factor)	= ☐ number of rows (factor)

Here are ways to write a division. The following all mean "15 divided by 5 equals 3."

$$15 \div 5 = 3 \qquad 15 / 5 = 3 \qquad \frac{15}{5} = 3$$

$$\begin{array}{r} 3 \\ 5{\overline{)15}} \end{array}$$

3 ← quotient
5)15 ← dividend
↑
divisor

The number you divide into is called the **dividend**. The number you divide by is called the **divisor**. The number that is the answer to a division problem is called the **quotient**.

CC SS Content Standards **3.OA.A.1, 3.OA.A.2, 3.OA.A.3, 3.OA.A.4, 3.OA.B.6, 3.OA.C.7**
Mathematical Practices **MP1, MP3, MP4, MP6, MP7**

The Meaning of Division **23**

Math Tools: Drawings and Equations

You can use equal shares drawings to help solve division problems. Here is how you might solve Problem 1 on page 23.

Start with the total, 15.

$15 \div ⑤ = \square$

Draw groups of 5, and connect them to the total. Count by 5s as you draw the groups. Stop when you reach 15, the total. Count how many groups you have: 3 groups.

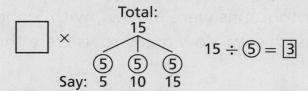

$\square \times$

Total: 15

⑤ ⑤ ⑤
Say: 5   10   15

$15 \div ⑤ = \boxed{3}$

You can use a similar type of drawing to find the number of rows or columns in an array. Here is how you might solve Problem 2 on page 23.

Start with the total, 10.

$10 \div ⑤ = \square$

Draw rows of 5, and connect them to the total. Count by 5s as you draw the rows. Stop when you reach 10, the total. Count how many rows you have: 2 rows.

5 ⟨ 5 ⟩
              Total:
10 ⟨ 5 ⟩   10 $10 \div ⑤ = \boxed{2}$

Write an equation and solve the problem.

3 At a bake sale, Luisa bought a lemon square for 35¢. If she paid using only nickels, how many nickels did she use?

_____

4 Mr. Su bought a sheet of 20 stamps. There were 5 stamps in each row. How many rows of stamps were there?

_____

The Meaning of Division

PATH to FLUENCY **Explore Patterns with 2s**

What patterns do you see below?

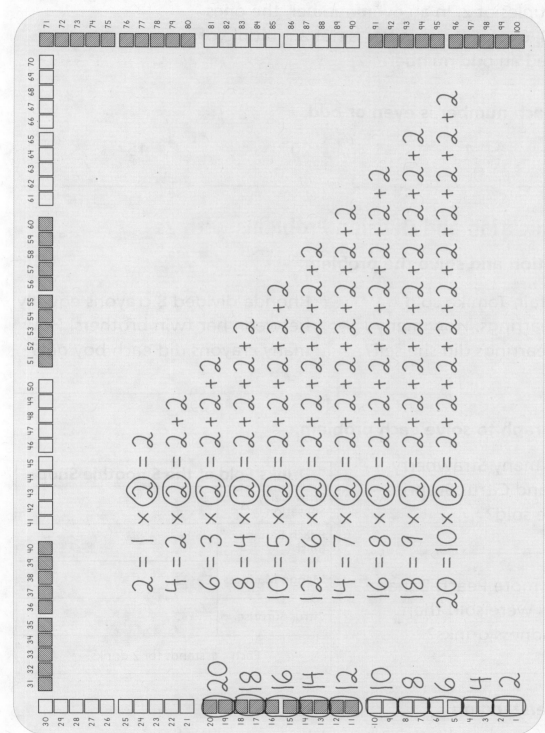

Content Standards **3.OA.A.1, 3.OA.A.2, 3.OA.A.3, 3.OA.A.4, 3.OA.B.6, 3.OA.C.7, 3.OA.D.9** Mathematical Practices **MP1, MP4, MP5, MP7**

Multiply and Divide with 2 **27**

© Houghton Mifflin Harcourt Publishing Company

Even and Odd Numbers

VOCABULARY
even number
odd number
pictograph

The 2s count-bys are called *even numbers* because they are multiples of 2. In an **even number**, the ones digit is 0, 2, 4, 6, or 8. If a number is not a multiple of two, it is called an **odd number**.

Tell whether each number is even or odd.

1 7   **2** 4   **3** 20   **4** 15

_____   _____   _____   _____

Solve Multiplication and Division Problems with 2s

Write an equation and solve the problem.

5 At the art fair, Tamika sold 9 pairs of earrings. How many individual earrings did she sell?

_____

6 Rhonda divided 8 crayons equally between her twin brothers. How many crayons did each boy get?

_____

Use the pictograph to solve each problem.

7 In all, how many Strawberry Sensation and Citrus Surprise drinks were sold?

_____

8 How many more Peach-Banana Blast drinks were sold than Mango Madness drinks?

_____

Drinks Sold at the Smoothie Shop	
Strawberry Sensation	🥤 🥤 🥤
Peach-Banana Blast	🥤 🥤 🥤 🥤 🥤 🥤 🥤
Mango Madness	🥤 🥤
Citrus Surprise	🥤 🥤 🥤 🥤 🥤
Each 🥤 stands for 2 drinks.	

✓ **Check Understanding**

Explain how patterns in the 2s count-bys and multiplications can help you when multiplying.

     Multiply and Divide with 2

Name _____

PATH to FLUENCY Check Sheet 1: 5s and 2s

5s Multiplications	5s Divisions	2s Multiplications	2s Divisions
$2 \times 5 = 10$	$30 / 5 = 6$	$4 \times 2 = 8$	$8 / 2 = 4$
$5 \cdot 6 = 30$	$5 \div 5 = 1$	$2 \cdot 8 = 16$	$18 \div 2 = 9$
$5 * 9 = 45$	$15 / 5 = 3$	$1 * 2 = 2$	$2 / 2 = 1$
$4 \times 5 = 20$	$50 \div 5 = 10$	$6 \times 2 = 12$	$16 \div 2 = 8$
$5 \cdot 7 = 35$	$20 / 5 = 4$	$2 \cdot 9 = 18$	$4 / 2 = 2$
$10 * 5 = 50$	$10 \div 5 = 2$	$2 * 2 = 4$	$20 \div 2 = 10$
$1 \times 5 = 5$	$35 / 5 = 7$	$3 \times 2 = 6$	$10 / 2 = 5$
$5 \cdot 3 = 15$	$40 \div 5 = 8$	$2 \cdot 5 = 10$	$12 \div 2 = 6$
$8 * 5 = 40$	$25 / 5 = 5$	$10 * 2 = 20$	$6 / 2 = 3$
$5 \times 5 = 25$	$45 / 5 = 9$	$2 \times 7 = 14$	$14 / 2 = 7$
$5 \cdot 8 = 40$	$20 \div 5 = 4$	$2 \cdot 10 = 20$	$4 \div 2 = 2$
$7 * 5 = 35$	$15 / 5 = 3$	$9 * 2 = 18$	$2 / 2 = 1$
$5 \times 4 = 20$	$30 \div 5 = 6$	$2 \times 6 = 12$	$8 \div 2 = 4$
$6 \cdot 5 = 30$	$25 / 5 = 5$	$8 \cdot 2 = 16$	$6 / 2 = 3$
$5 * 1 = 5$	$10 \div 5 = 2$	$2 * 3 = 6$	$20 \div 2 = 10$
$5 \times 10 = 50$	$45 / 5 = 9$	$2 \times 2 = 4$	$14 / 2 = 7$
$9 \cdot 5 = 45$	$35 \div 5 = 7$	$1 \cdot 2 = 2$	$10 \div 2 = 5$
$5 * 2 = 10$	$50 \div 5 = 10$	$2 * 4 = 8$	$16 \div 2 = 8$
$3 \times 5 = 15$	$40 / 5 = 8$	$5 \times 2 = 10$	$12 / 2 = 6$
$5 \cdot 5 = 25$	$5 \div 5 = 1$	$7 \cdot 2 = 14$	$18 \div 2 = 9$

Check Sheet 1: 5s and 2s

Write the correct answer.

① $5 \times 3 = $ ☐

② $18 \div 2 = $ ☐

③ Complete the multiplication sentence.

$5 \times 6 = 6 \times$ ☐

④ Andy uses 3 bananas in each of 5 loaves of banana bread he is baking. Write a multiplication expression to represent the total number of bananas Andy uses.

Show your work.

⑤ Solve to find the unknown number in the equation.

$5 \times$ ☐ $= 40$

Make a drawing. Write an equation. Solve.

1 Imaad has 5 bowls. He wants to serve 4 dumplings in each bowl. How many dumplings does he need in all?

_____

2 Marja arranges her toy cars so 7 toy cars are in each row. She makes 3 equal rows of toy cars. How many toy cars does Marja have?

_____

3 Noriko pastes stars on the first page of her book. She arranges the stars in 2 rows with 4 stars in each row. On the second page, she pastes 2 stars in a row. There are 4 rows of stars on the second page. How many stars are on each page?

_____

PATH to FLUENCY Check Sheet 2: 10s and 9s

10s Multiplications	10s Divisions	9s Multiplications	9s Divisions
$9 \times 10 = 90$	$100 / 10 = 10$	$3 \times 9 = 27$	$27 / 9 = 3$
$10 \cdot 3 = 30$	$50 \div 10 = 5$	$9 \cdot 7 = 63$	$9 \div 9 = 1$
$10 * 6 = 60$	$70 / 10 = 7$	$10 * 9 = 90$	$81 / 9 = 9$
$1 \times 10 = 10$	$40 \div 10 = 4$	$5 \times 9 = 45$	$45 \div 9 = 5$
$10 \cdot 4 = 40$	$80 / 10 = 8$	$9 \cdot 8 = 72$	$90 / 9 = 10$
$10 * 7 = 70$	$60 \div 10 = 6$	$9 * 1 = 9$	$36 \div 9 = 4$
$8 \times 10 = 80$	$10 / 10 = 1$	$2 \times 9 = 18$	$18 / 9 = 2$
$10 \cdot 10 = 100$	$20 \div 10 = 2$	$9 \cdot 9 = 81$	$63 \div 9 = 7$
$5 * 10 = 50$	$90 / 10 = 9$	$6 * 9 = 54$	$54 / 9 = 6$
$10 \times 2 = 20$	$30 / 10 = 3$	$9 \times 4 = 36$	$72 / 9 = 8$
$10 \cdot 5 = 50$	$80 \div 10 = 8$	$9 \cdot 5 = 45$	$27 \div 9 = 3$
$4 * 10 = 40$	$70 / 10 = 7$	$4 * 9 = 36$	$45 / 9 = 5$
$10 \times 1 = 10$	$100 \div 10 = 10$	$9 \times 1 = 9$	$63 \div 9 = 7$
$3 \cdot 10 = 30$	$90 / 10 = 9$	$3 \cdot 9 = 27$	$72 / 9 = 8$
$10 * 8 = 80$	$60 \div 10 = 6$	$9 * 8 = 72$	$54 \div 9 = 6$
$7 \times 10 = 70$	$30 / 10 = 3$	$7 \times 9 = 63$	$18 / 9 = 2$
$6 \cdot 10 = 60$	$10 \div 10 = 1$	$6 \cdot 9 = 54$	$90 \div 9 = 10$
$10 * 9 = 90$	$40 \div 10 = 4$	$9 * 9 = 81$	$9 \div 9 = 1$
$10 \times 10 = 100$	$20 / 10 = 2$	$10 \times 9 = 90$	$36 / 9 = 4$
$2 \cdot 10 = 20$	$50 \div 10 = 5$	$2 \cdot 9 = 18$	$81 \div 9 = 9$

Name

Math Tools: Quick 9s Multiplication

You can use the Quick 9s method to help you multiply by 9. Open your hands and turn them so they are facing you. Imagine that your fingers are numbered like this.

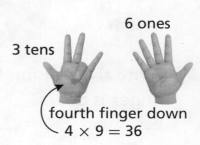

To find a number times 9, bend down the finger for that number. For example, to find 4×9, bend down your fourth finger.

The fingers to the left of your bent finger are the tens. The fingers to the right are the ones. For this problem, there are 3 tens and 6 ones, so $4 \times 9 = 36$.

Why does this work? Because $4 \times 9 = 4 \times (10 - 1) = 40 - 4 = 36$

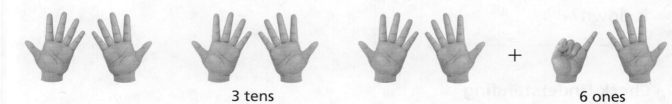

3 tens   +   6 ones

1 Write the multiplication that is shown when the seventh multiplier finger is down.

_____ × _____ = _____

2 Which multiplier finger will be down to show 5 tens and 4 ones?

_____

Math Tools: Quick 9s Division

You can also use Quick 9s to help you divide by 9.
For example, to find 72 ÷ 9, show 72 on your fingers.

7 tens 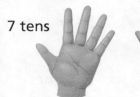 2 ones

Your eighth finger
is down, so 72 ÷ 9 = 8.
8 × 9 = 80 − 8 = 72

3 Write the division that is shown when the fifth multiplier
finger is down.

_____ ÷ _____ = _____

4 Which multiplier finger will be down to show 81 ÷ 9?

_____

5 Which multiplication is shown when the ninth finger
is down?

_____ × _____ = _____

Check Understanding

Use the picture below. Draw an X on the finger that you
would bend down to find 6 × 9.

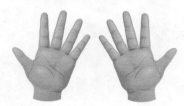

6 × 9 = ☐

Use the picture below. Draw an X on the finger that you
would bend down to find 27 ÷ 9.

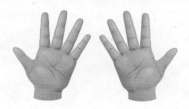

27 ÷ 9 = ☐

Multiply and Divide with 9

PATH to FLUENCY Check Sheet 3: 2s, 5s, 9s, and 10s

2s, 5s, 9s, 10s Multiplications	2s, 5s, 9s, 10s Multiplications	2s, 5s, 9s, 10s Divisions	2s, 5s, 9s, 10s Divisions
2 × 10 = 20	5 × 10 = 50	18 / 2 = 9	36 / 9 = 4
10 • 5 = 50	10 • 9 = 90	50 ÷ 5 = 10	70 ÷ 10 = 7
9 * 6 = 54	4 * 10 = 40	72 / 9 = 8	18 / 2 = 9
7 × 10 = 70	2 × 9 = 18	60 ÷ 10 = 6	45 ÷ 5 = 9
2 • 3 = 6	5 • 3 = 15	12 / 2 = 6	45 / 9 = 5
5 * 7 = 35	6 * 9 = 54	30 ÷ 5 = 6	30 ÷ 10 = 3
9 × 10 = 90	10 × 3 = 30	18 / 9 = 2	6 / 2 = 3
6 • 10 = 60	3 • 2 = 6	50 ÷ 10 = 5	50 ÷ 5 = 10
8 * 2 = 16	5 * 8 = 40	14 / 2 = 7	27 / 9 = 3
5 × 6 = 30	9 × 9 = 81	25 / 5 = 5	70 / 10 = 7
9 • 5 = 45	10 • 4 = 40	81 ÷ 9 = 9	20 ÷ 2 = 10
8 * 10 = 80	9 * 2 = 18	20 / 10 = 2	45 / 5 = 9
2 × 1 = 2	5 × 1 = 5	8 ÷ 2 = 4	54 ÷ 9 = 6
3 • 5 = 15	9 • 6 = 54	45 / 5 = 9	80 / 10 = 8
4 * 9 = 36	10 * 1 = 10	63 ÷ 9 = 7	16 ÷ 2 = 8
3 × 10 = 30	7 × 2 = 14	30 / 10 = 3	15 / 5 = 3
2 • 6 = 12	6 • 5 = 30	10 ÷ 2 = 5	90 ÷ 9 = 10
4 * 5 = 20	8 * 9 = 72	40 ÷ 5 = 8	100 ÷ 10 = 10
9 × 7 = 63	10 × 6 = 60	9 / 9 = 1	12 / 2 = 6
1 • 10 = 10	2 • 8 = 16	50 ÷ 10 = 5	35 ÷ 5 = 7

Check Sheet 3: 2s, 5s, 9s, and 10s

Make Sense of Problems with 2s, 5s, 9s, and 10s

Write an equation to represent each problem.   *Show your work.*
Then solve the problem.

1. Ian planted tulip bulbs in an array with 5 rows and 10 columns. How many bulbs did he plant?

2. Erin gave 30 basketball cards to her 5 cousins. Each cousin got the same number of cards. How many cards did each cousin get?

3. Martina bought 7 cans of racquetballs. There were 2 balls per can. How many racquetballs did she buy in all?

4. The 27 students in the orchestra stood in rows for their school picture. There were 9 students in every row. How many rows of students were there?

5. Lindsey needs 40 note cards. The note cards are packaged 10 to a box. How many boxes of cards should Lindsey buy?

6. There are 25 student desks in the classroom. The desks are arranged in 5 rows with the same number of desks in each row. How many desks are in each row?

© Houghton Mifflin Harcourt Publishing Company

Content Standards 3.OA.A.1, 3.OA.A.2, 3.OA.A.3, 3.OA.A.4, 3.OA.B.6, 3.OA.C.7
Mathematical Practices MP1, MP3, MP4, MP6

Build Fluency with 2s, 5s, 9s, and 10s **45**

Math Tools: Fast Array Drawings

A fast array drawing shows the number of items in each row and column, but does not show every single item.

Problem 1 on page 45:

Show the number of rows and the number of columns. Make a box in the center to show that you don't know the total.

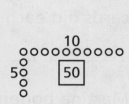

Here are three ways to find the total.

- Find 5×10.

- Use 10s count-bys to find the total in 5 rows of 10: 10, 20, 30, 40, 50.

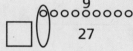

- Use 5s count-bys to find the total in 10 columns of 5: 5, 10, 15, 20, 25, 30, 35, 40, 45, 50.

Problem 4 on page 45:

Show the number in each row and the total. Make a box to show that you don't know the number of rows.

Here are two ways to find the number of rows.

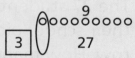

- Find $27 \div 9$ or solve $\square \times 9 = 27$.

- Count by 9s until you reach 27: 9, 18, 27.

Math Journal **Make a fast array drawing to solve each problem.**

7 Beth planted trees in 9 rows and 6 columns. How many trees did she plant?

8 The 36 boys stood in 4 rows for their team picture. How many boys were in each row?

✓ **Check Understanding**

Which problem has an unknown total?
Circle one: Problem 7 Problem 8

Write the correct answer.

1 $10 \cdot \boxed{} = 50$

2 $80 \div 10 = \boxed{}$

3 $2 \times \boxed{} = 16$

4 $4 \times 9 = \boxed{}$

5 $27 \div 9 = \boxed{}$

Complete the pattern below to show 9s multiplication.

1 $1 \times 9 = 10 - 1 = \boxed{}$

2 $2 \times 9 = 20 - 2 = \boxed{}$

3 $3 \times 9 = 30 - 3 = \boxed{}$

4 $4 \times 9 = 40 - \boxed{} = \boxed{}$

5 $5 \times 9 = \boxed{} - \boxed{} = \boxed{}$

6 $6 \times 9 = \boxed{} - \boxed{} = \boxed{}$

7 $7 \times 9 = \boxed{} - \boxed{} = \boxed{}$

8 $8 \times 9 = \boxed{} - \boxed{} = \boxed{}$

9 $9 \times 9 = \boxed{} - \boxed{} = \boxed{}$

10 $9 \times 10 = \boxed{} - \boxed{} = \boxed{}$

Name _____

Explore Patterns with 3s

What patterns do you see below?

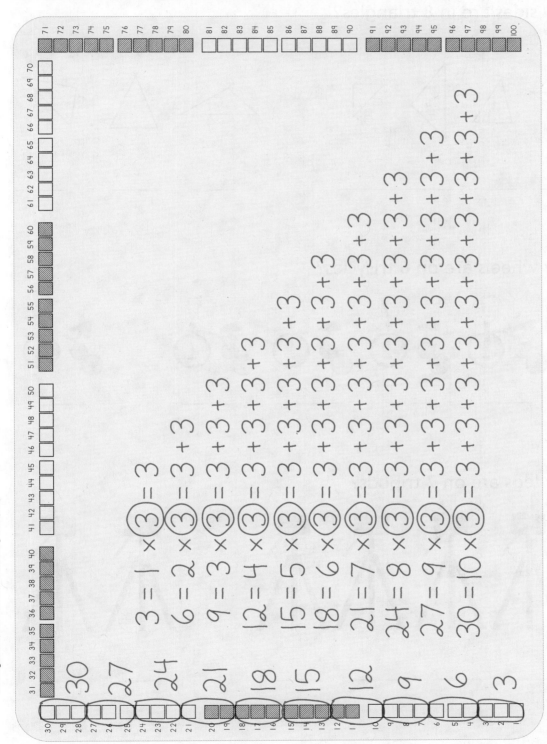

Content Standards 3.OA.A.1, 3.OA.A.2, 3.OA.A.3, 3.OA.A.4, 3.OA.B.6, 3.OA.C.7, 3.OA.D.9
Mathematical Practices MP1, MP2, MP3, MP4, MP5, MP6, MP7, MP8

PATH to FLUENCY Use the 5s Shortcut for 3s

Write the 3s count-bys to find the total.

1 How many sides are in 8 triangles?

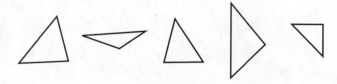
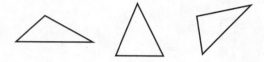

_____ _____ _____ _____ _____   _____ _____ _____

2 How many wheels are on 6 tricycles?

_____ _____ _____ _____ _____   _____

3 How many legs are on 7 tripods?

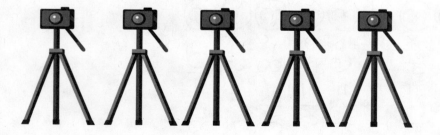

_____ _____ _____ _____ _____   _____ _____

Multiply and Divide with 3

PATH to FLUENCY

Study Sheet B

3s

Count-bys	Mixed Up ×	Mixed Up ÷
1 × 3 = 3	5 × 3 = 15	27 ÷ 3 = 9
2 × 3 = 6	1 × 3 = 3	6 ÷ 3 = 2
3 × 3 = 9	8 × 3 = 24	18 ÷ 3 = 6
4 × 3 = 12	10 × 3 = 30	30 ÷ 3 = 10
5 × 3 = 15	3 × 3 = 9	9 ÷ 3 = 3
6 × 3 = 18	7 × 3 = 21	3 ÷ 3 = 1
7 × 3 = 21	9 × 3 = 27	12 ÷ 3 = 4
8 × 3 = 24	2 × 3 = 6	24 ÷ 3 = 8
9 × 3 = 27	4 × 3 = 12	15 ÷ 3 = 5
10 × 3 = 30	6 × 3 = 18	21 ÷ 3 = 7

4s

Count-bys	Mixed Up ×	Mixed Up ÷
1 × 4 = 4	4 × 4 = 16	12 ÷ 4 = 3
2 × 4 = 8	1 × 4 = 4	36 ÷ 4 = 9
3 × 4 = 12	7 × 4 = 28	24 ÷ 4 = 6
4 × 4 = 16	3 × 4 = 12	4 ÷ 4 = 1
5 × 4 = 20	9 × 4 = 36	20 ÷ 4 = 5
6 × 4 = 24	10 × 4 = 40	28 ÷ 4 = 7
7 × 4 = 28	2 × 4 = 8	8 ÷ 4 = 2
8 × 4 = 32	5 × 4 = 20	40 ÷ 4 = 10
9 × 4 = 36	8 × 4 = 32	32 ÷ 4 = 8
10 × 4 = 40	6 × 4 = 24	16 ÷ 4 = 4

1s

Count-bys	Mixed Up ×	Mixed Up ÷
1 × 1 = 1	5 × 1 = 5	10 ÷ 1 = 10
2 × 1 = 2	7 × 1 = 7	8 ÷ 1 = 8
3 × 1 = 3	10 × 1 = 10	4 ÷ 1 = 4
4 × 1 = 4	1 × 1 = 1	9 ÷ 1 = 9
5 × 1 = 5	8 × 1 = 8	6 ÷ 1 = 6
6 × 1 = 6	4 × 1 = 4	7 ÷ 1 = 7
7 × 1 = 7	9 × 1 = 9	1 ÷ 1 = 1
8 × 1 = 8	3 × 1 = 3	2 ÷ 1 = 2
9 × 1 = 9	2 × 1 = 2	5 ÷ 1 = 5
10 × 1 = 10	6 × 1 = 6	3 ÷ 1 = 3

0s

Count-bys	Mixed Up ×
1 × 0 = 0	3 × 0 = 0
2 × 0 = 0	10 × 0 = 0
3 × 0 = 0	5 × 0 = 0
4 × 0 = 0	8 × 0 = 0
5 × 0 = 0	7 × 0 = 0
6 × 0 = 0	2 × 0 = 0
7 × 0 = 0	9 × 0 = 0
8 × 0 = 0	6 × 0 = 0
9 × 0 = 0	1 × 0 = 0
10 × 0 = 0	4 × 0 = 0

Study Sheet B

2×2

$\begin{array}{r} 2 \\ \times 3 \\ \hline \end{array}$ $\begin{array}{r} 3 \\ \times 2 \\ \hline \end{array}$

2×4
4×2

$\begin{array}{r} 2 \\ \times 5 \\ \hline \end{array}$ $\begin{array}{r} 5 \\ \times 2 \\ \hline \end{array}$

2×6
6×2

$\begin{array}{r} 2 \\ \times 7 \\ \hline \end{array}$ $\begin{array}{r} 7 \\ \times 2 \\ \hline \end{array}$

2×8
8×2

$\begin{array}{r} 2 \\ \times 9 \\ \hline \end{array}$ $\begin{array}{r} 9 \\ \times 2 \\ \hline \end{array}$

Card 1:
$10 = 2 \times 5$
$10 = 5 \times 2$

5	2
10	4
	6
	8
	10

5
2 [·····] 10

Card 2:
$\times \dfrac{\begin{array}{r}2 \\ 4\end{array}}{8}$ $\times \dfrac{\begin{array}{r}4 \\ 2\end{array}}{8}$

2	4
4	8
6	
8	

2
4 [··] 8

Card 3:
$6 = 2 \times 3$
$6 = 3 \times 2$

3	2
6	4
	6

3
2 [···] 6

Card 4:
$\times \dfrac{\begin{array}{r}2 \\ 2\end{array}}{4}$

2
4

2
2 [··] 4

Card 5:
$18 = 2 \times 9$
$18 = 9 \times 2$

9	2
18	4
	6
	8
	10
	12
	14
	16
	18

9
2 [·········] 18

Card 6:
$\times \dfrac{\begin{array}{r}2 \\ 8\end{array}}{16}$ $\times \dfrac{\begin{array}{r}8 \\ 2\end{array}}{16}$

8	2
16	4
	6
	8
	10
	12
	14
	16

2
8 [·] 16

Card 7:
$14 = 2 \times 7$
$14 = 7 \times 2$

7	2
14	4
	6
	8
	10
	12
	14

7
2 [·······] 14

Card 8:
$\times \dfrac{\begin{array}{r}2 \\ 6\end{array}}{12}$ $\times \dfrac{\begin{array}{r}6 \\ 2\end{array}}{12}$

6	2
12	4
	6
	8
	10
	12

2
6 [·] 12

Multiplication Strategy Cards

3×3

$3 \quad 4$
$\times 4 \quad \times 3$

3×5
5×3

$3 \quad 6$
$\times 6 \quad \times 3$

3×7
7×3

$3 \quad 8$
$\times 8 \quad \times 3$

3×9
9×3

4
$\times 4$

Card 1

$18 = 3 \times 6$

$18 = 6 \times 3$

6	3
12	6
18	9
	12
	15
	18

6
3 ○ 18

Card 2

3   5

$\times 5$ $\times 3$

15   15

5	3
10	6
15	9
	12
	15

3
5 ○ 15

Card 3

$12 = 3 \times 4$

$12 = 4 \times 3$

4	3
8	6
12	9
	12

4
3 ○ 12

Card 4

3

$\times 3$

9

3
6
9

3
3 ○ 9

Card 5

$16 = 4 \times 4$

4
8
12
16

4
4 ○ 16

Card 6

3   9

$\times 9$ $\times 3$

27   27

9	3
18	6
27	9
	12
	15
	18
	21
	24
	27

9
3 ○ 27

Card 7

$24 = 3 \times 8$

$24 = 8 \times 3$

8	3
16	6
24	9
	12
	15
	18
	21
	24

3
8 ○ 24

Card 8

3   7

$\times 7$ $\times 3$

21   21

7	3
14	6
21	9
	12
	15
	18
	21

7
3 ○ 21

Multiplication Strategy Cards

4×5
5×4

$\begin{array}{r} 4 \\ \times 6 \end{array}$ $\begin{array}{r} 6 \\ \times 4 \end{array}$

4×7
7×4

$\begin{array}{r} 4 \\ \times 8 \end{array}$ $\begin{array}{r} 8 \\ \times 4 \end{array}$

4×9
9×4

$\begin{array}{r} 5 \\ \times 5 \end{array}$

5×6
6×5

$\begin{array}{r} 5 \\ \times 7 \end{array}$ $\begin{array}{r} 7 \\ \times 5 \end{array}$

Card 1

$32 = 4 \times 8$

$32 = 8 \times 4$

8	4
16	8
24	12
32	16
	20
	24
	28
	32

4

8 | 32

Card 2

4   7

$\times 7$ $\times 4$

28   28

7	4
14	8
21	12
28	16
	20
	24
	28

7

4 | 28

Card 3

$24 = 4 \times 6$

$24 = 6 \times 4$

6	4
12	8
18	12
24	16
	20
	24

4

6 | 24

Card 4

4   5

$\times 5$ $\times 4$

20   20

5	4
10	8
15	12
20	16
	20

5

4 | 20

Card 5

$35 = 5 \times 7$

$35 = 7 \times 5$

7	5
14	10
21	15
28	20
35	25
	30
	35

7

5 | 35

Card 6

5   6

$\times 6$ $\times 5$

30   30

6	5
12	10
18	15
24	20
30	25
	30

5

6 | 30

Card 7

$25 = 5 \times 5$

5
10
15
20
25

5

5 | 25

Card 8

4   9

$\times 9$ $\times 4$

36   36

9	4
18	8
27	12
36	16
	20
	24
	28
	32
	36

9

4 | 36

5×8
8×5

5   9
×9   ×5

6×6

6   7
×7   ×6

6×8
8×6

6   9
×9   ×6

7×7

7   8
×8   ×7

Card 1

$42 = 7 \times 6$

$42 = 6 \times 7$

6	7
12	14
18	21
24	28
30	35
36	42
42	

7

6 · 42

Card 2

6

$\times 6$

36

6
12
18
24
30

36

6

6 · 36

Card 3

$45 = 9 \times 5$

$45 = 5 \times 9$

5	9
10	18
15	27
20	36
25	45

30
35
40
45

9

5 · 45

Card 4

8   5

$\times 5$ $\times 8$

40   40

5	8
10	16
15	24
20	32
25	40

30
35
40

5

8 · 40

Card 5

$56 = 7 \times 8$

$56 = 8 \times 7$

8	7
16	14
24	21
32	28
40	35
48	42
56	49
	56

8

7 · 56

Card 6

7

$\times 7$

49

7
14
21
28
35

42
49

7

7 · 49

Card 7

$54 = 9 \times 6$

$54 = 6 \times 9$

6	9
12	18
18	27
24	36
30	45
36	54
42	
48	
54	

9

6 · 54

Card 8

6   8

$\times 8$ $\times 6$

48   48

8	6
16	12
24	18
32	24
40	30
48	36
	42
	48

8

6 · 48

Multiplication Strategy Cards

7×9
9×7

$\begin{array}{r} 8 \\ \times\ 8 \\ \hline \end{array}$

9×8
8×9

$\begin{array}{r} 9 \\ \times\ 9 \\ \hline \end{array}$

Card 1

$81 = 9 \times 9$

9
18
27
36
45

54
63
72
81

9

9 | 81

Card 2

$$9 \atop \times\,8 \over 72$$

$$8 \atop \times\,9 \over 72$$

8
16
24
32
40

48
56
64
72

9
18
27
36
45

54
63
72

9

8 | 72

Card 3

$64 = 8 \times 8$

8
16
24
32
40

48
56
64

8

8 | 64

Card 4

$$7 \atop \times\,9 \over 63$$

$$9 \atop \times\,7 \over 63$$

9
18
27
36
45

54
63

7
14
21
28
35

42
49
56
63

9

7 | 63

Multiplication Strategy Cards

$2\overline{)4}$

$4 \div 2$

$2\overline{)6}$

$6 \div 2$

$2\overline{)8}$

$8 \div 2$

$2\overline{)10}$

$10 \div 2$

$2\overline{)12}$

$12 \div 2$

$2\overline{)14}$

$14 \div 2$

$2\overline{)16}$

$16 \div 2$

$2\overline{)18}$

$18 \div 2$

Card 1

5   2

$2\overline{)10}$ $5\overline{)10}$

2   5
4   10
6
8
10

     5
2 ∘∘∘∘∘
 ∘ 10

Card 2

4   2

$2\overline{)8}$ $4\overline{)8}$

2   4
4   8
6
8

   4
2 ∘∘∘∘
 ∘ 8

Card 3

3   2

$2\overline{)6}$ $3\overline{)6}$

2   3
4   6
6

   3
2 ∘∘∘
 ∘ 6

Card 4

2

$2\overline{)4}$

2
4

  2
2 ∘∘
 ∘4

Card 5

9   2

$2\overline{)18}$ $9\overline{)18}$

2   9
4   18
6
8
10

12
14
16
18

        9
2 ∘∘∘∘∘∘∘∘∘
 ∘   18

Card 6

8   2

$2\overline{)16}$ $8\overline{)16}$

2   8
4   16
6
8
10

12
14
16

       8
2 ∘∘∘∘∘∘∘∘
 ∘   16

Card 7

7   2

$2\overline{)14}$ $7\overline{)14}$

2   7
4   14
6
8
10

12
14

      7
2 ∘∘∘∘∘∘∘
 ∘   14

Card 8

6   2

$2\overline{)12}$ $6\overline{)12}$

2   6
4   12
6
8
10

12

     6
2 ∘∘∘∘∘∘
 ∘ 12

Division Strategy Cards

$3 \overline{)6}$

$6 \div 3$

$4 \overline{)8}$

$8 \div 4$

$5 \overline{)10}$

$10 \div 5$

$6 \overline{)12}$

$12 \div 6$

$7 \overline{)14}$

$14 \div 7$

$8 \overline{)16}$

$16 \div 8$

$9 \overline{)18}$

$18 \div 9$

$3 \overline{)9}$

$9 \div 3$

2 6	2 5	2 4	2 3
6)12 2)12	5)10 2)10	4)8 2)8	3)6 2)6

Card 1:
6)12   2)12
6   2
12   4
          6
          8
          10
          12

2
6 ○ 12

Card 2:
5)10   2)10
5   2
10   4
          6
          8
          10

2
5 ○ 10

Card 3:
4)8   2)8
4   2
8   4
          6
          8

2
4 ○ 8

Card 4:
3)6   2)6
3   2
6   4
          6

2
3 ○ 6

Card 5:
        3
3)9
3
6
9

3
3 ○ 9

Card 6:
9)18   2)18
9   2
18   4
          6
          8
          10
          12
          14
          16
          18

2
9 ○ 18

Card 7:
8)16   2)16
8   2
16   4
          6
          8
          10
          12
          14
          16

2
8 ○ 16

Card 8:
7)14   2)14
7   2
14   4
          6
          8
          10
          12
          14

2
7 ○ 14

Division Strategy Cards

$3\overline{)12}$

$12 \div 3$

$3\overline{)15}$

$15 \div 3$

$3\overline{)18}$

$18 \div 3$

$3\overline{)21}$

$21 \div 3$

$3\overline{)24}$

$24 \div 3$

$3\overline{)27}$

$27 \div 3$

$4\overline{)12}$

$12 \div 4$

$5\overline{)15}$

$15 \div 5$

Card 1

7
3⟌21

3
7⟌21

3	7
6	14
9	21
12	
15	
18	
21	

7
3 ∘ 21

Card 2

6
3⟌18

3
6⟌18

3	6
6	12
9	18
12	
15	
18	

6
3 ∘ 18

Card 3

5
3⟌15

3
5⟌15

3	5
6	10
9	15
12	
15	

5
3 ∘ 15

Card 4

4
3⟌12

3
4⟌12

3	4
6	8
9	12
12	

4
3 ∘ 12

Card 5

3
5⟌15

5
3⟌15

5	3
10	6
15	9
	12
	15

3
5 ∘ 15

Card 6

3
4⟌12

4
3⟌12

4	3
8	6
12	9
	12

3
4 ∘ 12

Card 7

9
3⟌27

3
9⟌27

3	9
6	18
9	27
12	
15	
18	
21	
24	
27	

9
3 ∘ 27

Card 8

8
3⟌24

3
8⟌24

3	8
6	16
9	24
12	
15	
18	
21	
24	

8
3 ∘ 24

Division Strategy Cards

$6 \overline{)18}$

$18 \div 6$

$7 \overline{)21}$

$21 \div 7$

$8 \overline{)24}$

$24 \div 8$

$9 \overline{)27}$

$27 \div 9$

$4 \overline{)16}$

$16 \div 4$

$4 \overline{)20}$

$20 \div 4$

$4 \overline{)24}$

$24 \div 4$

$4 \overline{)28}$

$28 \div 4$

Division Strategy Cards

3 **9**

$9\overline{)27}$ $3\overline{)27}$

9	3
18	6
27	9
	12
	15
	18
	21
	24
	27

3

9 ∘ 27

---

3 **8**

$8\overline{)24}$ $3\overline{)24}$

8	3
16	6
24	9
	12
	15
	18
	21
	24

3

8 ∘ 24

---

3 **7**

$7\overline{)21}$ $3\overline{)21}$

7	3
14	6
21	9
	12
	15
	18
	21

3

7 ∘ 21

---

3 **6**

$6\overline{)18}$ $3\overline{)18}$

6	3
12	6
18	9
	12
	15
	18

3

6 ∘ 18

---

7 **4**

$4\overline{)28}$ $7\overline{)28}$

4	7
8	14
12	21
16	28
20	
24	
28	

7

4 ∘ 28

---

6 **4**

$4\overline{)24}$ $6\overline{)24}$

4	6
8	12
12	18
16	24
20	
24	

6

4 ∘ 24

---

5 **4**

$4\overline{)20}$ $5\overline{)20}$

4	5
8	10
12	15
16	20
20	

5

4 ∘ 20

4

$4\overline{)16}$

4
8
12
16

4

4 ∘ 16

Division Strategy Cards

$4\overline{)32}$	$4\overline{)36}$	$5\overline{)20}$	$6\overline{)24}$
$32 \div 4$	$36 \div 4$	$20 \div 5$	$24 \div 6$

$7\overline{)28}$	$8\overline{)32}$	$9\overline{)36}$	$5\overline{)25}$
$28 \div 7$	$32 \div 8$	$36 \div 9$	$25 \div 5$

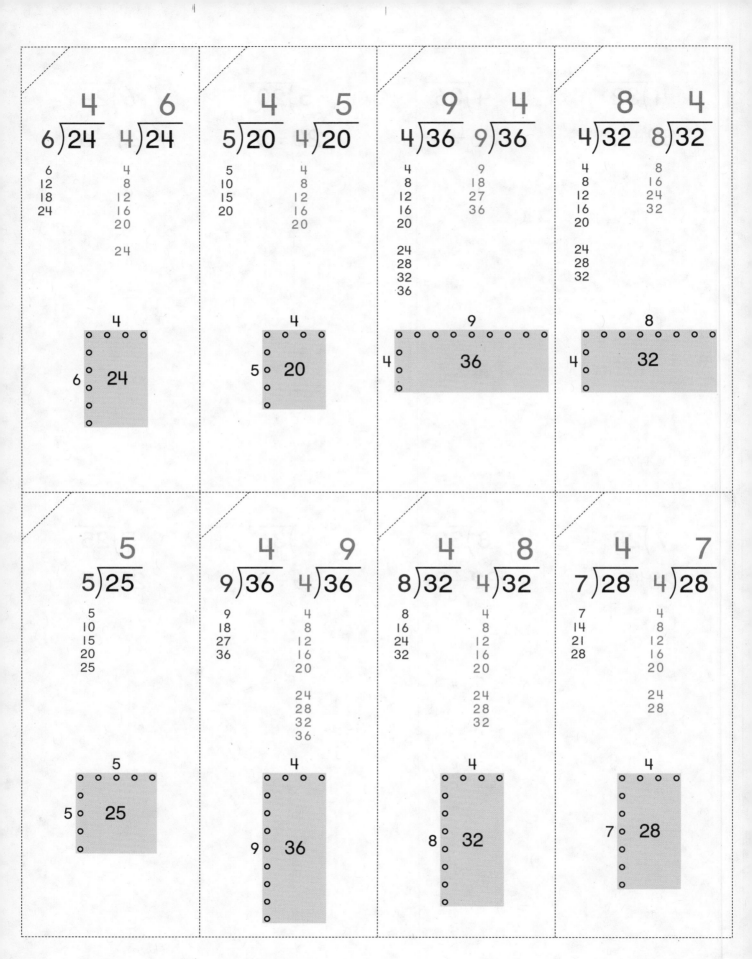

Division Strategy Cards

$5 \overline{)30}$

$30 \div 5$

$5 \overline{)35}$

$35 \div 5$

$5 \overline{)40}$

$40 \div 5$

$5 \overline{)45}$

$45 \div 5$

$6 \overline{)30}$

$30 \div 6$

$7 \overline{)35}$

$35 \div 7$

$8 \overline{)40}$

$40 \div 8$

$9 \overline{)45}$

$45 \div 9$

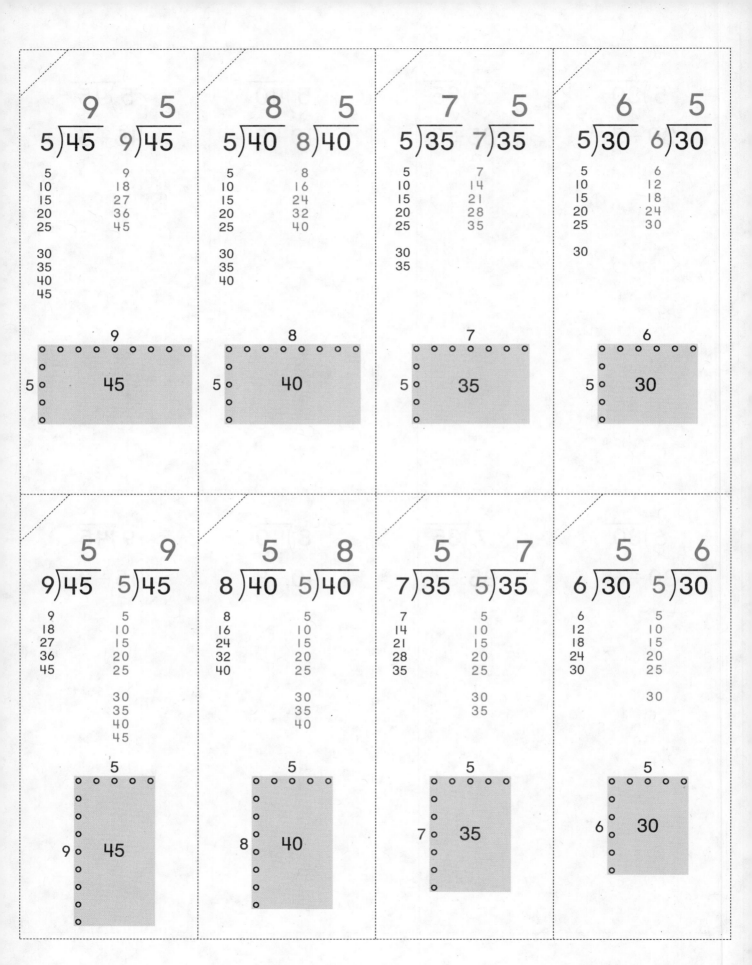

$6 \overline{)36}$

$36 \div 6$

$6 \overline{)42}$

$42 \div 6$

$6 \overline{)48}$

$48 \div 6$

$6 \overline{)54}$

$54 \div 6$

$7 \overline{)42}$

$42 \div 7$

$8 \overline{)48}$

$48 \div 8$

$9 \overline{)54}$

$54 \div 9$

$7 \overline{)49}$

$49 \div 7$

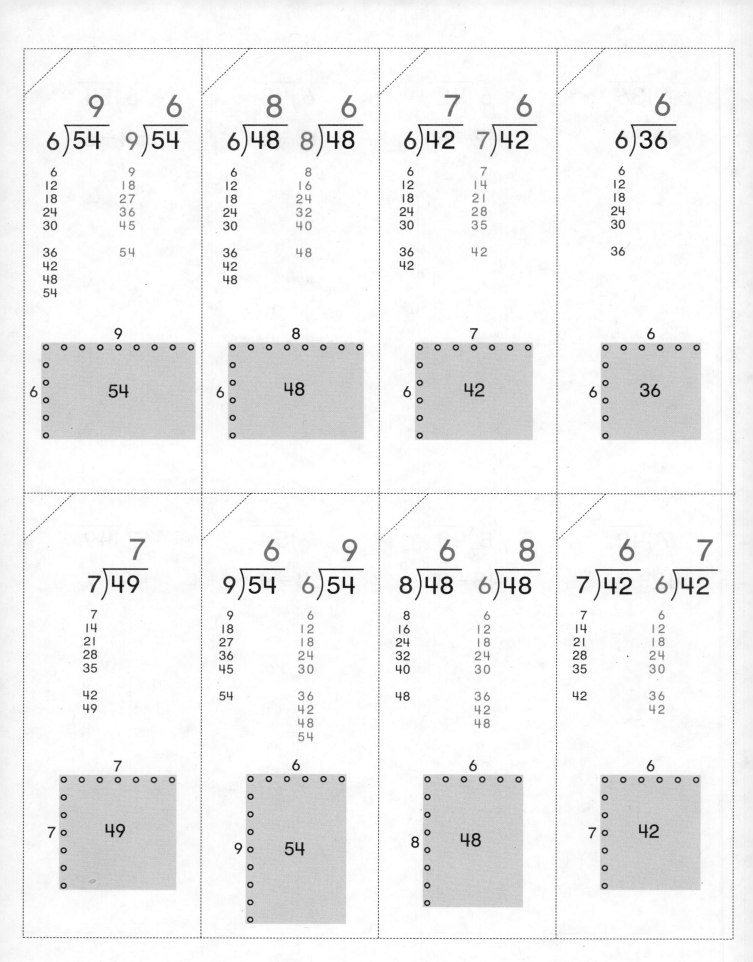

$7 \overline{)56}$	$7 \overline{)63}$	$8 \overline{)56}$	$9 \overline{)63}$
$56 \div 7$	$63 \div 7$	$56 \div 8$	$63 \div 9$

$8 \overline{)64}$	$8 \overline{)72}$	$9 \overline{)72}$	$9 \overline{)81}$
$64 \div 8$	$72 \div 8$	$72 \div 9$	$81 \div 9$

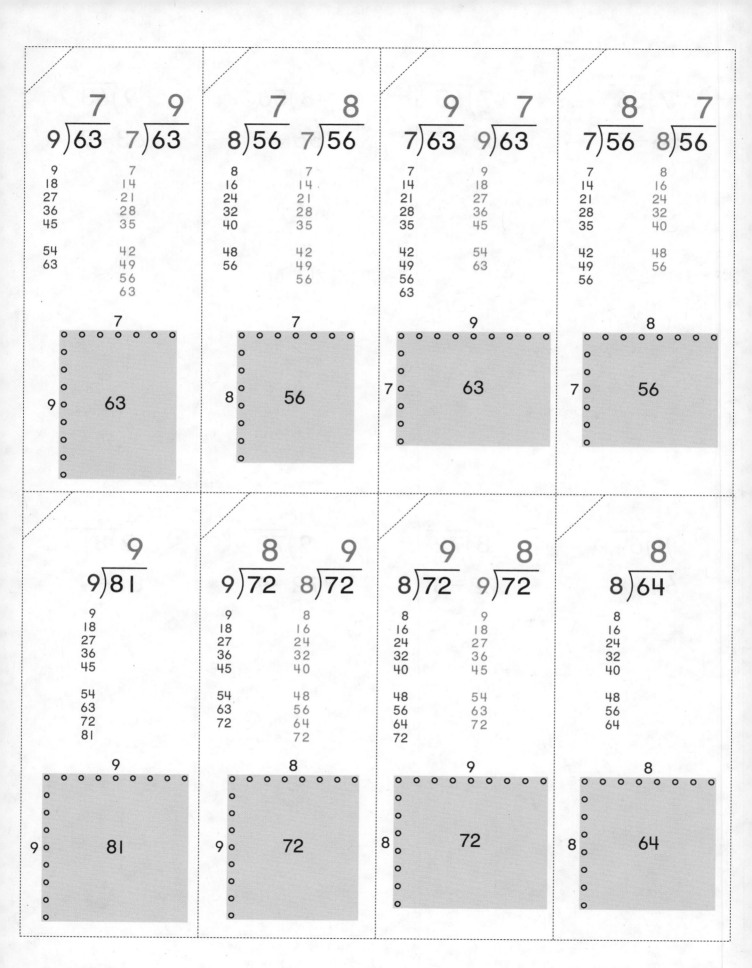

Division Strategy Cards

PATH to FLUENCY Check Sheet 4: 3s and 4s

3s Multiplications	3s Divisions	4s Multiplications	4s Divisions
8 × 3 = 24	9 / 3 = 3	1 × 4 = 4	40 / 4 = 10
3 • 2 = 6	21 ÷ 3 = 7	4 • 5 = 20	12 ÷ 4 = 3
3 * 5 = 15	27 / 3 = 9	8 * 4 = 32	24 / 4 = 6
10 × 3 = 30	3 ÷ 3 = 1	3 × 4 = 12	8 ÷ 4 = 2
3 • 3 = 9	18 / 3 = 6	4 • 6 = 24	4 / 4 = 1
3 * 6 = 18	12 ÷ 3 = 4	4 * 9 = 36	28 ÷ 4 = 7
7 × 3 = 21	30 / 3 = 10	10 × 4 = 40	32 / 4 = 8
3 • 9 = 27	6 ÷ 3 = 2	4 • 7 = 28	16 ÷ 4 = 4
4 * 3 = 12	24 / 3 = 8	4 * 4 = 16	36 / 4 = 9
3 × 1 = 3	15 / 3 = 5	2 × 4 = 8	20 / 4 = 5
3 • 4 = 12	21 ÷ 3 = 7	4 • 3 = 12	4 ÷ 4 = 1
3 * 3 = 9	3 / 3 = 1	4 * 2 = 8	32 / 4 = 8
3 × 10 = 30	9 ÷ 3 = 3	9 × 4 = 36	8 ÷ 4 = 2
2 • 3 = 6	27 / 3 = 9	1 • 4 = 4	16 / 4 = 4
3 * 7 = 21	30 ÷ 3 = 10	4 * 6 = 24	36 ÷ 4 = 9
6 × 3 = 18	18 / 3 = 6	5 × 4 = 20	12 / 4 = 3
5 • 3 = 15	6 ÷ 3 = 2	4 • 4 = 16	40 ÷ 4 = 10
3 * 8 = 24	15 ÷ 3 = 5	7 * 4 = 28	20 ÷ 4 = 5
9 × 3 = 27	12 / 3 = 4	8 × 4 = 32	24 / 4 = 6
2 • 3 = 6	24 ÷ 3 = 8	10 • 4 = 40	28 ÷ 4 = 7

Check Sheet 4: 3s and 4s

Name

Explore Patterns with 4s

What patterns do you see below?

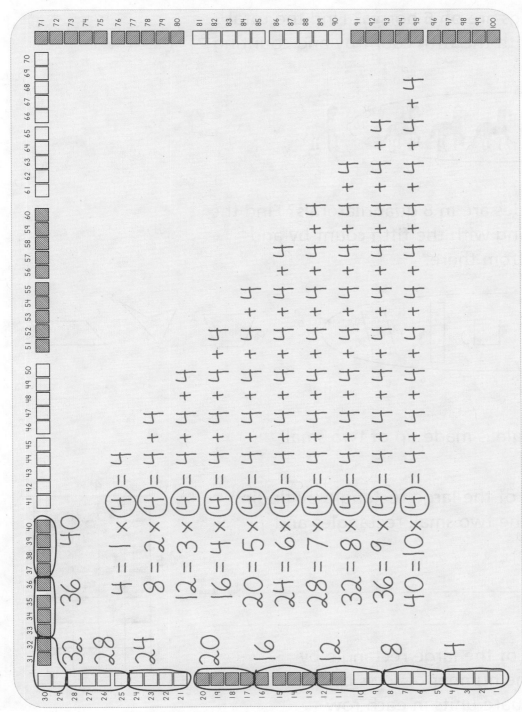

Content Standards 3.OA.A.1, 3.OA.A.2, 3.OA.A.4, 3.OA.B.5, 3.OA.C.7, 3.OA.D.9, 3 MD.C.7, 3.MD.C.7.b, 3.MD.C.7.c, 3.MD.C.7.d
Mathematical Practices MP1, MP2, MP3, MP6

PATH to FLUENCY Use the 5s Shortcut for 4s

Solve each problem.

1. How many legs are on 6 horses? Find the total by starting with the fifth count-by and counting up from there.

_____ _____

2. How many sides are in 8 quadrilaterals? Find the total by starting with the fifth count-by and counting up from there.

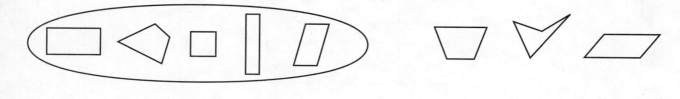

_____   _____   _____   _____

This large rectangle is made up of two small rectangles.

3. Find the area of the large rectangle by finding the areas of the two small rectangles and adding them.

_____

_____

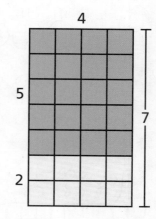

4. Find the area of the large rectangle by multiplying the number of rows by the number of square units in each row.

_____

Multiply and Divide with 4

Name _____

© Houghton Mifflin Harcourt Publishing Company

PATH to FLUENCY **Use Multiplications You Know**

You can combine multiplications to find other multiplications.

This equal shares drawing shows that 7 groups of 4 is the same as 5 groups of 4 plus 2 groups of 4.

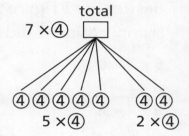

5 Find 5 ×④ and 2 ×④ and add the answers.

_____

6 Find 7 ×④. Did you get the same answer as in Exercise 5?

_____

7 Find this product: 5 × 4 = _____

8 Find this product: 4 × 4 = _____

9 Use your answers to Exercises 7 and 8 to show that (5 × 4) + (4 × 4) = 9 × 4 = _____

10 Make a drawing to show that your answers to Exercises 7–9 are correct.

What's the Error?

Dear Math Students,

Today I had to find 8 x 4. I didn't know the answer, but I figured it out by combining two multiplications I did know:

$5 \times 2 = 10$
$3 \times 2 = 6$
_____
$8 \times 4 = 16$

Is my answer right? If not, please correct my work and tell me why it is wrong.

Your friend,
The Puzzled Penguin

11 **Write an answer to the Puzzled Penguin.**

_____

_____

_____

Make Sense of Problems

Write an equation and solve the problem.

12 Galen has 20 pictures to place in his book. If he puts 4 pictures on each page, how many pages will he fill?

_____

13 Emery arranged tiles in an array with 4 columns and 7 rows. How many tiles were in the array?

_____

✔ **Check Understanding**

Draw a picture to show how you can use the answers to 5×4 and 3×4 to find 8×4.

Multiply and Divide with 4

Make Sense of Problems

Write an equation and solve the problem.

Show your work.

1 The garden shop received a shipment of 12 rose bushes. They arranged the rose bushes in 3 rows with the same number of bushes in each row. How many rose bushes were in each row?

_____

2 Eric saw 4 stop signs on the way to school. Each stop sign had 8 sides. How many sides were on all 4 stop signs?

_____

3 Ed needs 14 batteries. If he buys the batteries in packages of 2, how many packages of batteries will he need to buy?

_____

4 A flag has 5 rows of stars with the same number of stars in each row. There are 35 stars on the flag. How many stars are in each row?

_____

5 Melia learned in science class that insects have 6 legs. What is the total number of legs on 9 insects?

_____

6 Stan has 4 model car kits. Each kit comes with 5 tires. How many tires does Stan have altogether?

_____

Make Sense of Problems (continued)

Write an equation and solve the problem.

Show your work.

7 Maria bought a shoe rack. The shoe rack has 3 rows with places for 6 shoes on each row. How many shoes can be placed on the shoe rack?

_____

8 The park has 4 swing sets with the same number of swings on each set. There is a total of 16 swings at the park. How many swings are on each swing set?

_____

9 Amanda has 27 seashells in her collection. She displayed the seashells in 3 rows with the same number of seashells in each row. How many seashells are in each row?

_____

10 The art room has 4 round tables. There are 6 chairs around each table. Altogether, how many chairs are around the tables?

_____

11 Shanna is making bead necklaces for the craft fair. She can make 3 necklaces a day. She plans to make 21 necklaces. How many days will it take her to make the necklaces?

_____

✓ Check Understanding

What four equations can you write for this fast array drawing?

_____

```
          7
    o o o o o o o
3 o             21
    o
```

Use the Strategy Cards

Name _____

PATH to FLUENCY Play *Solve the Stack*

Read the rules for playing *Solve the Stack*. Then play the game with your group.

Rules for *Solve the Stack*

Number of players: 2–4

What you will need: 1 set of Multiplication and Division Strategy Cards

1. Shuffle the cards. Place them exercise side up in the center of the table.

2. Players take turns. On each turn, a player finds the answer to the multiplication or division on the top card and then turns the card over to check the answer.

3. If a player's answer is correct, he or she takes the card. If it is incorrect, the card is placed at the bottom of the stack.

4. Play ends when there are no more cards in the stack. The player with the most cards wins.

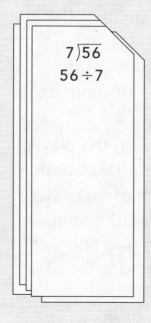

$$7\overline{)56}$$
$$56 \div 7$$

PATH to FLUENCY Play *High Card Wins*

Read the rules for playing *High Card Wins*. Then play the game with your partner.

Rules for *High Card Wins*

Number of players: 2

What you will need: 1 set of Multiplication and Division Strategy Cards for 2s, 3s, 4s, 5s, 9s

1. Shuffle the cards. Deal all the cards evenly between the two players.

2. Players put their stacks in front of them, exercise side up.

3. Each player takes the top card from his or her stack and puts it exercise side up in the center of the table.

4. Each player says the multiplication or division answer and then turns the card over to check. Then players do one of the following:

   • If one player says the wrong answer, the other player takes both cards and puts them at the bottom of his or her pile.

   • If both players say the wrong answer, both players take back their cards and put them at the bottom of their piles.

   • If both players say the correct answer, the player with the higher product or quotient takes both cards and puts them at the bottom of his or her pile. If the products or quotients are the same, the players set the cards aside and play another round. The winner of the next round takes all the cards.

5. Play continues until one player has all the cards.

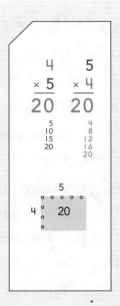

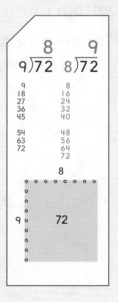

Play *High Card Wins*

PATH to FLUENCY Review Strategies

Answer the questions.

1 Emily knows that 4 × 10 = 40. How can she use subtraction and multiples of 9 to find 4 × 9?

_____

_____

2 Joey knows the multiplications 5 × 4 and 4 × 4. How can he use their products to find 9 × 4?

_____

3 Hannah knows that each division has a related multiplication. What related multiplication can she use to find 18 ÷ 3?

_____

4 Kyle knows that 5 × 3 = 15. How can he use the 5s shortcut to find 8 × 3?

_____

_____

5 Letitia knows that 5 × 4 = 20. How can she use the 5s shortcut to find 9 × 4?

_____

_____

6 Jorge knows that 6 × 9 = 54. How can he use the Commutative Property or arrays to find 9 × 6?

_____

_____

Make Sense of Problems

Write an equation and solve the problem.

Show your work.

7 Jordan has 32 peaches. He wants to divide them equally among 4 baskets. How many peaches will he put in each basket?

_____

8 A guitar has 6 strings. If Taylor replaces all the strings on 3 guitars, how many strings does he need?

_____

9 Kassler puts 5 strawberries in each bowl. Kassler has 40 strawberries. How many bowls will he fill?

_____

10 Ruel has a board 36 inches long. He wants to saw it into equal pieces 9 inches long. How many pieces will he get?

_____

Write a Word Problem

11 Write a word problem that can be solved using the equation $7 \times 10 = 70$.

_____

_____

_____

✔**Check Understanding**

What strategy did you use to solve Problem 10?

_____

Build Fluency with 2s, 3s, 4s, 5s, 9s, and 10s

Identify Types of Problems

Read each problem and decide what type of problem it is. Write the letter from the list below. Then write an equation to solve the problem.

a. Array Multiplication

b. Array Division

c. Equal Groups Multiplication

d. Equal Groups Division with an Unknown Group Size

e. Equal Groups Division with an Unknown Multiplier (number of groups)

f. None of the above

① Mrs. Ostrega has 3 children. She wants to buy 5 juice boxes for each child. How many juice boxes does she need?

_____

② Sophie picked 15 peaches from one tree and 3 peaches from another. How many peaches did she pick in all?

_____

③ Zamir brought 21 treats to the dog park. He divided the treats equally among the 7 dogs that were there. How many treats did each dog get?

_____

④ Art said he could make 12 muffins in his muffin pan. The pan has space for 3 muffins in a row. How many rows does the muffin pan have?

_____

⑤ Bia is helping with the lights for the school play. Each box of light bulbs has 6 rows, with 3 bulbs in each row. How many light bulbs are in each box?

_____

⑥ Tryouts were held to find triplets to act in a commercial for Triple-Crunch Cereal. If 24 children tried out for the commercial, how many sets of triplets tried out?

_____

Make Sense of Problems

Write an equation and solve the problem.

Show your work.

7 The produce market sells oranges in bags of 6. Santos bought 1 bag. How many oranges did he buy?

_____

8 Janine bought a jewelry organizer with 36 pockets. The pockets are arranged in 9 rows with the same number of pockets in each row. How many pockets are in each row?

_____

9 A parking lot has 9 rows of parking spaces. Each row has 7 spaces. How many cars can park in the lot?

_____

10 The pet store has 3 fish bowls on a shelf. There are 0 fish in each bowl. How many fish are in the bowls?

_____

Write a Word Problem

11 Write a word problem that can be solved using $0 \div 5$.

_____

_____

_____

✔ Check Understanding

Which of the problems on this page are array problems? _____

Solve and Create Word Problems

PATH to FLUENCY **Check Sheet 5: 1s and 0s**

1s Multiplications	1s Divisions	0s Multiplications
1 × 4 = 4	10 / 1 = 10	4 × 0 = 0
5 • 1 = 5	5 ÷ 1 = 5	2 • 0 = 0
7 * 1 = 7	7 / 1 = 7	0 * 8 = 0
1 × 8 = 8	9 ÷ 1 = 9	0 × 5 = 0
1 • 6 = 6	3 / 1 = 3	6 • 0 = 0
10 * 1 = 10	10 ÷ 1 = 10	0 * 7 = 0
1 × 9 = 9	2 / 1 = 2	0 × 2 = 0
3 • 1 = 3	8 ÷ 1 = 8	0 • 9 = 0
1 * 2 = 2	6 / 1 = 6	10 * 0 = 0
1 × 1 = 1	9 / 1 = 9	1 × 0 = 0
8 • 1 = 8	1 ÷ 1 = 1	0 • 6 = 0
1 * 7 = 7	5 / 1 = 5	9 * 0 = 0
1 × 5 = 5	3 ÷ 1 = 3	0 × 4 = 0
6 • 1 = 6	4 / 1 = 4	3 • 0 = 0
1 * 1 = 1	2 ÷ 1 = 2	0 * 3 = 0
1 × 10 = 10	8 / 1 = 8	8 × 0 = 0
9 • 1 = 9	4 ÷ 1 = 4	0 • 10 = 0
4 * 1 = 4	7 ÷ 1 = 7	0 * 1 = 0
2 × 1 = 2	1 / 1 = 1	5 × 0 = 0
1 • 3 = 3	6 ÷ 1 = 6	7 • 0 = 0

PATH to FLUENCY Check Sheet 6: Mixed 3s, 4s, 0s, and 1s

3s, 4s, 0s, 1s Multiplications	3s, 4s, 0s, 1s Multiplications	3s, 4s, 1s Divisions	3s, 4s, 1s Divisions
$5 \times 3 = 15$	$0 \times 5 = 0$	$18 / 3 = 6$	$4 / 1 = 4$
$6 \cdot 4 = 24$	$10 \cdot 1 = 10$	$20 \div 4 = 5$	$21 \div 3 = 7$
$9 * 0 = 0$	$6 * 3 = 18$	$1 / 1 = 1$	$16 / 4 = 4$
$7 \times 1 = 7$	$2 \times 4 = 8$	$21 \div 3 = 7$	$9 \div 1 = 9$
$3 \cdot 3 = 9$	$5 \cdot 0 = 0$	$12 / 4 = 3$	$15 / 3 = 5$
$4 * 7 = 28$	$1 * 2 = 2$	$5 \div 1 = 5$	$8 \div 4 = 2$
$0 \times 10 = 0$	$10 \times 3 = 30$	$15 / 3 = 5$	$5 / 1 = 5$
$1 \cdot 6 = 6$	$5 \cdot 4 = 20$	$24 \div 4 = 6$	$30 \div 3 = 10$
$3 * 4 = 12$	$0 * 8 = 0$	$7 / 1 = 7$	$12 / 4 = 3$
$5 \times 4 = 20$	$9 \times 1 = 9$	$12 / 3 = 4$	$8 / 1 = 8$
$0 \cdot 5 = 0$	$10 \cdot 3 = 30$	$36 \div 4 = 9$	$27 \div 3 = 9$
$9 * 1 = 9$	$9 * 4 = 36$	$6 / 1 = 6$	$40 / 4 = 10$
$2 \times 3 = 6$	$1 \times 0 = 0$	$12 \div 3 = 4$	$4 \div 1 = 4$
$3 \cdot 4 = 12$	$1 \cdot 6 = 6$	$16 / 4 = 4$	$9 / 3 = 3$
$0 * 9 = 0$	$3 * 6 = 18$	$7 \div 1 = 7$	$16 \div 4 = 4$
$1 \times 5 = 5$	$7 \times 4 = 28$	$9 / 3 = 3$	$10 / 1 = 10$
$2 \cdot 3 = 6$	$6 \cdot 0 = 0$	$8 \div 4 = 2$	$9 \div 3 = 3$
$4 * 4 = 16$	$8 * 1 = 8$	$2 \div 1 = 2$	$20 \div 4 = 5$
$9 \times 0 = 0$	$3 \times 9 = 27$	$6 / 3 = 2$	$6 / 1 = 6$
$1 \cdot 1 = 1$	$1 \cdot 4 = 4$	$32 \div 4 = 8$	$24 \div 3 = 8$

Name _____

© Houghton Mifflin Harcourt Publishing Company

(PATH to FLUENCY) Play *Multiplication Three-in-a-Row*

Read the rules for playing *Multiplication Three-in-a-Row*. Then play the game with a partner.

Rules for *Multiplication Three-in-a-Row*

Number of players: 2

What You Will Need: A set of Multiplication Strategy Cards, *Three-in-a-Row* Game Grids for each player (see page 83)

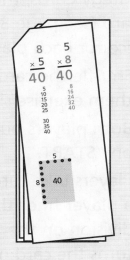

1. Each player looks through the cards and writes any nine of the products in the squares of a Game Grid. A player may write the same product more than once.

2. Shuffle the cards and place them exercise side up in the center of the table.

3. Players take turns. On each turn, a player finds the answer to the multiplication on the top card and then turns the card over to check the answer.

4. If the answer is correct, the player looks to see if the product is on the game grid. If it is, the player puts an X through that grid square. If the answer is wrong, or if the product is not on the grid, the player does not mark anything. The player then puts the card problem side up on the bottom of the stack.

5. The first player to mark three squares in a row (horizontally, vertically, or diagonally) wins.

⟨PATH to FLUENCY⟩ Play *Division Race*

Read the rules for playing *Division Race*. Then play the game with a partner.

Rules for *Division Race*

Number of players: 2

What You Will Need: a set of Division Strategy Cards, the *Division Race* game board (see page 84), a different game piece for each player

1. Shuffle the cards and then place them exercise side up on the table.

2. Both players put their game pieces on "START."

3. Players take turns. On each turn, a player finds the answer to the division on the top card and then turns the card over to check the answer.

4. If the answer is correct, the player moves *forward* that number of spaces. If a player's answer is wrong, the player moves *back* a number of spaces equal to the correct answer. Players cannot move back beyond the "START" square. The player puts the card on the bottom of the stack.

5. If a player lands on a space with special instructions, he or she should follow those instructions.

6. The game ends when everyone lands on or passes the "End" square.

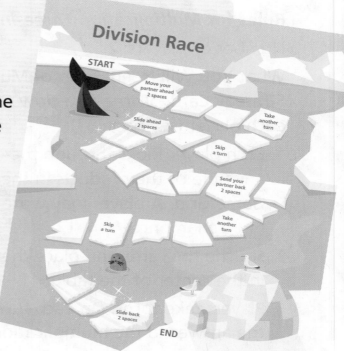

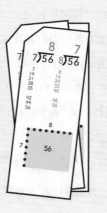

© Houghton Mifflin Harcourt Publishing Company

Name

Three-in-a-Row Game Grids **83**

Division Race

START

Move your partner ahead 2 spaces

Slide ahead 2 spaces

Take another turn

Skip a turn

Send your partner back 2 spaces

Take another turn

Skip a turn

Slide back 2 spaces

END

Division Race Game Board

Name _____

PATH to FLUENCY Dashes 1–4

Complete each Dash. Check your answers on page 89.

Dash 1 2s and 5s Multiplications	Dash 2 2s and 5s Divisions	Dash 3 9s and 10s Multiplications	Dash 4 9s and 10s Divisions
a. $2 \times 6 = $ _____	a. $18 / 2 = $ _____	a. $9 \times 10 = $ _____	a. $100 / 10 = $ _____
b. $9 * 5 = $ _____	b. $25 \div 5 = $ _____	b. $10 * 3 = $ _____	b. $9 \div 9 = $ _____
c. $7 \bullet 2 = $ _____	c. $8 / 2 = $ _____	c. $1 \bullet 9 = $ _____	c. $30 / 10 = $ _____
d. $5 \times 8 = $ _____	d. $45 \div 5 = $ _____	d. $2 \times 10 = $ _____	d. $81 \div 9 = $ _____
e. $2 * 4 = $ _____	e. $16 / 2 = $ _____	e. $9 * 9 = $ _____	e. $70 / 10 = $ _____
f. $3 \bullet 5 = $ _____	f. $20 \div 5 = $ _____	f. $10 \bullet 6 = $ _____	f. $45 \div 9 = $ _____
g. $1 \times 2 = $ _____	g. $4 / 2 = $ _____	g. $4 \times 9 = $ _____	g. $10 / 10 = $ _____
h. $5 * 7 = $ _____	h. $40 \div 5 = $ _____	h. $10 \times 10 = $ _____	h. $54 \div 9 = $ _____
i. $2 \bullet 9 = $ _____	i. $20 / 2 = $ _____	i. $9 * 2 = $ _____	i. $50 / 10 = $ _____
j. $4 \times 5 = $ _____	j. $35 \div 5 = $ _____	j. $1 \bullet 10 = $ _____	j. $27 \div 9 = $ _____
k. $5 * 2 = $ _____	k. $6 / 2 = $ _____	k. $7 \times 9 = $ _____	k. $20 / 10 = $ _____
l. $5 \bullet 1 = $ _____	l. $15 \div 5 = $ _____	l. $10 * 5 = $ _____	l. $72 \div 9 = $ _____
m. $2 \times 2 = $ _____	m. $14 / 2 = $ _____	m. $9 \bullet 8 = $ _____	m. $40 / 10 = $ _____
n. $10 \times 5 = $ _____	n. $5 \div 5 = $ _____	n. $7 \times 10 = $ _____	n. $18 \div 9 = $ _____
o. $10 * 2 = $ _____	o. $10 / 2 = $ _____	o. $3 * 9 = $ _____	o. $60 / 10 = $ _____
p. $5 \bullet 6 = $ _____	p. $10 \div 5 = $ _____	p. $10 \bullet 4 = $ _____	p. $90 \div 9 = $ _____
q. $2 \times 3 = $ _____	q. $6 / 2 = $ _____	q. $9 \times 5 = $ _____	q. $90 / 10 = $ _____
r. $5 * 5 = $ _____	r. $30 \div 5 = $ _____	r. $8 * 10 = $ _____	r. $63 \div 9 = $ _____
s. $8 \bullet 2 = $ _____	s. $2 / 2 = $ _____	s. $6 \bullet 9 = $ _____	s. $80 / 10 = $ _____
t. $6 \times 5 = $ _____	t. $45 \div 5 = $ _____	t. $10 \times 9 = $ _____	t. $36 \div 9 = $ _____

PATH to FLUENCY **Dashes 5–8**

Complete each Dash. Check your answers on page 89.

Dash 5 3s and 4s Multiplications	**Dash 6** 3s and 4s Divisions	**Dash 7** 0s and 1s Multiplications	**Dash 8** 1s and $n \div n$ Divisions
a. $3 \times 9 = $ _____	a. $12 / 4 = $ _____	a. $0 \times 6 = $ _____	a. $9 / 9 = $ _____
b. $4 * 2 = $ _____	b. $20 \div 4 = $ _____	b. $1 * 4 = $ _____	b. $8 \div 1 = $ _____
c. $6 \cdot 3 = $ _____	c. $21 / 3 = $ _____	c. $4 \cdot 0 = $ _____	c. $7 / 7 = $ _____
d. $10 \times 4 = $ _____	d. $16 \div 4 = $ _____	d. $8 \times 1 = $ _____	d. $6 \div 1 = $ _____
e. $3 * 1 = $ _____	e. $9 / 3 = $ _____	e. $0 * 2 = $ _____	e. $1 / 1 = $ _____
f. $4 \cdot 1 = $ _____	f. $32 \div 4 = $ _____	f. $1 \cdot 3 = $ _____	f. $4 \div 1 = $ _____
g. $10 \times 3 = $ _____	g. $24 / 4 = $ _____	g. $9 \times 0 = $ _____	g. $2 / 2 = $ _____
h. $5 * 4 = $ _____	h. $18 \div 3 = $ _____	h. $2 * 1 = $ _____	h. $2 \div 1 = $ _____
i. $3 \cdot 3 = $ _____	i. $40 / 4 = $ _____	i. $0 \cdot 8 = $ _____	i. $8 / 8 = $ _____
j. $4 \times 4 = $ _____	j. $12 \div 3 = $ _____	j. $1 \times 10 = $ _____	j. $9 \div 1 = $ _____
k. $8 * 3 = $ _____	k. $6 / 3 = $ _____	k. $7 * 0 = $ _____	k. $3 / 3 = $ _____
l. $7 \cdot 4 = $ _____	l. $28 \div 4 = $ _____	l. $1 \cdot 1 = $ _____	l. $5 \div 1 = $ _____
m. $3 \times 2 = $ _____	m. $24 / 3 = $ _____	m. $0 \times 0 = $ _____	m. $5 / 5 = $ _____
n. $4 * 9 = $ _____	n. $20 \div 4 = $ _____	n. $5 * 1 = $ _____	n. $10 / 10 = $ _____
o. $7 \cdot 3 = $ _____	o. $27 / 3 = $ _____	o. $1 \cdot 0 = $ _____	o. $7 \div 1 = $ _____
p. $3 \times 4 = $ _____	p. $15 \div 3 = $ _____	p. $1 \times 6 = $ _____	p. $4 / 4 = $ _____
q. $3 * 5 = $ _____	q. $27 / 3 = $ _____	q. $5 * 0 = $ _____	q. $10 \div 1 = $ _____
r. $4 \cdot 6 = $ _____	r. $36 \div 4 = $ _____	r. $0 \cdot 3 = $ _____	r. $6 / 6 = $ _____
s. $4 \times 3 = $ _____	s. $8 / 4 = $ _____	s. $7 \times 1 = $ _____	s. $3 \div 1 = $ _____
t. $8 * 4 = $ _____	t. $40 \div 4 = $ _____	t. $1 * 9 = $ _____	t. $1 / 1 = $ _____

© Houghton Mifflin Harcourt Publishing Company

PATH to FLUENCY Dashes 9–12

Complete each Dash. Check your answers on page 90.

Dash 9 **2s, 5s, 9s, 10s** **Multiplications**	**Dash 10** **2s, 5s, 9s, 10s** **Divisions**	**Dash 11** **3s, 4s, 0s, 1s** **Multiplications**	**Dash 12** **3s, 4s, 1s** **Divisions**
a. $4 \times 5 = $ ___	a. $8 / 2 = $ ___	a. $3 \times 0 = $ ___	a. $12 / 4 = $ ___
b. $10 \cdot 3 = $ ___	b. $50 \div 10 = $ ___	b. $4 \cdot 6 = $ ___	b. $5 \div 1 = $ ___
c. $8 * 9 = $ ___	c. $15 / 5 = $ ___	c. $9 * 1 = $ ___	c. $21 / 3 = $ ___
d. $6 \times 2 = $ ___	d. $63 \div 9 = $ ___	d. $3 \times 3 = $ ___	d. $1 \div 1 = $ ___
e. $5 \cdot 7 = $ ___	e. $90 / 10 = $ ___	e. $8 \cdot 4 = $ ___	e. $16 / 4 = $ ___
f. $10 * 5 = $ ___	f. $90 \div 9 = $ ___	f. $0 * 5 = $ ___	f. $9 \div 3 = $ ___
g. $8 \times 2 = $ ___	g. $35 / 5 = $ ___	g. $1 \times 6 = $ ___	g. $32 / 4 = $ ___
h. $6 \cdot 10 = $ ___	h. $14 \div 2 = $ ___	h. $4 \cdot 3 = $ ___	h. $8 \div 1 = $ ___
i. $9 * 3 = $ ___	i. $27 / 9 = $ ___	i. $7 * 4 = $ ___	i. $24 / 4 = $ ___
j. $2 \times 9 = $ ___	j. $45 / 5 = $ ___	j. $3 \times 7 = $ ___	j. $18 / 3 = $ ___
k. $5 \cdot 8 = $ ___	k. $10 \div 10 = $ ___	k. $0 \cdot 1 = $ ___	k. $10 \div 1 = $ ___
l. $10 * 7 = $ ___	l. $25 / 5 = $ ___	l. $10 * 1 = $ ___	l. $40 / 4 = $ ___
m. $5 \times 5 = $ ___	m. $54 \div 9 = $ ___	m. $4 \times 4 = $ ___	m. $12 \div 3 = $ ___
n. $1 \cdot 5 = $ ___	n. $6 / 2 = $ ___	n. $9 \cdot 3 = $ ___	n. $6 / 3 = $ ___
o. $9 * 6 = $ ___	o. $72 \div 9 = $ ___	o. $8 * 0 = $ ___	o. $4 \div 4 = $ ___
p. $10 \times 10 = $ ___	p. $40 / 5 = $ ___	p. $5 \times 4 = $ ___	p. $7 / 1 = $ ___
q. $4 \cdot 2 = $ ___	q. $80 \div 10 = $ ___	q. $1 \cdot 6 = $ ___	q. $28 \div 4 = $ ___
r. $10 * 8 = $ ___	r. $18 \div 2 = $ ___	r. $3 * 8 = $ ___	r. $24 \div 3 = $ ___
s. $3 \times 9 = $ ___	s. $36 / 9 = $ ___	s. $4 \times 9 = $ ___	s. $20 / 4 = $ ___
t. $9 \cdot 9 = $ ___	t. $30 \div 5 = $ ___	t. $0 \cdot 4 = $ ___	t. $27 \div 3 = $ ___

PATH to FLUENCY Dashes 9A–12A

Complete each Dash. Check your answers on page 90.

Dash 9A **2s, 5s, 9s, 10s** **Multiplications**	**Dash 10A** **2s, 5s, 9s, 10s** **Divisions**	**Dash 11A** **3s, 4s, 0s, 1s** **Multiplications**	**Dash 12A** **3s, 4s, 1s** **Divisions**
a. $9 \times 9 =$ _____	a. $30 / 5 =$ _____	a. $0 \times 4 =$ _____	a. $10 / 1 =$ _____
b. $4 * 5 =$ _____	b. $18 \div 2 =$ _____	b. $4 * 9 =$ _____	b. $40 \div 4 =$ _____
c. $10 \cdot 3 =$ _____	c. $40 / 5 =$ _____	c. $3 \cdot 8 =$ _____	c. $12 / 3 =$ _____
d. $3 \times 9 =$ _____	d. $6 \div 2 =$ _____	d. $3 \times 0 =$ _____	d. $6 \div 3 =$ _____
e. $10 * 8 =$ _____	e. $25 / 5 =$ _____	e. $4 * 6 =$ _____	e. $4 / 4 =$ _____
f. $6 \cdot 2 =$ _____	f. $45 \div 5 =$ _____	f. $9 \cdot 1 =$ _____	f. $7 \div 1 =$ _____
g. $8 \times 9 =$ _____	g. $14 / 2 =$ _____	g. $3 \times 3 =$ _____	g. $28 / 4 =$ _____
h. $4 * 2 =$ _____	h. $90 \div 9 =$ _____	h. $8 * 4 =$ _____	h. $24 \div 3 =$ _____
i. $10 \cdot 10 =$ _____	i. $63 / 9 =$ _____	i. $0 \cdot 5 =$ _____	i. $20 / 4 =$ _____
j. $9 \times 6 =$ _____	j. $50 \div 10 =$ _____	j. $1 \times 6 =$ _____	j. $27 \div 3 =$ _____
k. $5 * 7 =$ _____	k. $8 / 2 =$ _____	k. $5 * 4 =$ _____	k. $12 / 4 =$ _____
l. $10 \cdot 5 =$ _____	l. $15 \div 5 =$ _____	l. $8 \cdot 0 =$ _____	l. $5 \div 1 =$ _____
m. $8 \times 2 =$ _____	m. $90 / 10 =$ _____	m. $9 \times 3 =$ _____	m. $21 / 3 =$ _____
n. $6 * 10 =$ _____	n. $35 \div 5 =$ _____	n. $4 * 4 =$ _____	n. $1 \div 1 =$ _____
o. $2 * 9 =$ _____	o. $27 / 9 =$ _____	o. $10 \cdot 1 =$ _____	o. $16 / 4 =$ _____
p. $9 \cdot 6 =$ _____	p. $10 \div 10 =$ _____	p. $4 \times 3 =$ _____	p. $9 \div 3 =$ _____
q. $1 \times 5 =$ _____	q. $54 / 9 =$ _____	q. $7 * 4 =$ _____	q. $32 / 4 =$ _____
r. $5 * 5 =$ _____	r. $72 \div 9 =$ _____	r. $3 \cdot 7 =$ _____	r. $8 \div 1 =$ _____
s. $10 \cdot 7 =$ _____	s. $80 / 10 =$ _____	s. $0 \times 1 =$ _____	s. $24 / 4 =$ _____
t. $5 \times 8 =$ _____	t. $36 \div 9 =$ _____	t. $10 * 1 =$ _____	t. $18 \div 3 =$ _____

Name _____

PATH to FLUENCY Answers to Dashes 1–8

Use this sheet to check your answers to the Dashes on pages 85 and 86.

Dash 1 2s and 5s ×	Dash 2 2s and 5s ÷	Dash 3 9s and 10s ×	Dash 4 9s and 10s ÷	Dash 5 3s and 4s ×	Dash 6 3s and 4s ÷	Dash 7 0s and 1s ×	Dash 8 1s and $n \div n$ ÷
a. 12	a. 9	a. 90	a. 10	a. 27	a. 3	a. 0	a. 1
b. 45	b. 5	b. 30	b. 1	b. 8	b. 5	b. 4	b. 8
c. 14	c. 4	c. 9	c. 3	c. 18	c. 7	c. 0	c. 1
d. 40	d. 9	d. 20	d. 9	d. 40	d. 4	d. 8	d. 6
e. 8	e. 8	e. 81	e. 7	e. 3	e. 3	e. 0	e. 1
f. 15	f. 4	f. 60	f. 5	f. 4	f. 8	f. 3	f. 4
g. 2	g. 2	g. 36	g. 1	g. 30	g. 6	g. 0	g. 1
h. 35	h. 8	h. 100	h. 6	h. 20	h. 6	h. 2	h. 2
i. 18	i. 10	i. 18	i. 5	i. 9	i. 10	i. 0	i. 1
j. 20	j. 7	j. 10	j. 3	j. 16	j. 4	j. 10	j. 9
k. 10	k. 3	k. 63	k. 2	k. 24	k. 2	k. 0	k. 1
l. 5	l. 3	l. 50	l. 8	l. 28	l. 7	l. 1	l. 5
m. 4	m. 7	m. 72	m. 4	m. 6	m. 8	m. 0	m. 1
n. 50	n. 1	n. 70	n. 2	n. 36	n. 5	n. 5	n. 1
o. 20	o. 5	o. 27	o. 6	o. 21	o. 9	o. 0	o. 7
p. 30	p. 2	p. 40	p. 10	p. 12	p. 5	p. 6	p. 1
q. 6	q. 3	q. 45	q. 9	q. 15	q. 9	q. 0	q. 10
r. 25	r. 6	r. 80	r. 7	r. 24	r. 9	r. 0	r. 1
s. 16	s. 1	s. 54	s. 8	s. 12	s. 2	s. 7	s. 3
t. 30	t. 9	t. 90	t. 4	t. 32	t. 10	t. 9	t. 1

PATH to FLUENCY Answers to Dashes 9–12, 9A–12A

Use this sheet to check your answers to the Dashes on pages 87 and 88.

Dash 9 ×	Dash 10 ÷	Dash 11 ×	Dash 12 ÷	Dash 9A ×	Dash 10A ÷	Dash 11A ×	Dash 12A ÷
a. 20	a. 4	a. 0	a. 3	a. 81	a. 6	a. 0	a. 10
b. 30	b. 5	b. 24	b. 5	b. 20	b. 9	b. 36	b. 10
c. 72	c. 3	c. 9	c. 7	c. 30	c. 8	c. 24	c. 4
d. 12	d. 7	d. 9	d. 1	d. 27	d. 3	d. 0	d. 2
e. 35	e. 9	e. 32	e. 4	e. 80	e. 5	e. 24	e. 1
f. 50	f. 10	f. 0	f. 3	f. 12	f. 9	f. 9	f. 7
g. 16	g. 7	g. 6	g. 8	g. 72	g. 7	g. 9	g. 7
h. 60	h. 7	h. 12	h. 8	h. 8	h. 10	h. 32	h. 8
i. 27	i. 3	i. 28	i. 6	i. 100	i. 7	i. 0	i. 5
j. 18	j. 9	j. 21	j. 6	j. 54	j. 5	j. 6	j. 9
k. 40	k. 1	k. 0	k. 10	k. 35	k. 4	k. 20	k. 3
l. 70	l. 5	l. 10	l. 10	l. 50	l. 3	l. 0	l. 5
m. 25	m. 6	m. 16	m. 4	m. 16	m. 9	m. 27	m. 7
n. 5	n. 3	n. 27	n. 2	n. 60	n. 7	n. 16	n. 1
o. 54	o. 8	o. 0	o. 1	o. 18	o. 3	o. 10	o. 4
p. 100	p. 8	p. 20	p. 7	p. 54	p. 1	p. 12	p. 3
q. 8	q. 8	q. 6	q. 7	q. 5	q. 6	q. 28	q. 8
r. 80	r. 9	r. 24	r. 8	r. 25	r. 8	r. 21	r. 8
s. 27	s. 4	s. 36	s. 5	s. 70	s. 8	s. 0	s. 6
t. 81	t. 6	t. 0	t. 9	t. 40	t. 4	t. 10	t. 6

Solve Word Problems with 2s, 3s, 4s, 5s, and 9s

Write an equation and solve the problem.   *Show your work.*

1 Toni counted 36 chairs in the restaurant. Each table had 4 chairs. How many tables were there?

_____

2 One wall of an art gallery has 5 rows of paintings. Each row has row of 9 paintings. How many paintings are on the wall?

_____

3 Josh's muffin pan is an array with 4 rows and 6 columns. How many muffins can Josh make in the pan?

_____

4 To get ready for the school spelling bee, Tanya studied 3 hours each night for an entire week. How many hours did she study?

_____

5 The 14 trumpet players in the marching band lined up in 2 equal rows. How many trumpet players were in each row?

_____

6 The Sunnyside Riding Stable has 9 horses. The owners are going to buy new horseshoes for all the horses. How many horseshoes are needed?

_____

Make Sense of Problems

Write an equation and solve the problem.

Show your work.

7 Sadie plans to read 2 books every month for 6 months. How many books will she read during that time?

_____

8 A farmer sells pumpkins for $5 each. On Friday the farmer made $35 from the sale of pumpkins. How many pumpkins did the farmer sell on Friday?

_____

9 Each student collected 10 leaves for a group science project. If the group collected a total of 80 leaves, how many students are in the group?

_____

Write a Word Problem

10 Write and solve a word problem that can be solved using the equation $4 \times 1 = n$.

_____

_____

✓ **Check Understanding**

Write a related multiplication or division equation for the equation you wrote for Problem 9.

_____

Build Fluency with 0s, 1s, 2s, 3s, 4s, 5s, 9s, and 10s

(PATH to FLUENCY) **Math and Hobbies**

A hobby is something you do for fun. Owen's hobby is photography. He took pictures and displayed them on a poster.

Solve.

1 How many photos did Owen display on the poster? Explain the different strategies you can use to find the answer. Write an equation for each.

_____

_____

_____

_____

2 What other ways could Owen have arranged the photos in an array on a poster?

_____

_____

PATH to FLUENCY What is Your Hobby?

Carina asked some third graders, "What is your hobby?"
The answers are shown under the photos.

Dancing
Four third graders
said dancing.

Photography
Eight more than
dancing
said photography.

Reading
Six less than
photography said
reading.

Games
Eight third graders
said games.

3 Use the information above to complete the chart below.

What is Your Hobby?	
Hobby	Number of Students
Dancing	
Photography	
Games	
Reading	

4 Use the chart to complete the pictograph below.

Hobbies	
Dancing	
Photography	
Games	
Reading	

Each ☐ stands for 2 third graders.

5 How many third graders answered Carina's question?

_____

Focus on Mathematical Practices

Write an equation and solve the problem.

Show your work.

1 Mrs. Andrews divides 45 milliliters of water equally into 9 test tubes for her science class. How many milliliters of water does she place in each test tube?

_____

_____

2 The chorus members singing at a school concert stand in 3 rows, with 9 members in each row. How many chorus members are there singing altogether?

_____

3 The 32 students on a field trip are organized into groups of 4 for a tour. How many groups of students are there?

_____

Solve.

4 Susan arranges her model cars in 6 rows, with 3 cars in each row. How else can Susan arrange her model cars in equal rows?

_____

_____

5 Philip bakes 8 muffins and gives each of his friends 1 muffin. He has no muffins left over. To how many of his friends does Philip give a muffin?

_____

Fluency Check 1

Name ______________________ Date ______________________

Add.

1. $1 + 6 = \square$
2. $3 + 8 = \square$
3. $8 + 5 = \square$
4. $5 + 3 = \square$
5. $2 + 8 = \square$
6. $3 + 9 = \square$
7. $4 + 5 = \square$
8. $6 + 7 = \square$
9. $5 + 9 = \square$
10. $\begin{array}{r} 7 \\ +\ 5 \\ \hline \end{array}$
11. $\begin{array}{r} 6 \\ +\ 9 \\ \hline \end{array}$
12. $\begin{array}{r} 8 \\ +\ 0 \\ \hline \end{array}$
13. $\begin{array}{r} 9 \\ +\ 7 \\ \hline \end{array}$
14. $\begin{array}{r} 8 \\ +\ 6 \\ \hline \end{array}$
15. $\begin{array}{r} 7 \\ +\ 8 \\ \hline \end{array}$

1 Write a multiplication equation for the array.

_____

2 Write the numbers that complete the pattern.

| 6 | 7 | 8 | 9 | 72 | 81 |

4	×	9	=	36
5	×	9	=	45
☐	×	9	=	54
7	×	☐	=	63
8	×	9	=	☐

3 Read the problem. Choose the type of problem it is.
Then write an equation to solve the problem.

Pala is drawing tulips on posters. She draws
4 tulips each on 9 posters. How many tulips
does Pala draw on the posters?

The type of problem is

| array multiplication |
| array division |
| equal groups multiplication |

.

Equation: _____

_____ tulips

4 Draw a line to match the equation on the left with the
unknown number on the right.

$\frac{45}{5} = $ ▪ •   • 0

$9 \times$ ▪ $= 0$ •   • 5

▪ $\times 3 = 15$ •   • 8

▪ $\div 3 = 7$ •   • 9

$72 \div$ ▪ $= 9$ •   • 14

$7 \times 2 = $ ▪ •   • 21

8 Select the situation which could be represented by the multiplication expression 5 × 7. Mark all that apply.

Ⓐ total number of stamps on 5 pages with 7 stamps on each page

Ⓑ total number of stamps when there are 5 stamps on one page and 7 stamps on another page

Ⓒ 5 stamps divided evenly onto 7 pages

Ⓓ 5 more stamps than on a page with 7 stamps

Make a drawing for the problem. Then write an equation and solve it.

9 The 28 desks in Mr. Becker's class are arranged in 7 equal rows. How many desks are in each row?

10 Michelle's bookcase has 3 shelves. It holds 9 books on each shelf. How many books will fit in the bookcase?

11 Rami counts 6 birds sitting on each of 5 different wires. How many birds does Rami count?

12 Use properties of multiplication to solve.

12a. $9 \times 6 = \boxed{} \times 9$

12b. $\boxed{} \times 10 = 10$

12c. $\boxed{} \times 2 = 0$

12d. $(3 \times \boxed{}) \times 5 = 3 \times (4 \times 5)$

13 Chloe buys 10 balloons for her sisters. She gives 5 balloons to each sister and has none left.

Part A

How many sisters does Chloe have? Write an equation and solve the problem.

Equation: _____

_____ sisters

Part B

Solve the problem in a different way. Tell how the ways are alike and different.

Make Travel Plans

A group of 40 students is going to a science museum. Some parents have offered to drive the students. The table below shows the vehicles they can use.

Type of Vehicle	Number of Students the Vehicle Can Hold	Number of Vehicles Available
Small Car	2	3
Large Car	3	10
Crossover	4	4
Minivan	5	4
SUV	6	5

1. Plan two different ways the 40 students can ride to the museum. For each plan, be sure all the students have a ride. Describe the plan with words, pictures, equations, or a table. Explain which plan is better and tell why.

2. Plan a way to use the least number of vehicles. Describe the plan with words, pictures, equations, or a table. Explain why the plan uses the least number of vehicles.

3 If there is another trip, different parents will drive.
Will that change the least number of cars that
are needed? Explain your answer and show how
you know.

4 How would you change your strategy for planning
the trip if each vehicle needs to have an adult
other than the driver?

Dear Family:

In this unit, students learn multiplications and divisions for 6s, 7s, and 8s, while continuing to practice the rest of the basic multiplications and divisions covered in Unit 1.

Although students practice all the 6s, 7s, and 8s multiplications, they really have only six new multiplications to learn: 6×6, 6×7, 6×8, 7×7, 7×8, and 8×8. The lessons for these multiplications focus on strategies for finding the products using multiplications they know.

This unit also focuses on word problems. Students are presented with a variety of one-step and two-step word problems.

Here is an example of a two-step problem:

> A roller coaster has 7 cars. Each car has 4 seats. If there were 3 empty seats, how many people were on the roller coaster?

Students use the language and context of each problem to determine which operation or operations—multiplication, division, addition, or subtraction—they must use to solve it. Students use a variety of methods to solve two-step word problems.

Please continue to help your child get faster on multiplications and divisions. Use all of the practice materials that your child has brought home. Your support is crucial to your child's learning.

Please contact me if you have any questions or comments.

Thank you.

Sincerely,
Your child's teacher

CC SS Unit 2 addresses the following standards from the Common Core State Standards for Mathematics: **3.OA.A.1, 3.OA.A.2, 3.OA.A.3, 3.OA.A.4, 3.OA.B.5, 3.OA.B.6, 3.OA.C.7, 3.OA.D.8, 3.OA.D.9, 3.NBT.A.3, 3.MD.C.5, 3.MD.C.5.a, 3.MD.C.5.b, 3.MD.C.6, 3.MD.C.7, 3.MD.C.7.a, 3.MD.C.7.b, and all** Mathematical Practices.

Estimada familia:

En esta unidad los estudiantes aprenden las multiplicaciones y divisiones con el 6, el 7 y el 8, mientras siguen practicando las demás multiplicaciones y divisiones que se presentaron en la Unidad 1.

Aunque los estudiantes practican todas las multiplicaciones con el 6, el 7 y el 8, en realidad sólo tienen que aprender seis multiplicaciones nuevas: 6×6, 6×7, 6×8, 7×7, 7×8 y 8×8. Las lecciones acerca de estas multiplicaciones se centran en estrategias para hallar los productos usando multiplicaciones que ya se conocen.

Esta unidad también se centra en problemas verbales. A los estudiantes se les presenta una variedad de problemas de uno y de dos pasos.

> Este es un ejemplo de un problema de dos pasos:
> Una montaña rusa tiene 7 carros. Cada carro tiene 7 asientos. Si hay 3 asientos vacíos. Cuántas personas había en la montaña rusa?

Los estudiantes aprovechan el lenguaje y el contexto de cada problema para determinar qué operación u operaciones deben usar para resolverlo: multiplicación, división, suma o resta. Los estudiantes usan una variedad de métodos para resolver problemas de dos pasos.

Por favor continúe ayudando a su niño a practicar las multiplicaciones y las divisiones. Use todos los materiales de práctica que su niño ha llevado a casa. Su apoyo es importante para el aprendizaje de su niño.

Si tiene alguna duda o pregunta, por favor comuníquese conmigo.

Atentamente,
El maestro de su niño

En la Unidad 2 se aplican los siguientes estándares de los Estándares estatales comunes de matemáticas: **3.OA.A.1, 3.OA.A.2, 3.OA.A.3, 3.OA.A.4, 3.OA.B.5, 3.OA.B.6, 3.OA.C.7, 3.OA.D.8, 3.OA.D.9, 3.NBT.A.3, 3.MD.C.5, 3.MD.C.5.a, 3.MD.C.5.b, 3.MD.C.6, 3.MD.C.7, 3.MD.C.7.a, 3.MD.C.7.b, y todos los de** Prácticas matemáticas.

expression

Order of
Operations

square
number

A combination of numbers, variables, and/or operation signs. An expression does not have an equal sign.

Examples:
$4 + 7$ $a - 3$

A set of rules that state the order in which the operations in an expression should be done.

STEP 1: Perform operations inside parentheses first.
STEP 2: Multiply and divide from left to right.
STEP 3: Add and subtract from left to right.

The product of a whole number and itself.

Example:

$$4 \times 4 = 16$$

↑

square number

PATH to FLUENCY Explore Patterns with 6s

What patterns do you see below?

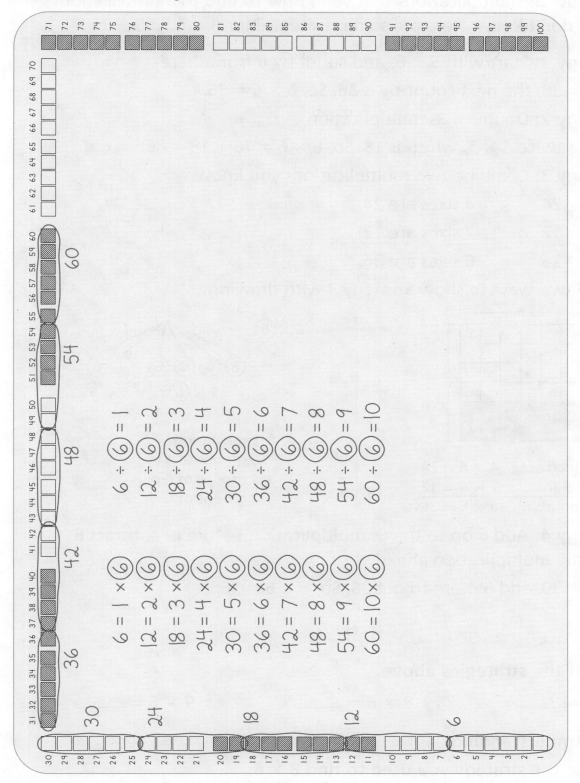

 Content Standards **3.OA.A.4, 3.OA.B.5, 3.OA.B.6, 3.OA.C.7, 3.OA.D.9, 3.MD.C.7, 3.MD.C.7.c** Mathematical Practices **MP1, MP5, MP6**

Multiply and Divide with 6 **107**

PATH to FLUENCY Strategies for Multiplying with 6

You can use 6s multiplications that you know to find 6s multiplications that you don't know. Here are some strategies for 6×6.

- **Strategy 1:** Start with 5×6, and count by 6 from there.

  $5 \times 6 = 30$, the next count-by is 36. So, $6 \times 6 = 36$.

- **Strategy 2:** Double a 3s multiplication.

  6×6 is twice 6×3, which is 18. So, $6 \times 6 = 18 + 18 = 36$.

- **Strategy 3:** Combine two multiplications you know.

$4 \times 6 = 24$	4 sixes are 24.
$2 \times 6 = 12$	2 sixes are 12.
$6 \times 6 = 36$	6 sixes are 36.

Here are two ways to show Strategy 3 with drawings.

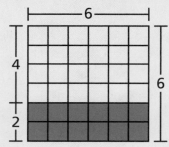

unshaded area: $4 \times 6 = 24$
shaded area: $2 \times 6 = 12$
total area: $6 \times 6 = 36$

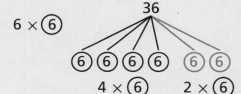

Explanation:
6 groups of 6 is
4 groups of 6 plus
2 groups of 6.

- **Strategy 4:** Add 6 on to the 6s multiplication before or subtract 6 from the multiplication ahead.

  $5 \times 6 = 30$, add 6 more to get 36. So, $6 \times 6 = 36$.

Apply Strategies for 6s Multiplications

Use any of the strategies above.

1 $7 \times 6 =$ _____   2 $8 \times 6 =$ _____   3 $9 \times 6 =$ _____

Check Understanding

Describe the strategy you used to find 8×6.

PATH to FLUENCY

Name _____

Study Sheet C

6s

Count-bys	Mixed Up ×	Mixed Up ÷
1 × 6 = 6	10 × 6 = 60	54 ÷ 6 = 9
2 × 6 = 12	8 × 6 = 48	30 ÷ 6 = 5
3 × 6 = 18	2 × 6 = 12	12 ÷ 6 = 2
4 × 6 = 24	6 × 6 = 36	60 ÷ 6 = 10
5 × 6 = 30	4 × 6 = 24	48 ÷ 6 = 8
6 × 6 = 36	1 × 6 = 6	36 ÷ 6 = 6
7 × 6 = 42	9 × 6 = 54	6 ÷ 6 = 1
8 × 6 = 48	3 × 6 = 18	42 ÷ 6 = 7
9 × 6 = 54	7 × 6 = 42	18 ÷ 6 = 3
10 × 6 = 60	5 × 6 = 30	24 ÷ 6 = 4

7s

Count-bys	Mixed Up ×	Mixed Up ÷
1 × 7 = 7	6 × 7 = 42	70 ÷ 7 = 10
2 × 7 = 14	8 × 7 = 56	14 ÷ 7 = 2
3 × 7 = 21	5 × 7 = 35	28 ÷ 7 = 4
4 × 7 = 28	9 × 7 = 63	56 ÷ 7 = 8
5 × 7 = 35	4 × 7 = 28	42 ÷ 7 = 6
6 × 7 = 42	10 × 7 = 70	63 ÷ 7 = 9
7 × 7 = 49	3 × 7 = 21	21 ÷ 7 = 3
8 × 7 = 56	1 × 7 = 7	49 ÷ 7 = 7
9 × 7 = 63	7 × 7 = 49	7 ÷ 7 = 1
10 × 7 = 70	2 × 7 = 14	35 ÷ 7 = 5

8s

Count-bys	Mixed Up ×	Mixed Up ÷
1 × 8 = 8	6 × 8 = 48	16 ÷ 8 = 2
2 × 8 = 16	10 × 8 = 80	40 ÷ 8 = 5
3 × 8 = 24	7 × 8 = 56	72 ÷ 8 = 9
4 × 8 = 32	2 × 8 = 16	32 ÷ 8 = 4
5 × 8 = 40	4 × 8 = 32	8 ÷ 8 = 1
6 × 8 = 48	8 × 8 = 64	80 ÷ 8 = 10
7 × 8 = 56	5 × 8 = 40	64 ÷ 8 = 8
8 × 8 = 64	9 × 8 = 72	24 ÷ 8 = 3
9 × 8 = 72	3 × 8 = 24	56 ÷ 8 = 7
10 × 8 = 80	1 × 8 = 8	48 ÷ 8 = 6

Squares

Count-bys	Mixed Up ×	Mixed Up ÷
1 × 1 = 1	3 × 3 = 9	25 ÷ 5 = 5
2 × 2 = 4	9 × 9 = 81	4 ÷ 2 = 2
3 × 3 = 9	4 × 4 = 16	81 ÷ 9 = 9
4 × 4 = 16	6 × 6 = 36	9 ÷ 3 = 3
5 × 5 = 25	2 × 2 = 4	36 ÷ 6 = 6
6 × 6 = 36	7 × 7 = 49	100 ÷ 10 = 10
7 × 7 = 49	10 × 10 = 100	16 ÷ 4 = 4
8 × 8 = 64	1 × 1 = 1	49 ÷ 7 = 7
9 × 9 = 81	5 × 5 = 25	1 ÷ 1 = 1
10 × 10 = 100	8 × 8 = 64	64 ÷ 8 = 8

Study Sheet C

PATH to FLUENCY Unknown Number Puzzles

Complete each Unknown Number puzzle.

1

×	5	2	
	30		48
4		8	32
	45		72

2

×		3	
6	30		42
4			28
	40	24	56

3

×	4		8
9		81	
	12		24
	20	45	40

4

×		3	
	60		20
6	36		
	18	9	6

5

×	8		2
7		28	
	16	8	
	32	16	8

6

×	9		
8		56	24
	54	42	18
5			15

7

×	8		7
8		40	
	32	20	28
	24	15	

8

×	3	4	
	27	36	81
7			63
			18

9

×			10
8	48	16	
7	42	14	
	36		60

Content Standards **3.OA.A.1, 3.OA.A.2, 3.OA.A.3, 3.OA.A.4, 3.OA.B.6, 3.OA.C.7, 3.MD.C.5, 3.MD.C.5.a, 3.MD.C.5.b, 3.MD.C.6, 3.MD.C.7.a, 3.MD.C.7.b**
Mathematical Practices **MP1, MP2, MP3, MP4, MP5, MP6**

Tiling and Multiplying to Find Area

Use inch tiles to find the area. Then label the side lengths and find the area using multiplication.

10

_____

Area: _____ _____

11

_____

_____

Area: _____ _____

12

_____

_____

Area: _____ _____

Solve Area Word Problems

PATH to FLUENCY Check Sheet 7: 6s and 8s

6s Multiplications	6s Divisions	8s Multiplications	8s Divisions
10 × 6 = 60	24 / 6 = 4	2 × 8 = 16	72 / 8 = 9
6 • 4 = 24	48 ÷ 6 = 8	8 • 10 = 80	16 ÷ 8 = 2
6 * 7 = 42	60 / 6 = 10	3 * 8 = 24	40 / 8 = 5
2 × 6 = 12	12 ÷ 6 = 2	9 × 8 = 72	8 ÷ 8 = 1
6 • 5 = 30	42 / 6 = 7	8 • 4 = 32	80 / 8 = 10
6 * 8 = 48	30 ÷ 6 = 5	8 * 7 = 56	48 ÷ 8 = 6
9 × 6 = 54	6 / 6 = 1	5 × 8 = 40	56 / 8 = 7
6 • 1 = 6	18 ÷ 6 = 3	8 • 6 = 48	24 ÷ 8 = 3
6 * 6 = 36	54 / 6 = 9	1 * 8 = 8	64 / 8 = 8
6 × 3 = 18	36 / 6 = 6	8 × 8 = 64	32 / 8 = 4
6 • 6 = 36	48 ÷ 6 = 8	4 • 8 = 32	80 ÷ 8 = 10
5 * 6 = 30	12 / 6 = 2	6 * 8 = 48	56 / 8 = 7
6 × 2 = 12	24 ÷ 6 = 4	8 × 3 = 24	8 ÷ 8 = 1
4 • 6 = 24	60 / 6 = 10	7 • 8 = 56	24 / 8 = 3
6 * 9 = 54	6 ÷ 6 = 1	8 * 2 = 16	64 ÷ 8 = 8
8 × 6 = 48	42 / 6 = 7	8 × 9 = 72	16 / 8 = 2
7 • 6 = 42	18 ÷ 6 = 3	8 • 1 = 8	72 ÷ 8 = 9
6 * 10 = 60	36 ÷ 6 = 6	8 * 8 = 64	32 ÷ 8 = 4
1 × 6 = 6	30 / 6 = 5	10 × 8 = 80	40 / 8 = 5
4 • 6 = 24	54 ÷ 6 = 9	5 • 8 = 40	48 ÷ 8 = 6

Check Sheet 7: 6s and 8s

Name _____

Explore Patterns with 8s

What patterns do you see below?

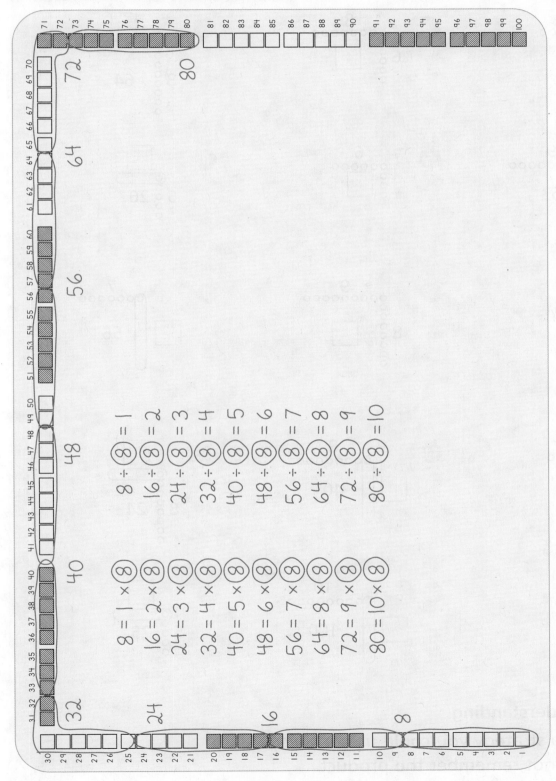

PATH to FLUENCY   Fast Array Drawings

Find the unknown number for each fast array drawing.

1 6
□ | 42

2 8
6 □

3 □
8 64

4 9
□ 63

5 6
4 □

6 □
5 20

7 □
9 45

8 9
8 □

9 7
□ 56

10 7
7 □

11 8
□ 40

12 □
8 24

13 6
6 □

14 10
□ 100

15 □
5 25

✓ Check Understanding

Describe a strategy you could use to find 9 × 8
if you do not remember the product.

Multiply and Divide with 8

Name _____

Identify the Type and Choose the Operation

Solve. Then circle what type of problem it is and what operation you use.

1. Students in Mr. Till's class hung their paintings on the wall. They made 6 rows, with 5 paintings in each row. How many paintings did the students hang?

   _____

   Circle one: array   equal groups   area
   Circle one: multiplication   division

2. Write your own problem that is the same type as Problem 1. _____

   _____

   _____

3. There are 8 goldfish in each tank at the pet store. If there are 56 goldfish in all, how many tanks are there?

   _____

   Circle one: array   equal groups   area
   Circle one: multiplication   division

4. Write your own problem that is the same type as Problem 3. _____

   _____

   _____

5. Pierre built a rectangular pen for his rabbits. The pen is 4 feet wide and 6 feet long. What is the area of the pen? _____

   Circle one: array   equal groups   area
   Circle one: multiplication   division

CC SS Content Standards **3.OA.A.1, 3.OA.A.2, 3.OA.A.3, 3.OA.A.4, 3.OA.B.6, 3.OA.C.7** Mathematical Practices **MP1, MP3, MP4, MP6**

Write Word Problems and Equations **119**

PATH to FLUENCY Identify the Type and Choose the Operation (continued)

6 Write your own problem that is the same type as Problem 5. _____

_____

_____

7 Paulo arranged 72 baseball cards in rows and columns. If there were 9 rows, into how many columns did he arrange the cards? _____

Circle one: array   equal groups   area
Circle one: multiplication   division

8 Write your own problem that is the same type as Problem 7. _____

_____

_____

9 The store sells bottles of juice in six-packs. Mr. Lee bought 9 six-packs for a picnic. How many bottles did he buy? _____

Circle one: array   equal groups   area
Circle one: multiplication   division

10 Write your own problem that is the same type as Problem 9. _____

_____

_____

11 **Math Journal** Write an area multiplication problem. Draw a fast array to solve it.

Name

What's the Error?

Dear Math Students,

Today my teacher asked me to find the answer to 8 × 6. Here is what I wrote:

8 × 6 = 14

Is my answer correct? If not, please correct my work and tell me what I did wrong.

Your friend,
Puzzled Penguin

12 Write an answer to the Puzzled Penguin.

_____

_____

Write and Solve Equations

Write an equation and solve the problem.

13 A large box of crayons holds 60 crayons. There are 10 crayons in each row. How many rows are there?

_____

_____

14 A sign covers 12 square feet. The sign is 4 feet long. How wide is the sign?

_____

_____

15 There are 28 students working on a project. There are 7 groups with an equal number of students in each group. How many students are in each group?

_____

_____

16 Amanda had 15 bracelets. She gave the same number of bracelets to 3 friends. How many bracelets did she give to each friend?

_____

_____

Write Word Problems and Equations **121**

Write and Solve Equations (continued)

Write an equation and solve the problem.

17 John has 24 baseball cards. He divided them equally among 6 friends. How many cards did each friend get?

_____

18 A third grade classroom has 3 tables for 24 students in the class. The same number of students sit at each table. How many students sit at a table?

_____

19 Marc bought 18 golf balls. The golf balls were packaged in boxes of 6. How many boxes of golf balls did Marc buy?

_____

20 Lara keeps her rock collection in a case that has 10 drawers. Each drawer can hold 6 rocks. How many rocks can the case hold?

_____

21 Write a problem that can be solved using the equation $54 \div 6 = n$, where n is the number in each group. Then solve the problem.

_____

_____

_____

✓ **Check Understanding**

Is Problem 19 an equal groups, array, or area problem?

_____

Write Word Problems and Equations

PATH to FLUENCY Check Sheet 8: 7s and Squares

7s Multiplications	7s Divisions	Squares Multiplications	Squares Divisions
4 × 7 = 28	14 / 7 = 2	8 × 8 = 64	81 / 9 = 9
7 • 2 = 14	28 ÷ 7 = 4	10 • 10 = 100	4 ÷ 2 = 2
7 * 8 = 56	70 / 7 = 10	3 * 3 = 9	25 / 5 = 5
7 × 7 = 49	56 ÷ 7 = 8	9 × 9 = 81	1 ÷ 1 = 1
7 • 1 = 7	42 / 7 = 6	4 • 4 = 16	100 / 10 = 10
7 * 10 = 70	63 ÷ 7 = 9	7 * 7 = 49	36 ÷ 6 = 6
3 × 7 = 21	7 / 7 = 1	5 × 5 = 25	49 / 7 = 7
7 • 6 = 42	49 ÷ 7 = 7	6 • 6 = 36	9 ÷ 3 = 3
5 * 7 = 35	21 / 7 = 3	1 * 1 = 1	64 / 8 = 8
7 × 9 = 63	35 / 7 = 5	5 * 5 = 25	16 / 4 = 4
7 • 4 = 28	7 ÷ 7 = 1	1 • 1 = 1	100 ÷ 10 = 10
9 * 7 = 63	63 / 7 = 9	3 • 3 = 9	49 / 7 = 7
2 × 7 = 14	14 ÷ 7 = 2	10 × 10 = 100	1 ÷ 1 = 1
7 • 5 = 35	70 / 7 = 10	4 × 4 = 16	9 / 3 = 3
8 * 7 = 56	21 ÷ 7 = 3	9 * 9 = 81	64 ÷ 8 = 8
7 × 3 = 21	49 / 7 = 7	2 × 2 = 4	4 / 2 = 2
6 • 7 = 42	28 ÷ 7 = 4	6 * 6 = 36	81 ÷ 9 = 9
10 * 7 = 70	56 ÷ 7 = 8	7 × 7 = 49	16 ÷ 4 = 4
1 × 7 = 7	35 / 7 = 5	5 • 5 = 25	25 / 5 = 5
7 • 7 = 49	42 ÷ 7 = 6	8 • 8 = 64	36 ÷ 6 = 6

Check Sheet 8: 7s and Squares

Name _____

PATH to FLUENCY Explore Square Numbers

Write an equation to show the area of each large square.

1 $1 \times 1 = 1$ **2** _____   **3** _____   **4** _____

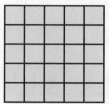   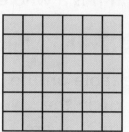

5 _____   **6** _____

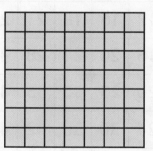   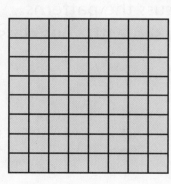

7 _____   **8** _____

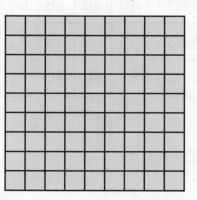   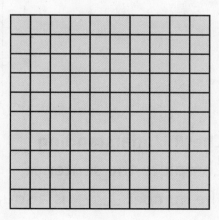

9 _____   **10** _____

CC SS Content Standards **3.OA.A.4, 3.OA.B.6, 3.OA.C.7, 3.OA.D.9, 3.MD.C.7.b**
Mathematical Practices **MP2, MP5, MP7**

Look for Patterns

VOCABULARY
square numbers

11 List the products in Exercises 1–10 in order.
Discuss the patterns you see with your class.

_____

The numbers you listed in Exercise 11 are called **square numbers** because they are the areas of squares with whole-number lengths of sides. A square number is the product of a whole number and itself. So, if n is a whole number, $n \times n$ is a square number.

Patterns on the Multiplication Table

12 In the table on the right, circle the products that are square numbers. Discuss the patterns you see with your class.

X	1	2	3	4	5	6	7	8	9	10
1	1	2	3	4	5	6	7	8	9	10
2	2	4	6	8	10	12	14	16	18	20
3	3	6	9	12	15	18	21	24	27	30
4	4	8	12	16	20	24	28	32	36	40
5	5	10	15	20	25	30	35	40	45	50
6	6	12	18	24	30	36	42	48	54	60
7	7	14	21	28	35	42	49	56	63	70
8	8	16	24	32	40	48	56	64	72	80
9	9	18	27	36	45	54	63	72	81	90
10	10	20	30	40	50	60	70	80	90	100

✓**Check Understanding**

Complete the sentence.

The number _____ is a square number because _____

_____

Square Numbers

PATH to FLUENCY **Check Sheet 9: 6s, 7s, and 8s**

6s, 7s, and 8s Multiplications	6s, 7s, and 8s Multiplications	6s, 7s, and 8s Divisions	6s, 7s, and 8s Divisions
$1 \times 6 = 6$	$0 \times 8 = 0$	$24 / 6 = 4$	$54 / 6 = 9$
$6 \cdot 7 = 42$	$6 \cdot 2 = 12$	$21 \div 7 = 3$	$24 \div 8 = 3$
$3 * 8 = 24$	$4 * 7 = 28$	$16 / 8 = 2$	$14 / 7 = 2$
$6 \times 2 = 12$	$8 \times 3 = 24$	$24 \div 8 = 3$	$32 \div 8 = 4$
$7 \cdot 5 = 35$	$5 \cdot 6 = 30$	$14 / 7 = 2$	$18 / 6 = 3$
$8 * 4 = 32$	$7 * 2 = 14$	$30 \div 6 = 5$	$56 \div 7 = 8$
$6 \times 6 = 36$	$3 \times 8 = 24$	$35 / 7 = 5$	$40 / 8 = 5$
$8 \cdot 7 = 56$	$6 \cdot 4 = 24$	$24 \div 8 = 3$	$35 \div 7 = 5$
$9 * 8 = 72$	$0 * 7 = 0$	$18 / 6 = 3$	$12 / 6 = 2$
$6 \times 10 = 60$	$8 \times 1 = 8$	$12 / 6 = 2$	$21 / 7 = 3$
$7 \cdot 1 = 7$	$8 \cdot 6 = 48$	$42 \div 7 = 6$	$16 \div 8 = 2$
$8 * 3 = 24$	$7 * 9 = 63$	$56 / 8 = 7$	$42 / 6 = 7$
$5 \times 6 = 30$	$10 \times 8 = 80$	$49 \div 7 = 7$	$80 \div 8 = 10$
$4 \cdot 7 = 28$	$6 \cdot 10 = 60$	$16 / 8 = 2$	$36 / 6 = 6$
$2 * 8 = 16$	$3 * 7 = 21$	$60 \div 6 = 10$	$7 \div 7 = 1$
$7 \times 7 = 49$	$8 \times 4 = 32$	$54 / 6 = 9$	$64 / 8 = 8$
$7 \cdot 6 = 42$	$6 \cdot 5 = 30$	$8 \div 8 = 1$	$24 \div 6 = 4$
$8 * 8 = 64$	$7 * 4 = 28$	$28 \div 7 = 4$	$21 \div 7 = 3$
$9 \times 6 = 54$	$8 \times 8 = 64$	$72 / 8 = 9$	$49 / 7 = 7$
$10 \cdot 7 = 70$	$6 \cdot 9 = 54$	$56 \div 7 = 8$	$24 \div 8 = 3$

PATH to FLUENCY **Check Sheet 10: 0s–10s**

0s–10s Multiplications	0s–10s Multiplications	0s–10s Divisions	0s–10s Divisions
9 × 0 = 0	9 × 4 = 36	9 / 1 = 9	90 / 10 = 9
1 • 1 = 1	5 • 9 = 45	12 ÷ 3 = 4	64 ÷ 8 = 8
2 * 3 = 6	6 * 10 = 60	14 / 2 = 7	15 / 5 = 3
1 × 3 = 3	7 × 3 = 21	20 ÷ 4 = 5	12 ÷ 6 = 2
5 • 4 = 20	5 • 3 = 15	10 / 5 = 2	14 / 7 = 2
7 * 5 = 35	4 * 1 = 4	48 ÷ 8 = 6	45 ÷ 9 = 5
6 × 9 = 54	7 × 5 = 35	35 / 7 = 5	8 / 1 = 8
4 • 7 = 28	6 • 3 = 18	60 ÷ 6 = 10	30 ÷ 3 = 10
1 * 8 = 8	8 * 7 = 56	81 / 9 = 9	16 / 4 = 4
9 × 8 = 72	5 × 8 = 40	20 / 10 = 2	8 / 2 = 4
2 • 10 = 20	9 • 9 = 81	16 ÷ 2 = 8	80 ÷ 10 = 8
0 * 7 = 0	9 * 10 = 90	30 / 5 = 6	36 / 4 = 9
4 × 1 = 4	0 × 0 = 0	49 ÷ 7 = 7	25 ÷ 5 = 5
2 • 4 = 8	1 • 0 = 0	60 / 6 = 10	42 / 7 = 6
10 * 3 = 30	1 * 6 = 6	30 ÷ 3 = 10	36 ÷ 6 = 6
8 × 4 = 32	7 × 2 = 14	8 / 1 = 8	90 / 9 = 10
5 • 8 = 40	6 • 3 = 18	16 ÷ 4 = 4	24 ÷ 8 = 3
4 * 6 = 24	4 * 5 = 20	16 ÷ 8 = 2	6 ÷ 2 = 3
7 × 6 = 42	6 × 6 = 36	40 / 10 = 4	9 / 3 = 3
1 • 8 = 8	10 • 7 = 70	36 ÷ 9 = 4	1 ÷ 1 = 1

© Houghton Mifflin Harcourt Publishing Company

Check Sheet 10: 0s–10s

PATH to FLUENCY Play Quotient Match and Division Blockout

Read the rules for playing a game.
Then play the game.

Rules for Quotient Match

Number of players: 2 or 3

What each player will need: Division Strategy Cards for 6s, 7s, and 8s

1. Shuffle the cards. Put the division cards, sides without answers, face up on the table in 6 rows of 4.

2. Players take turns. On each turn, a player chooses three cards that he or she thinks have the same quotient and turns them over.

3. If all three cards do have the same quotient the player takes them. If the cards do not have the same quotient, the player turns them back over so the without answers side is up.

4. Play continues until no cards remain.

Rules for Division Blockout

Number of players: 3

What each player will need: *Blockout* Game Board (TRB M70), Division Strategy Cards for 6s, 7s, and 8s

1. Players do not write anything on the game board. The first row is for 6s, the second row for 7s, and the third row for 8s, as indicated in the gray column on the left.

2. Each player shuffles his or her Division Strategy Cards for 6s, 7s, 8s, making sure the division sides without answers are face up.

3. Repeat Steps 2, 3, and 4 above. This time players will place the Strategy Cards in the appropriate row to indicate whether the unknown factor is 6, 7, or 8.

PATH to FLUENCY Play Multiplication Blockout

**Read the rules for playing *Multiplication Blockout*.
Then play the game.**

Rules for *Multiplication Block Out*

Number of players: 3

What each player will need: *Blockout* Game Board (TRB M70), Multiplication Strategy Cards for 6s, 7s, and 8s

1. Players choose any 5 factors from 2–9 and write them in any order in the gray spaces at the top of the game board. The players then write the products in the large white spaces. The result will be a scrambled multiplication table.

2. Once the table is complete, players cut off the gray row and gray column that show the factors so that only the products are showing. This will be the game board.

3. Each player shuffles his or her Multiplication Strategy Cards for 6s, 7s, and 8s, making sure the multiplication sides without answers are facing up.

4. One player says, "Go!" and everyone quickly places their Strategy Cards on the game board spaces showing the corresponding products. When a player's game board is completely filled, he or she calls out, "Blockout!"

5. Everyone stops and checks the player's work. If all the cards are placed correctly, that player is the winner. If the player has made a mistake, he or she sits out and waits for the next player to call out, "Blockout!"

PATH to FLUENCY Solve Word Problems with 6s, 7s, 8s

Write an equation and solve the problem.

1 Terri's class has 32 students. The students worked on an art project in groups of 4 students. How many groups were there?

_____

2 Kyle saw 9 ladybugs while he was camping. Each one had 6 legs. How many legs did the 9 ladybugs have in all?

_____

3 Adam walks 3 miles a day. How many miles does he walk in a week?

_____

4 Nancy's dog Rover eats 6 cups of food a day. In 8 days, how many cups of food does Rover eat?

_____

5 The school library has 72 books on the topic of weather. If Tanya arranged the books in 8 equal-sized stacks, how many books were in each stack?

_____

6 The 42 trumpet players in the marching band lined up in 6 equal rows. How many trumpet players were in each row?

_____

Solve Word Problems with 6s, 7s, and 8s (continued)

Write an equation and solve the problem.

7 Susan is having a party. She has 18 cups. She puts them in 6 equal stacks. How many cups are in each stack?

_____

8 Regina made an array with 7 rows of 9 blocks. How many blocks are in the array?

_____

9 Mr. Rodriguez plans to invite 40 students to a picnic. The invitations come in packs of 8. How many packs of invitations does Mr. Rodriguez need to buy?

_____

10 A classroom has 7 rows of 4 desks. How many desks are there in the classroom?

_____

11 Write a word problem for $48 \div 6$ where 6 is the size of the group.

_____

_____

12 Write a word problem for 7×9 where 9 is the number of items in one group.

_____

_____

✔ **Check Understanding**

Explain how you know when a word problem can be solved by using division.

Practice with 6s, 7s, and 8s

Name _____

Complete a Multiplication Table

1 Look at the factors to complete the Multiplication Table. Leave blanks for the products you do not know.

✕	1	2	3	4	5	6	7	8	9	10
1										
2										
3										
4										
5										
6										
7										
8										
9										
10										

2 Write the multiplications you need to practice.

_____

_____

_____

_____

_____

PATH to FLUENCY Scrambled Multiplication Tables

Complete each table.

A

×										
	6	30	54	60	42	24	18	12	48	36
	2	10	18	20	14	8	6	4	16	12
	10	50	90	100	70	40	30	20	80	60
	8	40	72	80	56	32	24	16	64	48
	5	25	45	50	35	20	15	10	40	30
	1	5	9	10	7	4	3	2	8	6
	9	45	81	90	63	36	27	18	72	54
	4	20	36	40	28	16	12	8	32	24
	7	35	63	70	49	28	21	14	56	42
	3	15	27	30	21	12	9	6	24	18

B

×										
	27	6	24	21	18	15	12	9	3	
	36	8	32	28	24		16	12	4	40
	9	2	8	7	6	5	4	3	1	10
	18	4	16	14		10	8	6	2	20
		14	56	49	42		28	21	7	
	72		64	56	48	40	32	24	8	80
	45	10	40		30	25	20	15	5	
	54	12	48	42	36	30	24	18	6	60
	90		80	70	60		40	30	10	100
	81	18	72		54	45	36	27	9	

C

×										
	100		20		70	50		90		10
	50	15		20	35		30		40	5
	10	3		4	7		6	9		1
		9		12	21	15		27	24	
		6	4	8			12	18	16	2
		12	8	16	28	20		36	32	
	90	27	18	36	63	45	54		72	
		18	12	24		30	36	54	48	6
		21		28	49		42		56	7
		24		32	56	40		72	64	8

D

×										
	48		42	12	36		18	6		30
	56	28		14		70	21		63	35
			70		60			10		50
		20	35		30		15	5	45	
	32			8		40			36	
	8	4		2			3	1		5
		8	14		12		6		18	10
	64		56		48	80	24	8		40
	72	36		18			27		81	
	24		21		18	30			3	27

© Houghton Mifflin Harcourt Publishing Company

✓ Check Understanding

Complete the sentences.

The numbers in the blue boxes are _____.

The numbers in the white boxes are _____.

Name

PATH to FLUENCY Dashes 13–16

Complete each Dash. Check your answers on page 141.

Dash 13 6s and 8s Multiplications	Dash 14 6s and 8s Divisions	Dash 15 7s and 8s Multiplications	Dash 16 7s and 8s Divisions
a. $6 \times 9 =$ _____	a. $72 / 8 =$ _____	a. $7 \times 3 =$ _____	a. $63 / 7 =$ _____
b. $8 * 2 =$ _____	b. $12 \div 6 =$ _____	b. $8 * 5 =$ _____	b. $80 \div 8 =$ _____
c. $4 \cdot 6 =$ _____	c. $16 / 8 =$ _____	c. $2 \cdot 7 =$ _____	c. $14 / 7 =$ _____
d. $7 \times 8 =$ _____	d. $24 \div 6 =$ _____	d. $1 \times 8 =$ _____	d. $16 \div 8 =$ _____
e. $6 * 1 =$ _____	e. $8 / 8 =$ _____	e. $7 * 9 =$ _____	e. $7 / 7 =$ _____
f. $8 \cdot 9 =$ _____	f. $6 \div 6 =$ _____	f. $8 \cdot 4 =$ _____	f. $48 \div 8 =$ _____
g. $3 \times 6 =$ _____	g. $40 / 8 =$ _____	g. $4 \times 7 =$ _____	g. $35 / 7 =$ _____
h. $4 * 8 =$ _____	h. $42 \div 6 =$ _____	h. $7 * 8 =$ _____	h. $32 \div 8 =$ _____
i. $6 \cdot 8 =$ _____	i. $24 / 8 =$ _____	i. $7 \cdot 1 =$ _____	i. $21 / 7 =$ _____
j. $8 \times 1 =$ _____	j. $18 \div 6 =$ _____	j. $8 \times 2 =$ _____	j. $8 \div 8 =$ _____
k. $2 * 6 =$ _____	k. $48 / 8 =$ _____	k. $5 * 7 =$ _____	k. $28 / 7 =$ _____
l. $3 \cdot 8 =$ _____	l. $48 \div 6 =$ _____	l. $9 \cdot 8 =$ _____	l. $40 \div 8 =$ _____
m. $6 \times 5 =$ _____	m. $64 / 8 =$ _____	m. $7 \times 6 =$ _____	m. $49 / 7 =$ _____
n. $8 * 8 =$ _____	n. $42 \div 6 =$ _____	n. $8 * 3 =$ _____	n. $72 \div 8 =$ _____
o. $6 \cdot 6 =$ _____	o. $56 / 8 =$ _____	o. $7 \cdot 7 =$ _____	o. $42 / 7 =$ _____
p. $5 \times 8 =$ _____	p. $30 \div 6 =$ _____	p. $8 \times 8 =$ _____	p. $24 \div 8 =$ _____
q. $6 * 7 =$ _____	q. $32 / 8 =$ _____	q. $7 * 0 =$ _____	q. $56 / 7 =$ _____
r. $8 \times 0 =$ _____	r. $54 \div 6 =$ _____	r. $6 \cdot 8 =$ _____	r. $64 \div 8 =$ _____
s. $0 * 6 =$ _____	s. $80 / 8 =$ _____	s. $8 \times 0 =$ _____	s. $70 / 7 =$ _____
t. $6 \cdot 10 =$ _____	t. $60 \div 6 =$ _____	t. $7 * 10 =$ _____	t. $56 \div 8 =$ _____

PATH to FLUENCY Dashes 17–20

Complete each Dash. Check your answers on page 141.

Dash 17 6s and 7s Multiplications	Dash 18 6s and 7s Divisions	Dash 19 6s, 7s, 8s Multiplications	Dash 20 6s, 7s, 8s Divisions
a. $6 \times 6 =$ _____	a. $70 / 7 =$ _____	a. $7 \times 7 =$ _____	a. $21 / 7 =$ _____
b. $7 * 7 =$ _____	b. $60 \div 6 =$ _____	b. $6 \cdot 3 =$ _____	b. $16 \div 8 =$ _____
c. $3 \cdot 6 =$ _____	c. $28 / 7 =$ _____	c. $8 * 6 =$ _____	c. $54 / 6 =$ _____
d. $8 \times 7 =$ _____	d. $30 \div 6 =$ _____	d. $6 \times 6 =$ _____	d. $48 \div 8 =$ _____
e. $6 * 1 =$ _____	e. $42 / 7 =$ _____	e. $7 \cdot 6 =$ _____	e. $64 / 8 =$ _____
f. $7 \cdot 2 =$ _____	f. $24 \div 6 =$ _____	f. $4 * 7 =$ _____	f. $42 \div 6 =$ _____
g. $9 \times 6 =$ _____	g. $35 / 7 =$ _____	g. $9 \times 7 =$ _____	g. $56 / 7 =$ _____
h. $9 * 7 =$ _____	h. $12 \div 6 =$ _____	h. $6 \cdot 9 =$ _____	h. $72 \div 8 =$ _____
i. $6 \cdot 8 =$ _____	i. $7 / 7 =$ _____	i. $6 * 4 =$ _____	i. $18 / 6 =$ _____
j. $7 \times 3 =$ _____	j. $36 \div 6 =$ _____	j. $8 \times 8 =$ _____	j. $28 / 7 =$ _____
k. $7 * 6 =$ _____	k. $21 / 7 =$ _____	k. $7 \cdot 3 =$ _____	k. $56 \div 8 =$ _____
l. $1 \cdot 7 =$ _____	l. $48 \div 6 =$ _____	l. $8 * 7 =$ _____	l. $30 / 6 =$ _____
m. $6 \times 2 =$ _____	m. $63 / 7 =$ _____	m. $6 \times 7 =$ _____	m. $63 \div 7 =$ _____
n. $7 * 5 =$ _____	n. $6 \div 6 =$ _____	n. $3 \cdot 6 =$ _____	n. $32 / 8 =$ _____
o. $4 \cdot 6 =$ _____	o. $56 / 7 =$ _____	o. $2 * 7 =$ _____	o. $48 \div 6 =$ _____
p. $6 \times 7 =$ _____	p. $18 \div 6 =$ _____	p. $9 \times 8 =$ _____	p. $49 / 7 =$ _____
q. $6 * 5 =$ _____	q. $49 / 7 =$ _____	q. $5 \cdot 6 =$ _____	q. $36 \div 6 =$ _____
r. $7 \cdot 4 =$ _____	r. $42 \div 6 =$ _____	r. $7 * 8 =$ _____	r. $24 \div 8 =$ _____
s. $6 \times 10 =$ _____	s. $14 / 7 =$ _____	s. $3 \times 7 =$ _____	s. $42 / 7 =$ _____
t. $7 \times 10 =$ _____	t. $54 \div 6 =$ _____	t. $9 \cdot 6 =$ _____	t. $24 \div 6 =$ _____

PATH to FLUENCY Dashes 9B–12B

Complete each multiplication and division Dash.
Check your answers on page 142.

Dash 9B 2s, 5s, 9s, 10s Multiplications	Dash 10B 2s, 5s, 9s, 10s Divisions	Dash 11B 0s, 1s, 3s, 4s Multiplications	Dash 12B 1s, 3s, 4s Divisions
a. $6 \times 2 =$ _____	a. $18 / 2 =$ _____	a. $7 \times 1 =$ _____	a. $2 / 1 =$ _____
b. $9 \cdot 4 =$ _____	b. $25 \div 5 =$ _____	b. $0 \cdot 6 =$ _____	b. $28 \div 4 =$ _____
c. $8 * 5 =$ _____	c. $70 / 10 =$ _____	c. $4 * 4 =$ _____	c. $3 / 3 =$ _____
d. $1 \times 10 =$ _____	d. $54 \div 9 =$ _____	d. $7 \times 3 =$ _____	d. $1 \div 1 =$ _____
e. $2 \cdot 7 =$ _____	e. $50 / 5 =$ _____	e. $3 \cdot 1 =$ _____	e. $40 / 4 =$ _____
f. $9 * 9 =$ _____	f. $81 \div 9 =$ _____	f. $4 * 7 =$ _____	f. $21 \div 3 =$ _____
g. $5 \times 6 =$ _____	g. $8 / 2 =$ _____	g. $9 \times 0 =$ _____	g. $5 / 1 =$ _____
h. $10 \cdot 4 =$ _____	h. $90 \div 10 =$ _____	h. $1 \cdot 1 =$ _____	h. $16 \div 4 =$ _____
i. $7 * 5 =$ _____	i. $35 / 5 =$ _____	i. $3 * 4 =$ _____	i. $15 / 3 =$ _____
j. $8 \times 2 =$ _____	j. $27 / 9 =$ _____	j. $4 \times 9 =$ _____	j. $6 / 1 =$ _____
k. $10 \cdot 10 =$ _____	k. $2 \div 2 =$ _____	k. $8 \cdot 1 =$ _____	k. $12 \div 4 =$ _____
l. $5 * 3 =$ _____	l. $36 / 9 =$ _____	l. $3 * 3 =$ _____	l. $27 / 3 =$ _____
m. $9 \times 7 =$ _____	m. $45 \div 5 =$ _____	m. $0 \times 4 =$ _____	m. $9 \div 1 =$ _____
n. $9 \cdot 2 =$ _____	n. $14 / 2 =$ _____	n. $10 \cdot 3 =$ _____	n. $8 / 4 =$ _____
o. $5 * 5 =$ _____	o. $20 \div 10 =$ _____	o. $6 * 4 =$ _____	o. $12 \div 3 =$ _____
p. $6 \times 9 =$ _____	p. $9 / 9 =$ _____	p. $1 \times 4 =$ _____	p. $3 / 1 =$ _____
q. $5 \cdot 2 =$ _____	q. $20 \div 5 =$ _____	q. $3 \cdot 6 =$ _____	q. $36 \div 4 =$ _____
r. $9 * 5 =$ _____	r. $45 \div 9 =$ _____	r. $4 * 8 =$ _____	r. $6 \div 3 =$ _____
s. $8 \times 10 =$ _____	s. $5 / 5 =$ _____	s. $7 \times 0 =$ _____	s. $4 / 1 =$ _____
t. $5 \cdot 10 =$ _____	t. $4 \div 2 =$ _____	t. $5 \cdot 3 =$ _____	t. $4 \div 4 =$ _____

PATH to FLUENCY Dashes 9C–12C

Complete each Dash. Check your answers on page 142.

Dash 9C 2s, 5 ,9s, 10s Multiplications	Dash 10C 2s, 5, 9s, 10s Divisions	Dash 11C 0s, 1s ,3s, 4s Multiplications	Dash 12C 1s, 3s, 4s Divisions
a. $5 \times 8 =$ _____	a. $36 \div 9 =$ _____	a. $0 \times 7 =$ _____	a. $4 / 1 =$ _____
b. $9 * 9 =$ _____	b. $30 / 5 =$ _____	b. $1 * 4 =$ _____	b. $15 \div 3 =$ _____
c. $10 \cdot 7 =$ _____	c. $18 \div 2 =$ _____	c. $3 \cdot 6 =$ _____	c. $24 / 4 =$ _____
d. $4 \times 5 =$ _____	d. $80 / 10 =$ _____	d. $4 \times 9 =$ _____	d. $9 \div 1 =$ _____
e. $5 * 5 =$ _____	e. $40 \div 5 =$ _____	e. $8 * 0 =$ _____	e. $21 / 3 =$ _____
f. $10 \cdot 3 =$ _____	f. $72 / 9 =$ _____	f. $7 * 1 =$ _____	f. $12 \div 4 =$ _____
g. $1 \times 5 =$ _____	g. $6 \div 2 =$ _____	g. $4 \cdot 3 =$ _____	g. $5 / 1 =$ _____
h. $3 * 9 =$ _____	h. $54 / 9 =$ _____	h. $4 \times 4 =$ _____	h. $3 \div 3 =$ _____
i. $9 \cdot 6 =$ _____	i. $25 \div 5 =$ _____	i. $0 * 5 =$ _____	i. $32 / 4 =$ _____
j. $10 \times 8 =$ _____	j. $10 / 10 =$ _____	j. $1 \cdot 6 =$ _____	j. $2 \div 1 =$ _____
k. $2 * 9 =$ _____	k. $45 \div 5 =$ _____	k. $3 \times 2 =$ _____	k. $18 / 3 =$ _____
l. $6 \cdot 2 =$ _____	l. $27 / 9 =$ _____	l. $4 * 7 =$ _____	l. $36 \div 4 =$ _____
m. $6 \times 10 =$ _____	m. $14 \div 2 =$ _____	m. $1 \cdot 0 =$ _____	m. $7 / 1 =$ _____
n. $8 * 9 =$ _____	n. $35 / 5 =$ _____	n. $2 \times 1 =$ _____	n. $24 \div 3 =$ _____
o. $8 \cdot 2 =$ _____	o. $90 \div 9 =$ _____	o. $9 * 3 =$ _____	o. $4 / 4 =$ _____
p. $4 \times 2 =$ _____	p. $90 / 10 =$ _____	p. $2 \cdot 4 =$ _____	p. $6 \div 1 =$ _____
q. $10 * 5 =$ _____	q. $63 \div 9 =$ _____	q. $0 \times 3 =$ _____	q. $12 / 3 =$ _____
r. $10 \cdot 10 =$ _____	r. $15 / 5 =$ _____	r. $1 * 1 =$ _____	r. $20 \div 4 =$ _____
s. $9 \times 6 =$ _____	s. $50 \div 10 =$ _____	s. $3 \cdot 9 =$ _____	s. $8 / 1 =$ _____
t. $5 * 7 =$ _____	t. $8 / 2 =$ _____	t. $4 \times 5 =$ _____	t. $27 \div 3 =$ _____

PATH to FLUENCY   Answers to Dashes 13–20

Use this sheet to check your answers to the Dashes on pages 137 and 138.

Dash 13 ×	Dash 14 ÷	Dash 15 ×	Dash 16 ÷	Dash 17 ×	Dash 18 ÷	Dash 19 ×	Dash 20 ÷
a. 54	a. 9	a. 21	a. 9	a. 36	a. 10	a. 49	a. 3
b. 16	b. 2	b. 40	b. 10	b. 49	b. 10	b. 18	b. 2
c. 24	c. 2	c. 14	c. 2	c. 18	c. 4	c. 48	c. 9
d. 56	d. 4	d. 8	d. 2	d. 56	d. 5	d. 36	d. 6
e. 6	e. 1	e. 63	e. 1	e. 6	e. 6	e. 42	e. 8
f. 72	f. 1	f. 32	f. 6	f. 14	f. 4	f. 28	f. 7
g. 18	g. 5	g. 28	g. 5	g. 54	g. 5	g. 63	g. 8
h. 32	h. 7	h. 56	h. 4	h. 63	h. 2	h. 54	h. 9
i. 48	i. 3	i. 7	i. 3	i. 48	i. 1	i. 24	i. 3
j. 8	j. 3	j. 16	j. 1	j. 21	j. 6	j. 64	j. 4
k. 12	k. 6	k. 35	k. 4	k. 42	k. 3	k. 21	k. 7
l. 24	l. 8	l. 72	l. 5	l. 7	l. 8	l. 56	l. 5
m. 30	m. 8	m. 42	m. 7	m. 12	m. 9	m. 42	m. 9
n. 64	n. 7	n. 24	n. 9	n. 35	n. 1	n. 18	n. 4
o. 36	o. 7	o. 49	o. 6	o. 24	o. 8	o. 14	o. 8
p. 40	p. 5	p. 64	p. 3	p. 42	p. 3	p. 72	p. 7
q. 42	q. 4	q. 0	q. 8	q. 30	q. 7	q. 30	q. 6
r. 0	r. 9	r. 48	r. 8	r. 28	r. 7	r. 56	r. 3
s. 0	s. 10	s. 0	s. 10	s. 60	s. 2	s. 21	s. 6
t. 60	t. 10	t. 70	t. 7	t. 70	t. 9	t. 54	t. 4

PATH to FLUENCY Answers to Dashes 9B–12B, 9C–12C

Use this sheet to check your answers to the Dashes on pages 139 and 140.

Dash 9B ×	Dash 10B ÷	Dash 11B ×	Dash 12B ÷	Dash 9C ×	Dash 10C ÷	Dash 11C ×	Dash 12C ÷
a. 12	a. 9	a. 7	a. 2	a. 40	a. 4	a. 0	a. 4
b. 36	b. 5	b. 0	b. 7	b. 81	b. 6	b. 4	b. 5
c. 40	c. 7	c. 16	c. 1	c. 70	c. 9	c. 18	c. 6
d. 10	d. 6	d. 21	d. 1	d. 20	d. 8	d. 36	d. 9
e. 14	e. 10	e. 3	e. 10	e. 25	e. 8	e. 0	e. 7
f. 81	f. 9	f. 28	f. 7	f. 30	f. 8	f. 7	f. 3
g. 30	g. 4	g. 0	g. 5	g. 5	g. 3	g. 12	g. 5
h. 40	h. 9	h. 1	h. 4	h. 27	h. 6	h. 16	h. 1
i. 35	i. 7	i. 12	i. 5	i. 54	i. 5	i. 0	i. 8
j. 16	j. 3	j. 36	j. 6	j. 80	j. 1	j. 6	j. 2
k. 100	k. 1	k. 8	k. 3	k. 18	k. 9	k. 6	k. 6
l. 15	l. 4	l. 9	l. 9	l. 12	l. 3	l. 28	l. 9
m. 63	m. 9	m. 0	m. 9	m. 60	m. 7	m. 0	m. 7
n. 18	n. 7	n. 30	n. 2	n. 72	n. 7	n. 2	n. 8
o. 25	o. 2	o. 24	o. 4	o. 16	o. 10	o. 27	o. 1
p. 54	p. 1	p. 4	p. 3	p. 8	p. 9	p. 8	p. 6
q. 10	q. 4	q. 18	q. 9	q. 50	q. 7	q. 0	q. 4
r. 45	r. 5	r. 32	r. 2	r. 100	r. 3	r. 1	r. 5
s. 80	s. 1	s. 0	s. 4	s. 54	s. 5	s. 27	s. 8
t. 50	t. 2	t. 15	t. 1	t. 35	t. 4	t. 20	t. 9

Write an equation and solve the problem.

Show your work.

1 The area of the rectangle shown is 42 square inches. What is the value of *n*?

Area = 42 square inches

6 inches

n

_____

2 There are 81 bottles of apple juice to be equally shared among 9 people. How many bottles will each of those 9 people receive?

_____

Solve.

3 7 × ▢ = 56

▢ = _____

4 9 × 9 = ▢

▢ = _____

5 Jaewon arranges his stamps in 6 equal rows. If he has 48 stamps, how many stamps will be in each row?

_____

Write an equation and solve the problem.

Show your work.

1 There are 7 rows of 9 mango trees in an orchard. How many mango trees are there in all?

_____

2 A carrot seed needs about 8 weeks to become a carrot. How many days is that?

_____

3 It takes a little more than 63 days for pea seeds to become peas that you can eat. How many weeks are 63 days?

_____

4 During harvest season each 24-hour day is split into 3 equal shifts. How long is each shift?

_____

5 Hal packs 6 boxes of oranges. Each box weighs 6 pounds. How much do the boxes weigh in all?

_____

Name _____

Choose the Operation

Write an equation and solve the problem.

1 Ernie helped his mother work in the yard for 3 days. He earned $6 each day. How much did he earn in all?

_____

2 Ernie helped his mother work in the yard for 3 days. He earned $6 the first day, $5 the second day, and $7 the third day. How much did he earn in all?

_____

3 Troy had $18. He gave $6 to each of his brothers and had no money left. How many brothers does Troy have?

_____

4 Troy gave $18 to his brothers. He gave $4 to Raj, $7 to Darnell, and the rest to Jai. How much money did Jai get?

_____

5 Jinja has 4 cousins. Grant has 7 more cousins than Jinja. How many cousins does Grant have?

_____

6 Jinja has 4 cousins. Grant has 7 times as many cousins as Jinja. How many cousins does Grant have?

_____

7 Camille has 15 fewer books than Jane has. Camille has 12 books. How many does Jane have?

_____

8 Camille has 4 more books than Jane has. Camille has 15 books. How many books does Jane have?

_____

Write an Equation

Write an equation and solve the problem.

Show your work.

9 Luke had a $5 bill. He spent $3 on a sandwich. How much change did he get?

10 Ramona is putting tiles on the kitchen floor. She will lay 8 rows of tiles, with 7 tiles in each row. How many tiles will Ramona use?

11 Josh earned a perfect score on 6 tests last year. Jenna earned a perfect score on 6 times as many tests. How many perfect scores did Jenna earn?

12 Sophie bought a stuffed animal for $3 and a board game for $7. How much money did Sophie spend?

13 Mr. Duarte buys 15 dog treats. He gives each of his 3 dogs the same number of treats. How many treats does each dog get?

14 Ahmed spent $9 on a book. Zal paid $6 more for the same book at a different store. How much did Zal spend on the book?

Equations and Word Problems

Write the Question

Write a question for the given information and solve.

15 Anna read 383 pages this month. Chris read 416 pages.

Question: _____

Solution: _____

16 Marisol had 128 beads in her jewelry box. She gave away 56 of them.

Question: _____

Solution: _____

17 Louis put 72 marbles in 8 bags. He put the same number of marbles in each bag.

Question: _____

Solution: _____

18 Geoff planted seeds in 4 pots. He planted 6 seeds in each pot.

Question: _____

Solution: _____

19 Marly put 10 books on each of 5 shelves in the library.

Question: _____

Solution: _____

Write the Problem

Write a problem that can be solved using the given equation. Then solve.

20 $9 \times 6 = $    **Solution:** _____

_____

_____

_____

21 $324 - 112 = $ 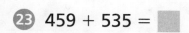   **Solution:** _____

_____

_____

_____

22 $56 \div 7 = $ **Solution:** _____

_____

_____

_____

23 $459 + 535 = $ **Solution:** _____

_____

_____

_____

✓ Check Understanding

Describe how you would begin to write a word problem for $42 \div 6 = n$.

Use Order of Operations

VOCABULARY
expression
Order of
Operations

This **expression** involves subtraction and multiplication:
$$10 - 3 \times 2$$

1 What do you get if you subtract first and then

multiply? _____

2 What do you get if you multiply first and then

subtract? _____

To make sure everyone has the same answer, people follow the **Order of Operations** rules. Using the Order of Operations, multiplication and division is done *before* addition and subtraction. The answer you found in question 2 is correct.

In the Order of Operations rules, using parentheses means "Do this first." For example, if you want people to subtract first in the exercise above, write it like this:
$$(10 - 3) \times 2$$

Find the answer.

3 $5 + 4 \times 2 =$ _____

4 $(9 - 3) \times 6 =$ _____

5 $8 \div 2 + 2 =$ _____

6 $6 \times (8 - 1) =$ _____

Rewrite each statement, using symbols and numbers instead of words.

7 Add 4 and 3, and multiply the total by 8. _____

8 Multiply 3 by 8, and add 4 to the total. _____

What's the Error?

Dear Math Students,

Today I found the answer to 6 + 3 x 2.
Here is how I found the answer.

6 + 3 x 2

9 x 2 = 18

Is my answer correct? If not, please correct
my work and tell me what I did wrong.

Your friend,
Puzzled Penguin

9 Write an answer to the Puzzled Penguin.

_____

_____

_____

Find the answer.

10 4 + 3 × 5 = _____

11 10 ÷ 2 + 3 = _____

12 12 − 9 ÷ 3 = _____

13 3 × 5 − 2 = _____

14 (4 + 3) × 5 = _____

15 10 ÷ (2 + 3) = _____

16 (12 − 9) ÷ 3 = _____

17 3 × (5 − 2) = _____

Write First-Step Questions for Two-Step Problems

Write First-Step Questions

**Write the first-step question and answer.
Then solve the problem.**

Show your work.

18 A roller coaster has 7 cars. Each car has 4 seats.
If there were 3 empty seats, how many people
were on the roller coaster?

_____

_____

19 Each week, Marta earns $10 babysitting. She
always spends $3 and saves the rest. How much
does she save in 8 weeks?

_____

_____

20 Abu bought 6 packs of stickers. Each pack had
8 stickers. Then Abu's friend gave him 10 more
stickers. How many stickers does Abu have now?

_____

_____

21 Zoe made some snacks. She put 4 apple slices and
2 melon slices on each plate. She prepared 5 plates.
How many slices of fruit did Zoe use in all?

_____

_____

22 Kyle ordered 8 pizzas for his party. Each pizza
was cut into 8 slices. 48 of the slices were plain
cheese, and the rest had mushrooms. How
many slices of pizza had mushrooms?

_____

_____

Write First-Step Questions (continued)

Write the first-step question and answer.
Then solve the problem.

Show your work.

23 Kagami baked 86 blueberry muffins. Her sisters ate 5 of them. Kagami divided the remaining muffins equally among 9 plates. How many muffins did she put on each plate?

_____

_____

24 Lucia had 42 plums. Jorge had 12 more plums than Lucia. Jorge divided his plums equally among 6 people. How many plums did each person get?

_____

_____

25 On his way to school, Kevin counted 5 mountain bikes and 3 road bikes. How many wheels were on the bikes altogether?

_____

_____

26 Juana has 21 shirts. Leslie had 7 fewer shirts than Juana, but then she bought 4 more. How many shirts does Leslie have now?

_____

_____

Check Understanding

Describe the difference between solving
$6 + 4 \times 2 = n$ and $(6 + 4) \times 2 = n$.

Write First-Step Questions for Two-Step Problems

Name _____

Multiply with Multiples of 10

When a number of ones is multiplied by 10, the ones become tens.

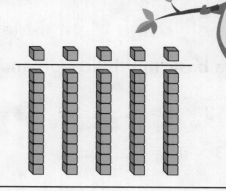

1 ten × 5 ones = 5 tens

$\quad$ 10 × 5 = _____

To multiply with multiples of 10, use place value and properties.

2 × 3 $\quad$= (2 × 1) × (3 × 1) $\quad$= (2 × 3) × (1 × 1) $\quad$= 6 × 1 $\quad$= 6

2 × 30 = (2 × 1) × (3 × 10) = (2 × 3) × (1 × 10) = 6 × 10 = 60

Use a shortcut.

Find the basic multiplication product.
Then multiply by 10.

$\quad$ 2 × 30

$\qquad$ 6 × 10 = 60

Multiply.

1 6 × 40

$\quad$ ☐ × 10 = _____

2 4 × 50

$\quad$ ☐ × 10 = _____

3 70 × 8

$\quad$ ☐ × 10 = _____

4 90 × 3

$\quad$ ☐ × 10 = _____

© Houghton Mifflin Harcourt Publishing Company

Multiply Using Mental Math

Use a basic multiplication and mental math to complete.

5   $3 \times 4 =$ _____

$3 \times 40 =$ _____

6   $1 \times 2 =$ _____

$10 \times 2 =$ _____

7   $9 \times 8 =$ _____

$9 \times 80 =$ _____

8   $2 \times 9 =$ _____

$2 \times 90 =$ _____

9   $5 \times 5 =$ _____

$5 \times 50 =$ _____

10   $3 \times 5 =$ _____

$3 \times 50 =$ _____

11   $1 \times 1 =$ _____

$10 \times 1 =$ _____

12   $2 \times 3 =$ _____

$20 \times 3 =$ _____

13   $5 \times 6 =$ _____

$5 \times 60 =$ _____

14   $2 \times 4 =$ _____

$2 \times 40 =$ _____

15   $6 \times 3 =$ _____

$6 \times 30 =$ _____

16   $9 \times 2 =$ _____

$9 \times 20 =$ _____

17   $2 \times 30 =$ _____

18   $5 \times 40 =$ _____

19   $9 \times 60 =$ _____

20   $3 \times 80 =$ _____

21   $2 \times 70 =$ _____

22   $5 \times 90 =$ _____

23   $9 \times 50 =$ _____

24   $5 \times 20 =$ _____

25   $3 \times 30 =$ _____

26   $5 \times 80 =$ _____

27   $9 \times 90 =$ _____

28   $5 \times 60 =$ _____

29   $70 \times 5 =$ _____

30   $8 \times 50 =$ _____

31   $60 \times 4 =$ _____

✓**Check Understanding**

Describe how you can use a multiplication strategy
to find 7×40.

Multiply with Multiples of 10

PATH to FLUENCY Dashes 21–22, 19A–20A

Complete each Dash. Check your answers on page 161.

Dash 21 2s, 3s, 4s, 5s, 9s Multiplications	Dash 22 2s, 3s, 4s, 5s, 9s Divisions	Dash 19A 6s, 7s, 8s Multiplications	Dash 20A 6s, 7s, 8s Divisions
a. 6 × 3 = ___	a. 16 / 4 = ___	a. 9 × 6 = ___	a. 24 ÷ 6 = ___
b. 4 • 7 = ___	b. 54 ÷ 9 = ___	b. 7 * 7 = ___	b. 21 / 7 = ___
c. 8 * 2 = ___	c. 4 / 2 = ___	c. 3 • 7 = ___	c. 42 ÷ 7 = ___
d. 5 × 3 = ___	d. 28 ÷ 4 = ___	d. 6 × 3 = ___	d. 16 / 8 = ___
e. 4 • 4 = ___	e. 25 / 5 = ___	e. 7 * 8 = ___	e. 24 ÷ 8 = ___
f. 3 • 9 = ___	f. 21 ÷ 3 = ___	f. 8 • 6 = ___	f. 54 / 6 = ___
g. 9 × 9 = ___	g. 40 / 4 = ___	g. 5 × 6 = ___	g. 36 ÷ 6 = ___
h. 8 • 9 = ___	h. 81 ÷ 9 = ___	h. 6 * 6 = ___	h. 48 / 8 = ___
i. 6 * 4 = ___	i. 35 / 5 = ___	i. 9 • 8 = ___	i. 49 ÷ 7 = ___
j. 3 × 3 = ___	j. 12 / 3 = ___	j. 7 × 6 = ___	j. 64 / 8 = ___
k. 2 • 7 = ___	k. 2 ÷ 2 = ___	k. 2 * 7 = ___	k. 48 ÷ 6 = ___
l. 8 • 5 = ___	l. 63 / 9 = ___	l. 4 • 7 = ___	l. 42 / 6 = ___
m. 4 × 9 = ___	m. 36 ÷ 4 = ___	m. 3 × 6 = ___	m. 32 ÷ 8 = ___
n. 9 • 5 = ___	n. 18 / 2 = ___	n. 9 * 7 = ___	n. 56 / 7 = ___
o. 7 * 3 = ___	o. 9 ÷ 3 = ___	o. 6 • 7 = ___	o. 63 ÷ 7 = ___
p. 2 × 2 = ___	p. 36 / 9 = ___	p. 6 × 9 = ___	p. 72 / 8 = ___
q. 8 • 4 = ___	q. 40 ÷ 5 = ___	q. 8 * 7 = ___	q. 30 ÷ 6 = ___
r. 5 * 1 = ___	r. 12 ÷ 4 = ___	r. 6 • 4 = ___	r. 18 / 6 = ___
s. 5 × 5 = ___	s. 9 / 9 = ___	s. 7 × 3 = ___	s. 56 ÷ 8 = ___
t. 6 • 9 = ___	t. 14 ÷ 2 = ___	t. 8 * 8 = ___	t. 28 / 7 = ___

PATH to FLUENCY Dashes 21A–22A,19B–20B

Complete each Dash. Check your answers on page 161.

Dash 21A 2s, 3s, 4s, 5s, 9s Multiplications	Dash 22A 2s, 3s, 4s, 5s, 9s Divisions	Dash 19B 6s, 7s, 8s Multiplications	Dash 20B 6s, 7s, 8s Divisions
a. 6×9 = ____	a. $14 \div 2$ = ____	a. 6×2 = ____	a. $36 \div 6$ = ____
b. $6 * 3$ = ____	b. $16 / 4$ = ____	b. $7 * 7$ = ____	b. $63 / 7$ = ____
c. $4 \cdot 7$ = ____	c. $9 \div 9$ = ____	c. $8 \cdot 5$ = ____	c. $24 \div 8$ = ____
d. 5×5 = ____	d. $54 / 9$ = ____	d. 4×6 = ____	d. $18 / 6$ = ____
e. $8 * 2$ = ____	e. $12 \div 4$ = ____	e. $3 * 7$ = ____	e. $28 \div 7$ = ____
f. $5 \cdot 1$ = ____	f. $4 / 2$ = ____	f. $1 \cdot 8$ = ____	f. $48 / 8$ = ____
g. 5×3 = ____	g. $40 \div 5$ = ____	g. 6×9 = ____	g. $54 \div 6$ = ____
h. $8 * 4$ = ____	h. $28 / 4$ = ____	h. $7 * 5$ = ____	h. $42 / 7$ = ____
i. $4 \cdot 4$ = ____	i. $36 \div 9$ = ____	i. $8 \cdot 3$ = ____	i. $72 \div 8$ = ____
j. 2×2 = ____	j. $25 / 5$ = ____	j. 4×6 = ____	j. $6 / 6$ = ____
k. $3 * 9$ = ____	k. $9 \div 3$ = ____	k. $9 * 7$ = ____	k. $14 \div 7$ = ____
l. $7 \cdot 3$ = ____	l. $21 / 3$ = ____	l. $8 \cdot 8$ = ____	l. $56 / 8$ = ____
m. 9×9 = ____	m. $18 \div 2$ = ____	m. 6×1 = ____	m. $12 \div 6$ = ____
n. $9 * 5$ = ____	n. $40 / 4$ = ____	n. $7 * 4$ = ____	n. $7 / 7$ = ____
o. $8 \cdot 9$ = ____	o. $36 \div 4$ = ____	o. $8 \cdot 6$ = ____	o. $16 \div 8$ = ____
p. 4×9 = ____	p. $81 / 9$ = ____	p. 7×6 = ____	p. $30 / 6$ = ____
q. $6 * 4$ = ____	q. $63 \div 9$ = ____	q. $2 * 7$ = ____	q. $56 \div 7$ = ____
r. $8 \cdot 5$ = ____	r. $35 / 5$ = ____	r. $9 \cdot 8$ = ____	r. $8 / 8$ = ____
s. 2×7 = ____	s. $12 \div 3$ = ____	s. 6×5 = ____	s. $48 \div 6$ = ____
t. $3 * 3$ = ____	t. $2 / 2$ = ____	t. $7 * 6$ = ____	t. $21 / 7$ = ____

PATH to FLUENCY Dashes 21B–22B, 19C–20C

Complete each Dash. Check your answers on page 162.

Dash 21B 2s, 3s, 4s, 5s, 9s Multiplications	Dash 22B 2s, 3s, 4s, 5s, 9s Divisions	Dash 19C 6s, 7s, 8s Multiplications	Dash 20C 6s, 7s, 8s Divisions
a. 2 × 3 = _____	a. 8 ÷ 2 = _____	a. 6 × 8 = _____	a. 54 ÷ 6 = _____
b. 3 * 8 = _____	b. 18 / 3 = _____	b. 7 * 3 = _____	b. 49 / 7 = _____
c. 4 • 4 = _____	c. 12 ÷ 4 = _____	c. 8 • 6 = _____	c. 24 ÷ 8 = _____
d. 5 × 6 = _____	d. 25 / 5 = _____	d. 2 × 6 = _____	d. 6 / 6 = _____
e. 9 * 8 = _____	e. 63 ÷ 9 = _____	e. 8 * 7 = _____	e. 35 ÷ 7 = _____
f. 9 • 2 = _____	f. 16 / 2 = _____	f. 9 • 8 = _____	f. 72 / 8 = _____
g. 3 × 3 = _____	g. 3 ÷ 3 = _____	g. 6 × 4 = _____	g. 18 ÷ 6 = _____
h. 4 * 2 = _____	h. 28 / 4 = _____	h. 7 * 1 = _____	h. 28 / 7 = _____
i. 9 • 5 = _____	i. 45 ÷ 5 = _____	i. 8 • 3 = _____	i. 8 ÷ 8 = _____
j. 9 × 4 = _____	j. 27 / 9 = _____	j. 5 × 6 = _____	j. 30 / 6 = _____
k. 2 * 7 = _____	k. 12 ÷ 2 = _____	k. 9 * 7 = _____	k. 21 ÷ 7 = _____
l. 3 • 5 = _____	l. 12 / 3 = _____	l. 4 • 8 = _____	l. 40 / 8 = _____
m. 4 × 8 = _____	m. 20 ÷ 4 = _____	m. 6 × 6 = _____	m. 42 ÷ 6 = _____
n. 5 * 3 = _____	n. 40 / 5 = _____	n. 7 * 5 = _____	n. 63 / 7 = _____
o. 9 • 6 = _____	o. 54 ÷ 9 = _____	o. 8 • 8 = _____	o. 32 ÷ 8 = _____
p. 2 × 8 = _____	p. 2 / 2 = _____	p. 1 × 6 = _____	p. 36 / 6 = _____
q. 3 * 7 = _____	q. 9 ÷ 3 = _____	q. 2 * 7 = _____	q. 14 ÷ 7 = _____
r. 4 • 1 = _____	r. 36 / 4 = _____	r. 5 • 8 = _____	r. 56 / 8 = _____
s. 5 × 8 = _____	s. 15 ÷ 5 = _____	s. 6 × 9 = _____	s. 24 ÷ 6 = _____
t. 9 * 9 = _____	t. 9 / 9 = _____	t. 7 * 7 = _____	t. 42 / 7 = _____

PATH to FLUENCY Dashes 21C–22C, 19D–20D

Complete each Dash. Check your answers on page 162.

Dash 21C 2s, 3s, 4s, 5s, 9s **Multiplications**	**Dash 22C** 2s, 3s, 4s, 5s, 9s **Divisions**	**Dash 19D** 6s, 7s, 8s **Multiplications**	**Dash 20D** 6s, 7s, 8s **Divisions**
a. $2 \times 9 =$ ____	a. $8 \div 2 =$ ____	a. $6 \times 9 =$ ____	a. $18 / 6 =$ ____
b. $3 * 7 =$ ____	b. $6 / 3 =$ ____	b. $7 * 6 =$ ____	b. $42 \div 7 =$ ____
c. $4 \cdot 5 =$ ____	c. $4 \div 4 =$ ____	c. $8 \cdot 2 =$ ____	c. $32 / 8 =$ ____
d. $5 \times 3 =$ ____	d. $20 / 5 =$ ____	d. $3 \times 6 =$ ____	d. $54 \div 6 =$ ____
e. $9 * 1 =$ ____	e. $63 \div 9 =$ ____	e. $4 * 7 =$ ____	e. $49 / 7 =$ ____
f. $1 \cdot 2 =$ ____	f. $16 / 2 =$ ____	f. $9 \cdot 8 =$ ____	f. $8 / 8 =$ ____
g. $4 \times 3 =$ ____	g. $15 \div 3 =$ ____	g. $6 \times 6 =$ ____	g. $30 \div 6 =$ ____
h. $4 * 1 =$ ____	h. $32 / 4 =$ ____	h. $7 * 2 =$ ____	h. $35 / 7 =$ ____
i. $7 \cdot 5 =$ ____	i. $30 \div 5 =$ ____	i. $8 \cdot 1 =$ ____	i. $48 \div 8 =$ ____
j. $9 \times 9 =$ ____	j. $45 / 9 =$ ____	j. $2 \times 6 =$ ____	j. $24 / 6 =$ ____
k. $2 * 3 =$ ____	k. $2 \div 2 =$ ____	k. $8 * 7 =$ ____	k. $14 \div 7 =$ ____
l. $3 \cdot 8 =$ ____	l. $21 / 3 =$ ____	l. $3 \cdot 8 =$ ____	l. $56 / 8 =$ ____
m. $4 \times 4 =$ ____	m. $12 \div 4 =$ ____	m. $6 \times 4 =$ ____	m. $6 \div 6 =$ ____
n. $5 * 2 =$ ____	n. $10 / 5 =$ ____	n. $7 * 5 =$ ____	n. $21 / 7 =$ ____
o. $9 \cdot 6 =$ ____	o. $9 \div 9 =$ ____	o. $8 \cdot 8 =$ ____	o. $40 \div 8 =$ ____
p. $6 \times 2 =$ ____	p. $12 / 2 =$ ____	p. $1 \times 6 =$ ____	p. $48 / 6 =$ ____
q. $9 * 3 =$ ____	q. $27 \div 3 =$ ____	q. $3 * 7 =$ ____	q. $56 \div 7 =$ ____
r. $6 \cdot 4 =$ ____	r. $20 / 4 =$ ____	r. $4 \cdot 8 =$ ____	r. $64 / 8 =$ ____
s. $5 \times 5 =$ ____	s. $40 \div 8 =$ ____	s. $6 \times 7 =$ ____	s. $36 \div 6 =$ ____
t. $3 * 9 =$ ____	t. $81 / 9 =$ ____	t. $7 * 7 =$ ____	t. $7 / 7 =$ ____

Name

Answers to Dashes 21–22, 19A–22A, 19B–20B

Use this sheet to check your answers to the Dashes on pages 157 and 158.

Dash 21 ×	Dash 22 ÷	Dash 19A ×	Dash 20A ÷	Dash 21A ×	Dash 22A ÷	Dash 19B ×	Dash 20B ÷
a. 18	a. 4	a. 54	a. 4	a. 54	a. 7	a. 12	a. 6
b. 28	b. 6	b. 49	b. 3	b. 18	b. 4	b. 49	b. 9
c. 16	c. 2	c. 21	c. 6	c. 28	c. 1	c. 40	c. 3
d. 15	d. 7	d. 18	d. 2	d. 25	d. 6	d. 24	d. 3
e. 16	e. 5	e. 56	e. 3	e. 16	e. 3	e. 21	e. 4
f. 27	f. 7	f. 48	f. 9	f. 5	f. 2	f. 8	f. 6
g. 81	g. 10	g. 30	g. 6	g. 15	g. 8	g. 54	g. 9
h. 72	h. 9	h. 36	h. 6	h. 32	h. 7	h. 35	h. 6
i. 24	i. 7	i. 72	i. 7	i. 16	i. 4	i. 24	i. 9
j. 9	j. 4	j. 42	j. 8	j. 4	j. 5	j. 24	j. 1
k. 14	k. 1	k. 14	k. 8	k. 27	k. 3	k. 63	k. 2
l. 40	l. 7	l. 28	l. 7	l. 21	l. 7	l. 64	l. 7
m. 36	m. 9	m. 18	m. 4	m. 81	m. 9	m. 6	m. 2
n. 45	n. 9	n. 63	n. 8	n. 45	n. 10	n. 28	n. 1
o. 21	o. 3	o. 42	o. 9	o. 72	o. 9	o. 48	o. 2
p. 4	p. 4	p. 54	p. 9	p. 36	p. 9	p. 42	p. 5
q. 32	q. 8	q. 56	q. 5	q. 24	q. 7	q. 14	q. 8
r. 5	r. 3	r. 24	r. 3	r. 40	r. 7	r. 72	r. 1
s. 25	s. 1	s. 21	s. 7	s. 14	s. 4	s. 30	s. 8
t. 54	t. 7	t. 64	t. 4	t. 9	t. 1	t. 42	t. 3

Answers to Dashes 21B–22B, 19C–22C, 19D–20D

Use this sheet to check your answers to the Dashes on pages 159 and 160.

Dash 21B ×	Dash 22B ÷	Dash 19C ×	Dash 20C ÷	Dash 21C ×	Dash 22C ÷	Dash 19D ×	Dash 20D ÷
a. 6	a. 4	a. 48	a. 9	a. 18	a. 4	a. 54	a. 3
b. 24	b. 6	b. 21	b. 7	b. 21	b. 2	b. 42	b. 6
c. 16	c. 3	c. 48	c. 3	c. 20	c. 1	c. 16	c. 4
d. 30	d. 5	d. 12	d. 1	d. 15	d. 4	d. 18	d. 9
e. 72	e. 7	e. 56	e. 5	e. 9	e. 7	e. 28	e. 7
f. 18	f. 8	f. 72	f. 9	f. 2	f. 8	f. 72	f. 1
g. 9	g. 1	g. 24	g. 3	g. 12	g. 5	g. 36	g. 5
h. 8	h. 7	h. 7	h. 4	h. 4	h. 8	h. 14	h. 5
i. 45	i. 9	i. 24	i. 1	i. 35	i. 6	i. 8	i. 6
j. 36	j. 3	j. 30	j. 5	j. 81	j. 5	j. 12	j. 4
k. 14	k. 6	k. 63	k. 3	k. 6	k. 1	k. 56	k. 2
l. 15	l. 4	l. 32	l. 5	l. 24	l. 7	l. 24	l. 7
m. 32	m. 5	m. 36	m. 7	m. 16	m. 3	m. 24	m. 1
n. 15	n. 8	n. 35	n. 9	n. 10	n. 2	n. 35	n. 3
o. 54	o. 6	o. 64	o. 4	o. 54	o. 1	o. 64	o. 5
p. 16	p. 1	p. 6	p. 6	p. 12	p. 6	p. 6	p. 8
q. 21	q. 3	q. 14	q. 2	q. 27	q. 9	q. 21	q. 8
r. 4	r. 9	r. 40	r. 7	r. 24	r. 5	r. 32	r. 8
s. 40	s. 3	s. 54	s. 4	s. 25	s. 5	s. 42	s. 6
t. 81	t. 1	t. 49	t. 6	t. 27	t. 9	t. 49	t. 1

Name _____

Solve Two-Step Word Problems

Write an equation and solve the problem.   *Show your work.*

1 Raul spent 10 minutes doing homework for each
of 5 subjects and 15 minutes for another subject.
How many minutes did Raul spend on his homework?

_____

2 At Sonya's cello recital, there were 8 rows of chairs,
with 6 chairs in each row. There was a person in each
chair, and there were 17 more people standing. How
many people were in the audience altogether?

_____

3 Jana played a game with a deck of cards.
She placed the cards on the floor in 3 rows of 10.
If the deck has 52 cards, how many cards did
Jana leave out?

_____

4 Mukesh was making 7 salads. He opened a can
of olives and put 6 olives on each salad. Then he
ate the rest of the olives in the can. If there
were 51 olives to start with, how many olives
did Mukesh eat?

_____

5 Peter wallpapered a wall that was 8 feet wide
and 9 feet high. He had 28 square feet of
wallpaper left over. How many square feet of
wallpaper did he start with?

_____

CC SS Content Standards **3.OA.A.1, 3.OA.A.2, 3.OA.A.3, 3.OA.A.4, 3.OA.B.6, 3.OA.C.7, 3.OA.D.8**
Mathematical Practices **MP1, MP2, MP3, MP4, MP5, MP6**

PATH to FLUENCY **What's My Rule?**

A function table is a table of ordered pairs. For every input number, there is only one output number. The rule describes what to do to the input number to get the output number.

Write the rule and then complete the function table.

6 Rule: _____

Input	Output
7	42
8	_____
_____	54
6	36
4	24
5	_____

7 Rule: _____

Input	Output
81	9
45	5
72	_____
_____	7
27	_____
54	6

8 Rule: _____

Input	Output
21	7
27	9
_____	6
15	_____
_____	8
9	3

9 Rule: _____

Input	Output
5	25
_____	40
9	_____
3	15
7	35
_____	20

 Check Understanding

Explain how you chose the rule for the table in Exercise 9.

Play Multiplication and Division Games

PATH to FLUENCY Play *Division Three-in-a-Row*

Rules for *Division Three-in-a-Row*

Number of players: 2
What You Will Need: Product Cards, one
Three-in-a-Row Game Grid for each player

1. Players write a number in each of the
   squares on their game grids. They may
   use only numbers from 1 to 9, but they
   may use the same number more than once.

2. Shuffle the cards. Place them division side
   up in a stack in the center of the table.

3. Players take turns. On each turn, a player
   completes the division on the top card
   and then partners check the answer.

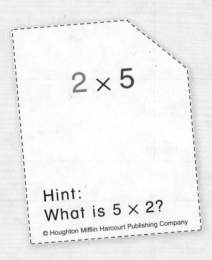

4. For a correct answer, if the quotient is on
   the game grid, the player puts an X
   through that grid square. If the answer
   is wrong, or if the quotient is not on the
   grid, the player doesn't mark anything.
   The player puts the card division
   side up on the bottom of the stack.

5. The first player to mark three squares
   in a row (horizontally, vertically, or
   diagonally) wins.

Three-in-a-Row Game Grids

2×2

$2 \cdot 3$

Hint:
What is $3 \cdot 2$?

$2 * 4$

Hint:
What is $4 * 2$?

2×5

Hint:
What is 5×2?

2×6

Hint:
What is 6×2?

$2 \cdot 7$

Hint:
What is $7 \cdot 2$?

$2 * 8$

Hint:
What is $8 * 2$?

2×9

Hint:
What is 9×2?

5×2

Hint:
What is 2×5?

$5 \cdot 3$

Hint:
What is $3 \cdot 5$?

$5 * 4$

Hint:
What is $4 * 5$?

5×5

5×6

Hint:
What is 6×5?

$5 \cdot 7$

Hint:
What is $7 \cdot 5$?

$5 * 8$

Hint:
What is $8 * 5$?

5×9

Hint:
What is 9×5?

Product Cards: 2s, 5s, 9s

$2\overline{)10}$

Hint: What is

☐ × 2 = 10?

$2\overline{)8}$

Hint: What is

☐ × 2 = 8?

$2\overline{)6}$

Hint: What is

☐ × 2 = 6?

$2\overline{)4}$

Hint: What is

☐ × 2 = 4?

$2\overline{)18}$

Hint: What is

☐ × 2 = 18?

$2\overline{)16}$

Hint: What is

☐ × 2 = 16?

$2\overline{)14}$

Hint: What is

☐ × 2 = 14?

$2\overline{)12}$

Hint: What is

☐ × 2 = 12?

$5\overline{)25}$

Hint: What is

☐ × 5 = 25?

$5\overline{)20}$

Hint: What is

☐ × 5 = 20?

$5\overline{)15}$

Hint: What is

☐ × 5 = 15?

$5\overline{)10}$

Hint: What is

☐ × 5 = 10?

$5\overline{)45}$

Hint: What is

☐ × 5 = 45?

$5\overline{)40}$

Hint: What is

☐ × 5 = 40?

$5\overline{)35}$

Hint: What is

☐ × 5 = 35?

$5\overline{)30}$

Hint: What is

☐ × 5 = 30?

Product Cards: 2s, 5s, 9s

9×2

Hint:
What is 2×9?
© Houghton Mifflin Harcourt Publishing Company

$9 \bullet 3$

Hint:
What is $3 \cdot 9$?
© Houghton Mifflin Harcourt Publishing Company

$9 * 4$

Hint:
What is $4 * 9$?
© Houghton Mifflin Harcourt Publishing Company

9×5

Hint:
What is 5×9?
© Houghton Mifflin Harcourt Publishing Company

9×6

Hint:
What is 6×9?
© Houghton Mifflin Harcourt Publishing Company

$9 \bullet 7$

Hint:
What is $7 \cdot 9$?
© Houghton Mifflin Harcourt Publishing Company

$9 * 8$

Hint:
What is $8 * 9$?
© Houghton Mifflin Harcourt Publishing Company

9×9

© Houghton Mifflin Harcourt Publishing Company

$\times$

$\bullet$

$*$

$\times$

$\times$

$\bullet$

$*$

$\times$

You can write any numbers on the last 8 cards. Use them to practice difficult problems or if you lose a card.

$9\overline{)45}$

Hint: What is
$\square \times 9 = 45$?

$9\overline{)36}$

Hint: What is
$\square \times 9 = 36$?

$9\overline{)27}$

Hint: What is
$\square \times 9 = 27$?

$9\overline{)18}$

Hint: What is
$\square \times 9 = 18$?

$9\overline{)81}$

Hint: What is
$\square \times 9 = 81$?

$9\overline{)72}$

Hint: What is
$\square \times 9 = 72$?

$9\overline{)63}$

Hint: What is
$\square \times 9 = 63$?

$9\overline{)54}$

Hint: What is
$\square \times 9 = 54$?

You can write any numbers on the last 8 cards. Use them to practice difficult problems or if you lose a card.

Product Cards: 2s, 5s, 9s

3 × 2

Hint:
What is 2 × 3?
© Houghton Mifflin Harcourt Publishing Company

3 • 3

Hint:
What is 3 × 3?
© Houghton Mifflin Harcourt Publishing Company

3 * 4

Hint:
What is 4 * 3?
© Houghton Mifflin Harcourt Publishing Company

3 × 5

Hint:
What is 5 × 3?
© Houghton Mifflin Harcourt Publishing Company

3 × 6

Hint:
What is 6 × 3?
© Houghton Mifflin Harcourt Publishing Company

3 • 7

Hint:
What is 7 • 3?
© Houghton Mifflin Harcourt Publishing Company

3 * 8

Hint:
What is 8 * 3?
© Houghton Mifflin Harcourt Publishing Company

3 × 9

Hint:
What is 9 × 3?
© Houghton Mifflin Harcourt Publishing Company

4 × 2

Hint:
What is 2 × 4?
© Houghton Mifflin Harcourt Publishing Company

4 • 3

Hint:
What is 3 • 4?
© Houghton Mifflin Harcourt Publishing Company

4 * 4

© Houghton Mifflin Harcourt Publishing Company

4 × 5

Hint:
What is 5 × 4?
© Houghton Mifflin Harcourt Publishing Company

4 × 6

Hint:
What is 6 × 4?
© Houghton Mifflin Harcourt Publishing Company

4 • 7

Hint:
What is 7 • 4?
© Houghton Mifflin Harcourt Publishing Company

4 * 8

Hint:
What is 8 * 4?
© Houghton Mifflin Harcourt Publishing Company

4 × 9

Hint:
What is 9 × 4?
© Houghton Mifflin Harcourt Publishing Company

$3 \overline{)15}$

Hint: What is
☐ × 3 = 15?
© Houghton Mifflin Harcourt Publishing Company

$3 \overline{)12}$

Hint: What is
☐ × 3 = 12?
© Houghton Mifflin Harcourt Publishing Company

$3 \overline{)9}$

Hint: What is
☐ × 3 = 9?
© Houghton Mifflin Harcourt Publishing Company

$3 \overline{)6}$

Hint: What is
☐ × 3 = 6?
© Houghton Mifflin Harcourt Publishing Company

$3 \overline{)27}$

Hint: What is
☐ × 3 = 27?
© Houghton Mifflin Harcourt Publishing Company

$3 \overline{)24}$

Hint: What is
☐ × 3 = 24?
© Houghton Mifflin Harcourt Publishing Company

$3 \overline{)21}$

Hint: What is
☐ × 3 = 21?
© Houghton Mifflin Harcourt Publishing Company

$3 \overline{)18}$

Hint: What is
☐ × 3 = 18?
© Houghton Mifflin Harcourt Publishing Company

$4 \overline{)20}$

Hint: What is
☐ × 4 = 20?
© Houghton Mifflin Harcourt Publishing Company

$4 \overline{)16}$

Hint: What is
☐ × 4 = 16?
© Houghton Mifflin Harcourt Publishing Company

$4 \overline{)12}$

Hint: What is
☐ × 4 = 12?
© Houghton Mifflin Harcourt Publishing Company

$4 \overline{)8}$

Hint: What is
☐ × 4 = 8?
© Houghton Mifflin Harcourt Publishing Company

$4 \overline{)36}$

Hint: What is
☐ × 4 = 36?
© Houghton Mifflin Harcourt Publishing Company

$4 \overline{)32}$

Hint: What is
☐ × 4 = 32?
© Houghton Mifflin Harcourt Publishing Company

$4 \overline{)28}$

Hint: What is
☐ × 4 = 28?
© Houghton Mifflin Harcourt Publishing Company

$4 \overline{)24}$

Hint: What is
☐ × 4 = 24?
© Houghton Mifflin Harcourt Publishing Company

Product Cards: 3s, 4s

6×2	$6 \cdot 3$	$6 * 4$	6×5
Hint: What is 2×6?	**Hint:** What is $3 \cdot 6$?	**Hint:** What is $4 * 6$?	**Hint:** What is 5×6?

© Houghton Mifflin Harcourt Publishing Company

6×6	$6 \cdot 7$	$6 * 8$	6×9
	Hint: What is $7 \cdot 6$?	**Hint:** What is $8 * 6$?	**Hint:** What is 9×6?

© Houghton Mifflin Harcourt Publishing Company

7×2	$7 \cdot 3$	$7 * 4$	7×5
Hint: What is 2×7?	**Hint:** What is $3 \cdot 7$?	**Hint:** What is $4 * 7$?	**Hint:** What is 5×7?

© Houghton Mifflin Harcourt Publishing Company

7×6	$7 \cdot 7$	$7 * 8$	7×9
Hint: What is 6×7?		**Hint:** What is $8 * 7$?	**Hint:** What is 9×7?

© Houghton Mifflin Harcourt Publishing Company

© Houghton Mifflin Harcourt Publishing Company

UNIT 2 LESSON 13

Product Cards: 6s, 7s, 8s **167G**

$6\overline{)30}$

Hint: What is
☐ × 6 = 30?

$6\overline{)24}$

Hint: What is
☐ × 6 = 24?

$6\overline{)18}$

Hint: What is
☐ × 6 = 18?

$6\overline{)12}$

Hint: What is
☐ × 6 = 12?

$6\overline{)54}$

Hint: What is
☐ × 6 = 54?

$6\overline{)48}$

Hint: What is
☐ × 6 = 48?

$6\overline{)42}$

Hint: What is
☐ × 6 = 42?

$6\overline{)36}$

Hint: What is
☐ × 6 = 36?

$7\overline{)35}$

Hint: What is
☐ × 7 = 35?

$7\overline{)28}$

Hint: What is
☐ × 7 = 28?

$7\overline{)21}$

Hint: What is
☐ × 7 = 21?

$7\overline{)14}$

Hint: What is
☐ × 7 = 14?

$7\overline{)63}$

Hint: What is
☐ × 7 = 63?

$7\overline{)56}$

Hint: What is
☐ × 7 = 56?

$7\overline{)49}$

Hint: What is
☐ × 7 = 49?

$7\overline{)42}$

Hint: What is
☐ × 7 = 42?

Product Cards: 6s, 7s, 8s

8×2

Hint:
What is 2×8?

$8 \cdot 3$

Hint:
What is $3 \cdot 8$?

$8 * 4$

Hint:
What is $4 * 8$?

8×5

Hint:
What is 5×8?

8×6

Hint:
What is 6×8?

$8 \cdot 7$

Hint:
What is $7 \cdot 8$?

$8 * 8$

8×9

Hint:
What is 9×8?

$\times$

$\bullet$

$*$

$\times$

$\times$

$\bullet$

$*$

$\times$

You can write any numbers on the last 8 cards. Use them to practice difficult problems or if you lose a card.

$8\overline{)40}$ Hint: What is $\square \times 8 = 40$? © Houghton Mifflin Harcourt Publishing Company	$8\overline{)32}$ Hint: What is $\square \times 8 = 32$? © Houghton Mifflin Harcourt Publishing Company	$8\overline{)24}$ Hint: What is $\square \times 8 = 24$? © Houghton Mifflin Harcourt Publishing Company	$8\overline{)16}$ Hint: What is $\square \times 8 = 16$? © Houghton Mifflin Harcourt Publishing Company
$8\overline{)72}$ Hint: What is $\square \times 8 = 72$? © Houghton Mifflin Harcourt Publishing Company	$8\overline{)64}$ Hint: What is $\square \times 8 = 64$? © Houghton Mifflin Harcourt Publishing Company	$8\overline{)56}$ Hint: What is $\square \times 8 = 56$? © Houghton Mifflin Harcourt Publishing Company	$8\overline{)48}$ Hint: What is $\square \times 8 = 48$? © Houghton Mifflin Harcourt Publishing Company
$\overline{)}$	$\overline{)}$	$\overline{)}$	$\overline{)}$
$\overline{)}$	$\overline{)}$	$\overline{)}$	$\overline{)}$

You can write any numbers on the last 8 cards. Use them to practice difficult problems or if you lose a card.

Name

PATH to FLUENCY Diagnostic Checkup for Basic Multiplication

1. $7 \times 5 = $ _____

2. $2 \times 3 = $ _____

3. $9 \times 9 = $ _____

4. $9 \times 6 = $ _____

5. $6 \times 2 = $ _____

6. $3 \times 0 = $ _____

7. $3 \times 4 = $ _____

8. $6 \times 8 = $ _____

9. $5 \times 9 = $ _____

10. $3 \times 3 = $ _____

11. $2 \times 9 = $ _____

12. $5 \times 7 = $ _____

13. $6 \times 10 = $ _____

14. $4 \times 1 = $ _____

15. $6 \times 4 = $ _____

16. $4 \times 8 = $ _____

17. $5 \times 2 = $ _____

18. $1 \times 3 = $ _____

19. $3 \times 9 = $ _____

20. $7 \times 6 = $ _____

21. $7 \times 2 = $ _____

22. $9 \times 0 = $ _____

23. $8 \times 9 = $ _____

24. $8 \times 7 = $ _____

25. $8 \times 10 = $ _____

26. $6 \times 3 = $ _____

27. $4 \times 4 = $ _____

28. $3 \times 8 = $ _____

29. $5 \times 5 = $ _____

30. $6 \times 0 = $ _____

31. $7 \times 9 = $ _____

32. $6 \times 6 = $ _____

33. $9 \times 2 = $ _____

34. $8 \times 3 = $ _____

35. $5 \times 4 = $ _____

36. $7 \times 7 = $ _____

37. $5 \times 10 = $ _____

38. $5 \times 1 = $ _____

39. $10 \times 9 = $ _____

40. $5 \times 6 = $ _____

41. $6 \times 5 = $ _____

42. $9 \times 3 = $ _____

43. $4 \times 2 = $ _____

44. $7 \times 8 = $ _____

45. $8 \times 2 = $ _____

46. $5 \times 0 = $ _____

47. $4 \times 9 = $ _____

48. $6 \times 7 = $ _____

49. $9 \times 5 = $ _____

50. $6 \times 1 = $ _____

51. $7 \times 4 = $ _____

52. $9 \times 8 = $ _____

53. $4 \times 10 = $ _____

54. $5 \times 3 = $ _____

55. $6 \times 9 = $ _____

56. $8 \times 6 = $ _____

57. $8 \times 5 = $ _____

58. $8 \times 0 = $ _____

59. $8 \times 4 = $ _____

60. $4 \times 7 = $ _____

61. $3 \times 5 = $ _____

62. $7 \times 3 = $ _____

63. $5 \times 9 = $ _____

64. $3 \times 6 = $ _____

65. $7 \times 10 = $ _____

66. $8 \times 1 = $ _____

67. $0 \times 4 = $ _____

68. $9 \times 7 = $ _____

69. $4 \times 5 = $ _____

70. $4 \times 3 = $ _____

71. $1 \times 9 = $ _____

72. $8 \times 8 = $ _____

Content Standards 3.OA.A.4, 3.OA.B.6, 3.OA.C.7, 3.OA.D.9
Mathematical Practices MP3, MP5, MP6, MP7, MP8

Name _____

PATH to FLUENCY **Diagnostic Checkup for Basic Division**

1 $12 \div 2 =$ _____　　**2** $8 \div 1 =$ _____　　**3** $36 \div 9 =$ _____　　**4** $35 \div 7 =$ _____

5 $20 \div 5 =$ _____　　**6** $24 \div 3 =$ _____　　**7** $12 \div 4 =$ _____　　**8** $6 \div 6 =$ _____

9 $6 \div 2 =$ _____　　**10** $3 \div 3 =$ _____　　**11** $18 \div 9 =$ _____　　**12** $63 \div 7 =$ _____

13 $20 \div 10 =$ _____　　**14** $0 \div 1 =$ _____　　**15** $40 \div 4 =$ _____　　**16** $48 \div 8 =$ _____

17 $18 \div 2 =$ _____　　**18** $6 \div 3 =$ _____　　**19** $8 \div 4 =$ _____　　**20** $36 \div 6 =$ _____

21 $8 \div 2 =$ _____　　**22** $9 \div 1 =$ _____　　**23** $9 \div 9 =$ _____　　**24** $56 \div 7 =$ _____

25 $40 \div 5 =$ _____　　**26** $9 \div 3 =$ _____　　**27** $36 \div 4 =$ _____　　**28** $56 \div 8 =$ _____

29 $80 \div 10 =$ _____　　**30** $7 \div 1 =$ _____　　**31** $45 \div 9 =$ _____　　**32** $48 \div 6 =$ _____

33 $5 \div 5 =$ _____　　**34** $30 \div 3 =$ _____　　**35** $16 \div 4 =$ _____　　**36** $72 \div 8 =$ _____

37 $10 \div 2 =$ _____　　**38** $1 \div 1 =$ _____　　**39** $54 \div 9 =$ _____　　**40** $21 \div 7 =$ _____

41 $25 \div 5 =$ _____　　**42** $15 \div 3 =$ _____　　**43** $32 \div 4 =$ _____　　**44** $24 \div 8 =$ _____

45 $90 \div 10 =$ _____　　**46** $18 \div 3 =$ _____　　**47** $63 \div 9 =$ _____　　**48** $54 \div 6 =$ _____

49 $45 \div 5 =$ _____　　**50** $6 \div 1 =$ _____　　**51** $20 \div 4 =$ _____　　**52** $49 \div 7 =$ _____

53 $15 \div 5 =$ _____　　**54** $0 \div 3 =$ _____　　**55** $28 \div 4 =$ _____　　**56** $30 \div 6 =$ _____

57 $16 \div 2 =$ _____　　**58** $21 \div 3 =$ _____　　**59** $81 \div 9 =$ _____　　**60** $64 \div 8 =$ _____

61 $30 \div 5 =$ _____　　**62** $12 \div 3 =$ _____　　**63** $27 \div 9 =$ _____　　**64** $42 \div 7 =$ _____

65 $40 \div 10 =$ _____　　**66** $10 \div 1 =$ _____　　**67** $24 \div 4 =$ _____　　**68** $18 \div 6 =$ _____

69 $35 \div 5 =$ _____　　**70** $27 \div 3 =$ _____　　**71** $72 \div 9 =$ _____　　**72** $42 \div 6 =$ _____

　　　　Diagnostic Division Checkup

PATH to FLUENCY Patterns With 10s, 5s, and 9s

These multiplication tables help us see some patterns that make recalling basic multiplications easier.

1 What pattern do you see in the 10s count-bys?

_____

2 Look at the 5s and the 10s together. What patterns do you see?

_____

3 Look at the 9s count-bys. How does each 9s count-by relate to the 10s count-by in the next row?

_____

How could this pattern help you remember the 9s count-bys?

_____

_____

4 Look at the digits in each 9s product. What is the sum of the digits in each 9s product?

_____

How could you use this knowledge to check your answers when you multiply by 9?

_____

5s and 10s

×	1	2	3	4	5	6	7	8	9	10
1	1	2	3	4	5	6	7	8	9	10
2	2	4	6	8	10	12	14	16	18	20
3	3	6	9	12	15	18	21	24	27	30
4	4	8	12	16	20	24	28	32	36	40
5	5	10	15	20	25	30	35	40	45	50
6	6	12	18	24	30	36	42	48	54	60
7	7	14	21	28	35	42	49	56	63	70
8	8	16	24	32	40	48	56	64	72	80
9	9	18	27	36	45	54	63	72	81	90
10	10	20	30	40	50	60	70	80	90	100

9s

×	1	2	3	4	5	6	7	8	9	10
1	1	2	3	4	5	6	7	8	9	10
2	2	4	6	8	10	12	14	16	18	20
3	3	6	9	12	15	18	21	24	27	30
4	4	8	12	16	20	24	28	32	36	40
5	5	10	15	20	25	30	35	40	45	50
6	6	12	18	24	30	36	42	48	54	60
7	7	14	21	28	35	42	49	56	63	70
8	8	16	24	32	40	48	56	64	72	80
9	9	18	27	36	45	54	63	72	81	90
10	10	20	30	40	50	60	70	80	90	100

(PATH to FLUENCY) **Patterns With Other Numbers**

On these grids, find patterns with 2s, 4s, 6s, and 8s.

5 Look at the ones digits in all the 2s, 4s, 6s, and 8s count-bys. What pattern do you see?

_____

2s, 4s, 6s, 8s

×	1	2	3	4	5	6	7	8	9
1	1	2	3	4	5	6	7	8	9
2	2	4	6	8	10	12	14	16	18
3	3	6	9	12	15	18	21	24	27
4	4	8	12	16	20	24	28	32	36
5	5	10	15	20	25	30	35	40	45
6	6	12	18	24	30	36	42	48	54
7	7	14	21	28	35	42	49	56	63
8	8	16	24	32	40	48	56	64	72
9	9	18	27	36	45	54	63	72	81
10	10	20	30	40	50	60	70	80	90

6 Are the 2s, 4s, 6s, and 8s products even numbers or odd numbers?

_____

On the multiplication table labeled Doubles, look for rows that have products that are double the products in other rows.

7 Name the factors that have products that are double the products of another factor.

_____

_____

_____

_____

Doubles

×	1	2	3	4	5	6	7	8	9
1	1	2	3	4	5	6	7	8	9
2	2	4	6	8	10	12	14	16	18
3	3	6	9	12	15	18	21	24	27
4	4	8	12	16	20	24	28	32	36
5	5	10	15	20	25	30	35	40	45
6	6	12	18	24	30	36	42	48	54
7	7	14	21	28	35	42	49	56	63
8	8	16	24	32	40	48	56	64	72
9	9	18	27	36	45	54	63	72	81
10	10	20	30	40	50	60	70	80	90

8 How can you find 6×8 if you know 3×8?

_____

Rewrite each list so that the count-by list is correct.

9 4, 8, 12, 18, 20, 24, 28 _____

10 18, 28, 36, 45, 54, 63, 70 _____

✔ **Check Understanding**

Cross out the number that does not belong in this count-by list:
16, 24, 28, 32, 40, 48, 56, 64, 72.

Build Fluency with 0s–10s

Name _____

Math and Recipes

The animal keepers at zoos feed and care for the animals. The animal keepers consult a zoo nutritionist to decide what and how much to feed the animals. In the zoo kitchens there are recipes posted for each type of animal such as the one shown below.

Gorilla's Zoo Stew	
32 carrots	8 yams
32 oranges	8 eggs
24 apples	16 bananas
64 ounces Monkey's Chow	72 grapes
48 ounces primate-diet food	56 stalks of celery
8 heads lettuce, any variety	bales of hydroponic grass to taste

Toss all ingredients lightly. Divide among 8 trays.
The recipe makes 8 gorilla servings.

Write an equation and solve the problem.

1 How much of each ingredient is in 1 gorilla serving?

_____

_____

_____

2 How much of each ingredient in the Gorilla's Zoo Stew recipe is needed to serve 6 gorillas?

_____

_____

_____

_____

Content Standards 3.OA.A.1, 3.OA.A.2, 3.OA.A.3, 3.OA.A.4, 3.OA.B.5
Mathematical Practices **MP1, MP2, MP3, MP4, MP5, MP6, MP7**

Focus on Mathematical Practices **171**

Favorite Zoo Animals

The students in third grade took a field trip to a zoo. The students were asked to name their favorite zoo animal. The pictograph below shows the animals the students chose.

Favorite Zoo Animal

Bear	☺ ☺ ☺ ☺ ☺ ☺ ☺
Elephant	☺ ☺ ☺ ☺ ☺ ☺ ☺ ☺
Giraffe	☺ ☺ ☺ ☺
Gorilla	☺ ☺ ☺ ☺ ☺ ☺
Lion	☺ ☺

Each ☺ stands for 7 students.

3 Use the information in the pictograph to complete the chart to show the number of students that chose each zoo animal.

Favorite Zoo Animal

Zoo Animal	Number of Students
Bear	
Elephant	
Giraffe	
Gorilla	
Lion	

Solve.

4 If 63 students chose a zebra as their favorite zoo animal, how many symbols would you use to show that on the pictograph?

Focus on Mathematical Practices

Name _____ **Date** _____

Solve.

1 $6 + 8 \div 4 =$ ▣

▣ = _____

2 $3 \times 40 =$ ▣

▣ = _____

Write an equation and solve the problem.

Show your work.

3 The pet shop had 8 cages of mice, with 4 mice in each cage. 5 mice escaped. How many mice were left in cages?

_____

4 Ingrid baked 47 cookies, but 5 were burned and thrown away. The rest were shared equally among 6 people. How many cookies did each person get?

_____

5 Maria had $4. Then she earned $7 each day for 8 days. How much money does she have now?

_____

Fluency Check 2 **Name** ______________________ **Date** ______

PATH to FLUENCY

Subtract.

1. $8 - 6 = \square$
2. $6 - 4 = \square$
3. $5 - 5 = \square$
4. $11 - 6 = \square$
5. $12 - 8 = \square$
6. $10 - 1 = \square$
7. $13 - 8 = \square$
8. $14 - 7 = \square$
9. $15 - 9 = \square$
10. $\begin{array}{r} 17 \\ -\ 8 \\ \hline \end{array}$
11. $\begin{array}{r} 12 \\ -\ 6 \\ \hline \end{array}$
12. $\begin{array}{r} 15 \\ -\ 7 \\ \hline \end{array}$
13. $\begin{array}{r} 19 \\ -\ 9 \\ \hline \end{array}$
14. $\begin{array}{r} 14 \\ -\ 9 \\ \hline \end{array}$
15. $\begin{array}{r} 16 \\ -\ 8 \\ \hline \end{array}$

Solve.

1 Write the numbers that complete the unknown number puzzle.

| 3 | 5 | 8 | 10 | 12 | 54 |

×	9		2
6		18	
	45	15	◯
	72	24	16

Explain how you found the number in the circle.

2 There are 56 books on a library cart. Each student helper puts 7 books on a shelf. How many student helpers are there?

For numbers 2a–2d, choose Yes or No to tell whether the equation could be used to solve the problem.

2a. $56 \times 7 = \boxed{}$ ○ Yes   ○ No

2b. $56 \div 7 = \boxed{}$ ○ Yes   ○ No

2c. $7 \times \boxed{} = 56$ ○ Yes   ○ No

2d. $7 \div \boxed{} = 56$ ○ Yes   ○ No

3. Raul makes a sign for the school fair. It has a length of 9 inches and a width of 8 inches. What is the area of the sign?

Draw a rectangle to help solve the problem. Label your drawing.

Write an equation to solve the problem.

Area of the sign: _____ square inches

4. For numbers 4a–4c, select True or False for each statement.

4a. The first step to solve $3 + 2 \times 4$ is $3 + 2$. ○ True ○ False

4b. The first step to solve $5 \times 4 \div 2$ is 5×4. ○ True ○ False

4c. The first step to solve $(9 - 6) \div 3$ is $9 - 6$. ○ True ○ False

5. Write a problem that can be solved using the given equation. Then solve.

$$7 \times 6 = \boxed{}$$

Solution: _____ tickets

6 Select the equation below where the unknown number is 8. Select all that apply.

(A) $7 \times \blacksquare = 63$

(D) $\blacksquare \times 9 = 72$

(B) $4 \times \blacksquare = 32$

(E) $24 \div \blacksquare = 3$

(C) $36 \div 4 = \blacksquare$

(F) $18 \div 2 = \blacksquare$

7 For numbers 7a–7d, choose Yes or No to tell whether the product is correct.

7a. $3 \times 30 = 900$ ○ Yes ○ No

7b. $5 \times 40 = 200$ ○ Yes ○ No

7c. $2 \times 40 = 800$ ○ Yes ○ No

7d. $9 \times 60 = 540$ ○ Yes ○ No

8 Carrie finds 7 seashells at the beach. Her brother finds 8 seashells. They divide the seashells equally among 3 people. How many seashells did each person get? Write an equation to solve the problem.

Equation: _____

_____ seashells

9 A toy store sells 7 different model cars. Each model car comes in 5 different colors. How many different model cars are there?

Part A

Solve the problem.

_____ different model cars

Part B

Choose the type of problem and the operation you use to solve.

The type is | array
equal groups
area | . The operation is | multiplication
division | .

Write another problem that is the same type.

```


```

10 Write a question for the given information. Then write an equation and solve.

A museum has 297 visitors on Friday. It has 468 visitors on Saturday.

```


```

Solution: _____ visitors

11 How can you use a pattern to find 6 × 9 if you know 3 × 9? Complete the given part of the multiplication table to help you explain.

×	1	2	3	4	5	6	7	8	9
3									
6									

12 Select the equations that show square numbers. Select all that apply.

(A) 2 × 5 = 10   (D) 6 × 6 = 36

(B) 4 × 4 = 16   (E) 8 × 4 = 32

(C) 8 × 8 = 64   (F) 5 × 5 = 25

Draw a picture for one of the equations you chose. Explain why it is a square number.

13 Read the problem. Write the first step question and answer.
Then write an equation to solve the problem.

A school buys games for 6 classrooms. It buys 3 board games,
4 puzzles games, and 1 video game for each classroom.
How many games does the school buy?

_____ games

14 Draw a line to match each expression on the left with
an expression on the right that has the same value.

7 × 40   •   • 5 × 6

2 × 4 × 4 •   • 7 × 5 + 7 × 2

7 × 7   •   • 2 + 2

2 + 2 × 4 •   • 28 × 10

5 × 3 × 2 •   • 8 × 4

8 ÷ 4 + 2 •   • 2 + 8

15 Choose the equations that make the statements true.

You know that

| 3 × 9 = 27 |
| 3 × 5 = 15 |
| 8 × 6 = 48 |
| 4 × 7 = 28 |

. So, you know that

| 24 ÷ 3 = 8 |
| 18 ÷ 9 = 2 |
| 36 ÷ 6 = 6 |
| 48 ÷ 8 = 6 |

.

Play a Target Game

The object of this target game is to score 100 points, or as close to 100 points as possible without going over.

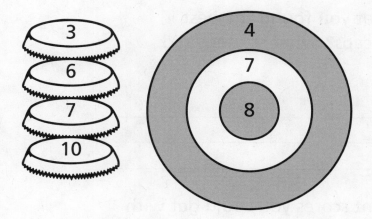

- You may drop two, three, or four bottle caps onto the target. To calculate the points for each drop, multiply the points on the cap by the points on the ring. For example, if the 3 cap lands on the 4 ring, the score would be 3 × 4 = 12.

- To find your final score, add the points for all your drops.

  Example: If the 3 bottle cap lands on the 4 ring, and the 7 bottle cap lands on the 8 ring, you could calculate your score using this equation.

  (3 × 4) + (7 × 8) =

     12   +   56   = 68

- Repeat the process by tossing other caps. Keep track of your scores and your equations for finding your scores.

1 What is the best possible score you can get with 2 bottle caps? Show your work.

_____

_____

2 How do you know that you found the best possible score with 2 caps? What strategy did you use?

_____

_____

_____

3 What are two different scores you could get with the same 3 caps? Show your work.

_____

_____

_____

_____

4 Can you score exactly 100 points with 3 caps? Show your work.

_____

_____

_____

5 Michael says that he can score exactly 100 points with 4 bottle caps. Is that true? Show your work.

_____

_____

_____

Dear Family:

Your child is currently participating in math activities that help him or her to understand place value, rounding, and addition and subtraction of 3-digit numbers.

- **Place Value Drawings:** Students learn to represent numbers with drawings that show how many hundreds, tens, and ones are in the numbers. Hundreds are represented by boxes. Tens are represented by vertical line segments, called ten sticks. Ones are represented by small circles. The drawings are also used to help students understand regrouping in addition and subtraction. Here is a place value drawing for the number 178.

1 hundred   7 tens   8 ones

The 7 ten sticks and 8 circles are grouped in 5s so students can see the quantities easily and avoid errors.

- **Secret Code Cards:** Secret Code Cards are a set of cards for hundreds, tens, and ones. Students learn about place value by assembling the cards to show two- and three-digit numbers. Here is how the number 148 would be assembled.

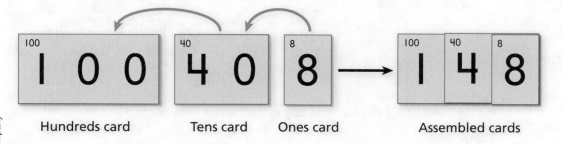

Hundreds card   Tens card Ones card   Assembled cards

Estimate Sums and Differences Students learn to estimate sums and differences by rounding numbers. They also use estimates to check that their actual answers are reasonable.

	Rounded to the nearest hundred	Rounded to the nearest ten
493	500	490
129	100	130
+ 369	+ 400	+ 370
991	Estimate: 1,000	Estimate: 990

© Houghton Mifflin Harcourt Publishing Company

Addition Methods: Students may use the common U.S. method, referred to as the New Groups Above Method, as well as two alternative methods. In the New Groups Below Method, students add from right to left and write the new ten and new hundred on the line. In the Show All Totals Method, students add in either direction, write partial sums and then add the partial sums to get the total. Students also use proof drawings to demonstrate grouping 10 ones to make a new ten and grouping 10 tens to make a new hundred.

The New Groups Below Method shows the teen number 13 better than the New Groups Above Method, where the 1 and 3 are separated. Also, addition is easier in New Groups Below, where you add the two numbers you see and just add 1.

New Groups Above:

1 ← the new ten
46
+ 37
83

New Groups Below:

46
+ 37
83 ← the new ten

Add right to left.

Show All Totals:

46
+ 37
70
13
83

Add left to right.

Proof Drawing:

8 tens   3 ones   the new ten

Subtraction Methods: Students may use the common U.S. method in which the subtraction is done right to left, with the ungrouping done before each column is subtracted. They also learn an alternative method in which all the ungrouping is done *before* the subtracting. If they do all the ungrouping first, students can subtract either from left to right or from right to left.

The Ungroup First Method helps students avoid the common error of subtracting a smaller top number from a larger bottom number.

1. Ungroup first.
2. Subtract (from left to right or from right to left).

15
3 5 13
4̶6̶3̶
− 275
188

Ungroup 1 hundred to make 10 tens.

Ungroup 1 ten to make 10 ones.

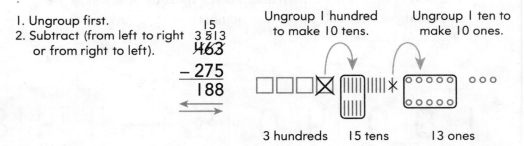

3 hundreds   15 tens   13 ones

Please contact me if you have any questions or comments.

Thank you.

Sincerely,
Your child's teacher

CC SS **Unit 3 addresses the following standards from the** Common Core State Standards for Mathematics: **3.OA.D.8, 3.OA.D.9, 3.NBT.A.1, 3.NBT.A.2, and all** Mathematical Practices.

Estimada familia:

Su niño está participando en actividades matemáticas que le servirán para comprender el valor posicional, el redondeo y la suma y resta de números de 3 dígitos.

- **Dibujos de valor posicional:** Los estudiantes aprenden a representar números por medio de dibujos que muestran cuántas centenas, decenas y unidades contienen. Las centenas están representadas con casillas, las decenas con segmentos verticales, llamados palitos de decenas, y las unidades con círculos pequeños. Los dibujos también se usan para ayudar a los estudiantes a comprender cómo se reagrupa en la suma y en la resta. Este es un dibujo de valor posicional para el número 178.

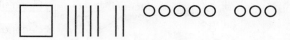

    1 centena   7 decenas   8 unidades

Los palitos de decenas y los círculos se agrupan en grupos de 5 para que las cantidades se puedan ver más fácilmente y se eviten errores.

- **Tarjetas de código secreto:** Las tarjetas de código secreto son un conjunto de tarjetas con centenas, decenas y unidades. Los estudiantes aprenden acerca del valor posicional organizando las tarjetas de manera que muestren números de dos y de tres dígitos. Así se puede formar el número 148:

   Tarjeta   Tarjeta   Tarjeta   Tarjetas organizadas
de centenas de decenas de unidades

Estimar sumas y diferencias: Los estudiantes aprenden a estimar sumas y diferencias redondeando números. También usan las estimaciones para comprobar que sus respuestas son razonables.

	Redondear a la centena más próxima	Redondear a la decena más próxima
493	500	490
129	100	130
+ 369	+ 400	+ 370
991	Estimación: 1,000	Estimación: 990

Métodos de suma: Los estudiantes pueden usar el método común de EE. UU., conocido como Grupos nuevos arriba, y otros dos métodos alternativos. En el método de Grupos nuevos abajo, los estudiantes suman de derecha a izquierda y escriben la nueva decena y la nueva centena en el renglón. En el método de Mostrar todos los totales, los estudiantes suman en cualquier dirección, escriben sumas parciales y luego las suman para obtener el total. Los estudiantes también usan dibujos de comprobación para demostrar cómo se agrupan 10 unidades para formar una nueva decena, y 10 decenas para formar una nueva centena.

El método de Grupos nuevos abajo muestra el número 13 mejor que el método de Grupos nuevos arriba, en el que se separan los números 1 y 3. Además, es más fácil sumar con Grupos nuevos abajo, donde se suman los dos números que se ven y simplemente se añade 1.

Grupos nuevos arriba:

$$
\begin{array}{r}
\overset{1}{4}6 \\
+\ 37 \\
\hline
83
\end{array}
$$

← la decena nueva

Grupos nuevos abajo:

$$
\begin{array}{r}
46 \\
+\ 37 \\
\hline
\underset{1}{8}3
\end{array}
$$

Sumar de derecha a izquierda.

← la decena nueva

Mostrar todos los totales:

$$
\begin{array}{r}
46 \\
+\ 37 \\
\hline
70 \\
13 \\
\hline
83
\end{array}
$$

Sumar de izquierda a derecha.

Dibujo de comprobación:

8 decenas 3 unidades

la decena nueva

Métodos de resta: Los estudiantes pueden usar el método común de EE. UU., en el cual la resta se hace de derecha a izquierda, desagrupando antes de restar cada columna. También aprenden un método alternativo en el que desagrupan todo *antes* de restar. Si los estudiantes desagrupan todo primero, pueden restar de izquierda a derecha o de derecha a izquierda.

El método de Desagrupar primero ayuda a los estudiantes a evitar el error común de restar un número pequeño de arriba, de un número más grande de abajo.

1. Desagrupar primero.
2. Restar (de izquierda a derecha o de derecha a izquierda).

$$
\begin{array}{r}
15 \\
3\ \overset{\cancel{5}}{} \overset{\cancel{1}}{}3 \\
\cancel{463} \\
-\ 275 \\
\hline
188
\end{array}
$$

Desagrupar 1 centena para formar 10 decenas.

Desagrupar 1 decena para formar 10 unidades.

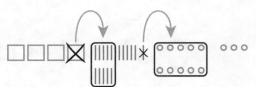

3 centenas   15 decenas   13 unidades

Si tiene alguna pregunta o algún comentario, por favor comuníquese conmigo. Gracias.

Atentamente,
El maestro de su niño

© Houghton Mifflin Harcourt Publishing Company

En la Unidad 3 se aplican los siguientes estándares de los Estándares estatales comunes de matemáticas: **3.OA.D.8, 3.OA.D.9, 3.NBT.A.1, 3.NBT.A.2, y todos los de** Prácticas matemáticas.

Make Place Value Drawings

estimate

ones

expanded
form

place value

hundreds

round

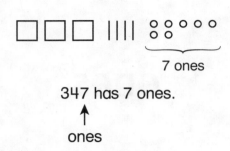

347 has 7 ones.

↑
ones

A reasonable guess about how many or about how much.

The value assigned to the place that a digit occupies in a number.

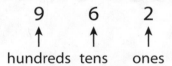

9   6   2

↑   ↑   ↑

hundreds tens ones

A number written to show the value of each of its digits.

Examples:
347 = 300 + 40 + 7
347 = 3 hundreds + 4 tens + 7 ones

To find about how many or how much by expressing a number to the nearest ten, hundred, thousand, and so on.

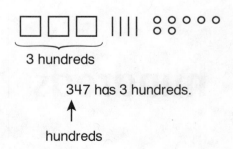

347 has 3 hundreds.

↑
hundreds

standard form

tens

thousands

The name of a number written using digits.

Example:
1,829

4 tens

347 has 4 tens.

↑
tens

Thousands	Hundreds	Tens	Ones
6	7	8	2

There are 6 thousands in 6,782.

Name _____

Practice Place Value Drawings to 999

VOCABULARY
place value

Write the number for each dot drawing.

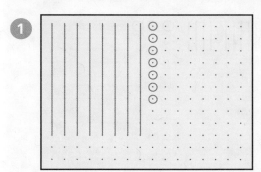

1

2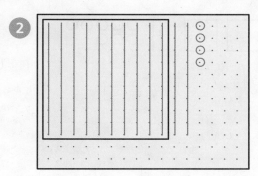

_____   _____

Write the number for each place value drawing.

3 ☐ ☐ ||||| || ○○○○○ ○○

4 ☐ ☐ ☐ ||||| | ○

_____   _____

5 ☐ ☐ ☐ || ○○○
☐ ☐ ☐

6 ☐ ☐ ☐ |||| ○○○○○ ○○○○
☐

_____   _____

Make a place value drawing for each number.

7 86

8 587

Practice with the Thousand Model

Write the number for each place value drawing.

9

_____

10

_____

Make a place value drawing for each number.

11 2,368

12 5,017

Write Numbers for Word Names

Write the number for the words.

13 eighty-two _____

14 ninety-nine _____

15 four hundred sixty-seven _____

16 nine hundred six _____

17 one thousand, fifteen _____

18 eight thousand, one hundred twenty _____

✓**Check Understanding**

Use place value drawings to show how the numbers 251 and 521 are different.

Make Place Value Drawings

1	2	10	20
1	2	1 0	2 0

3	4	30	40
3	4	3 0	4 0

5	6	50	60
5	6	5 0	6 0

7	8	70	80
7	8	7 0	8 0

9	90	100
9	9 0	1 0 0

Secret Code Cards 1–100 **189A**

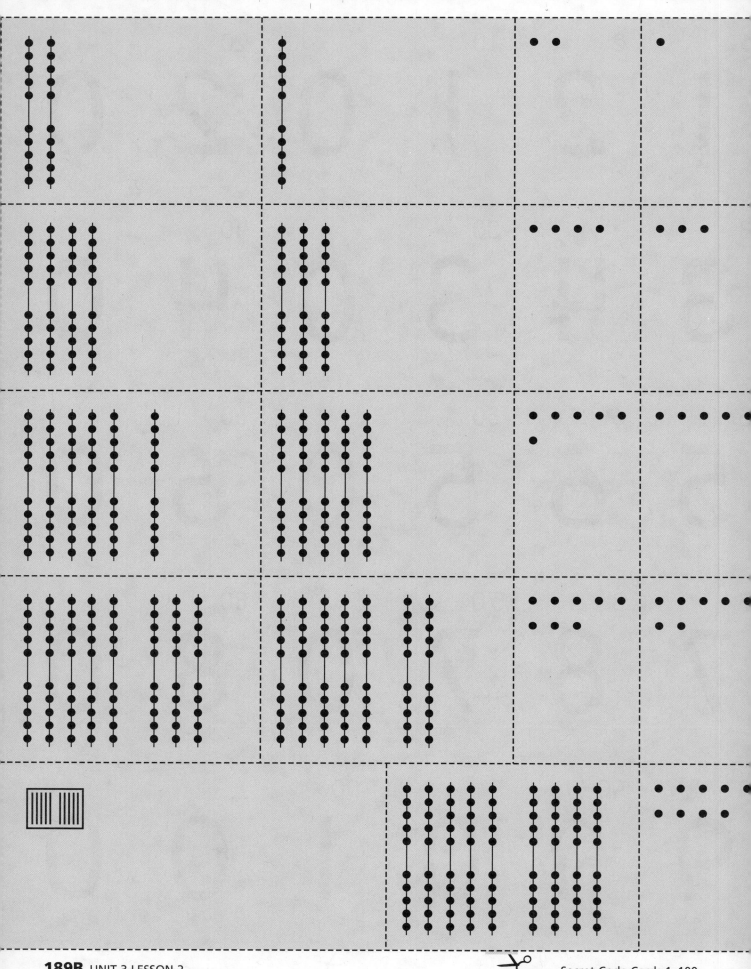

Secret Code Cards 1–100

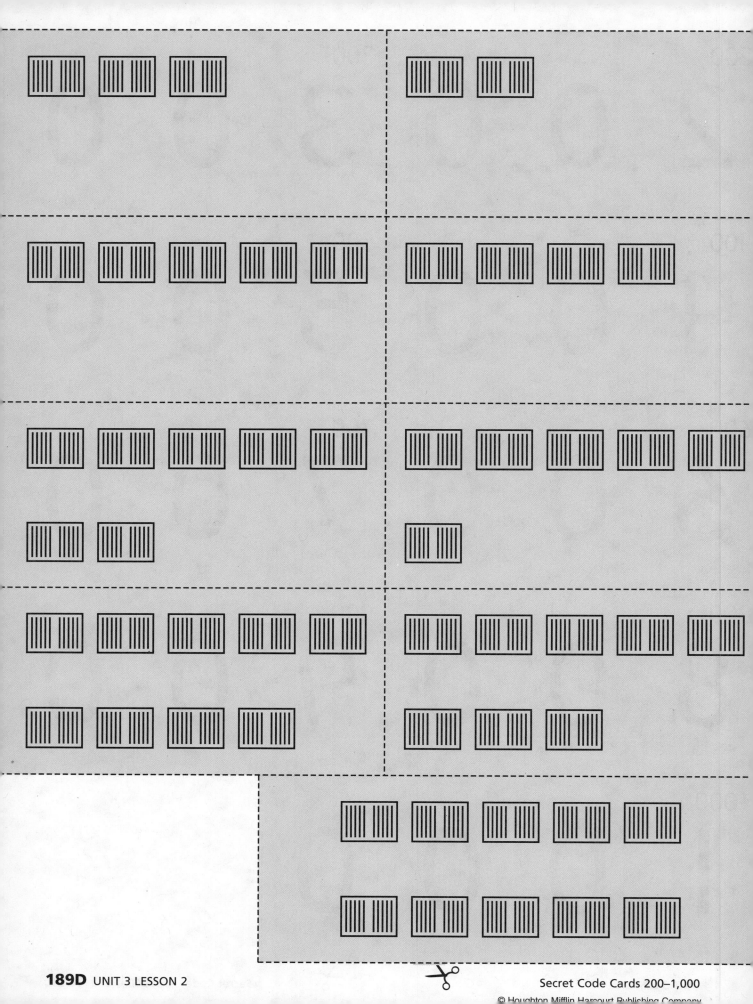

Secret Code Cards 200–1,000

Name _____

VOCABULARY
hundreds
tens
ones
thousands
expanded form

Build and Discuss Other Numbers

Write the number.

1 700 + 20 + 9 = _____

2 1,000 + 600 + 80 + 4 = _____

3 400 + 5 = _____

4 3 **hundreds** + 4 **tens** + 7 **ones** = _____

5 8 hundreds + 1 ten = _____

6 1 **thousand** + 9 hundreds + 1 ten + 8 ones = _____

Write the number in expanded form in two ways.

7 585

_____

_____

8 1,367

_____

_____

9 213

_____

_____

What's the Error?

Dear Math Students,

I was asked to build the number 238 with Secret Code Cards. I made the number with these cards.

| 200 | 3 | 8 |
| 2 0 0 | 3 | 8 |

| 200 | 3 | 8 |
| 2 | 3 | 8 |

My teacher says that what I showed is not correct. Can you help me?

Your friend,
Puzzled Penguin

10 Write an answer to Puzzled Penguin.

_____

_____

_____

_____

✔ Check Understanding

Use the number 456 to complete the sentences. Build the number with Secret Code Cards to check your answer.

The value of the digit 4 is _____.

The value of the digit 5 is _____.

The value of the digit 6 is _____.

Build Numbers

Read and Write Numbers

VOCABULARY
standard form

Write the number for the words.

1 two hundred twelve _____

2 two thousand, eight _____

3 nine hundred ninety-one _____

4 six thousand, fifty-one _____

5 four hundred sixteen _____

6 six hundred nine _____

7 nine hundred eighty-seven

_____

8 five thousand, thirty _____

9 four thousand, seventeen

_____

10 eight thousand, six hundred

_____

Write the word name for each number.

11 783

_____

12 907

_____

13 3,001

_____

14 8,043

_____

Write each number in expanded form.

15 314 _____

16 2,148 _____

17 7,089 _____

18 8,305 _____

Write each number in standard form.

19 5 thousands + 8 tens + 7 ones

_____

20 6 thousands + 4 hundreds + 5 ones

_____

Solve and Discuss

Use a place value drawing to help you solve each problem. Label your answers.

Show your work.

21 Scott baked a batch of rolls. He gave a bag of 10 rolls to each of 7 friends. He kept 1 roll for himself. How many rolls did he bake in all?

_____

22 Sixty-two bags of hot dog buns were delivered to the school cafeteria. Each bag had 10 buns. How many buns were delivered?

_____

Mario and Rosa baked 89 corn muffins. They put the muffins in boxes of 10.

23 How many boxes did they fill?

_____

24 How many muffins were left over?

_____

Zoe's scout troop collected 743 cans of food to donate to a shelter. They put the cans in boxes of 10.

25 How many boxes did they fill?

_____

26 How many cans were left over?

_____

✔ **Check Understanding**

Write the number 4,250 in expanded form in two different ways.

4,250 = _____ hundreds + _____ tens or

_____ thousands + _____ hundreds + _____ ones

Place Value in Word Problems

Scrambled Place Value Names

Unscramble the place values and write the number.

1 8 ones + 6 hundreds + 4 tens

_____

2 9 hundreds + 7 tens + 1 one

_____

3 5 ones + 0 tens + 7 hundreds

_____

4 5 tens + 4 ones + 3 hundreds

_____

5 2 tens + 2 hundreds + 2 ones

_____

6 8 hundreds + 3 ones + 6 tens

_____

Unscramble the place values and write the number.
Then, make a place value drawing for the number.

7 6 hundreds + 9 ones + 3 tens

_____

8 9 ones + 3 tens + 8 hundreds

_____

9 8 ones + 3 hundreds + 4 tens

_____

10 2 hundreds + 9 tens + 1 one

_____

Solve and Discuss

Solve each problem. Label your answer.

11 The bookstore received 35 boxes of books. Each box held 10 books. How many books did the store receive?

_____

> Maya's family picked 376 apples and put them in baskets. Each basket held 10 apples.

12 How many baskets did they fill?   13 How many apples were left over?

_____   _____

> Aidee had 672 digital photos. She put them in folders of 100 each.

14 How many folders did Aidee fill?   15 How many photos were left over?

_____   _____

> Joe had 543 pennies in his coin bank. He grouped the pennies into piles of 100.

16 How many piles of 100 did Joe make?   17 How many extra pennies did he have?

_____   _____

✓ **Check Understanding**

Make a place value drawing to represent the 543 pennies in Joe's coin bank.

Practice with Place Value

Name _____

VOCABULARY
estimate
round

Estimate

Solve the problem.

1. Tasha read three books over the summer. Here is the number of pages in each book:

Watership Down	494 pages
Sounder	128 pages
The Secret Garden	368 pages

   About how many pages did Tasha read? Explain how you made your **estimate**.

   _____

   _____

Practice Rounding

Round each number to the nearest hundred. Use drawings or Secret Code Cards, if they help you.

2. 128 _____

3. 271 _____

4. 376 _____

5. 649 _____

6. 415 _____

7. 550 _____

8. 62 _____

9. 1,481 _____

10. 2,615 _____

11. **Explain Your Thinking** When you round a number to the nearest hundred, how do you know whether to round up or round down?

   _____

   _____

   _____

   _____

Solve Problems by Estimating

Solve by rounding to the nearest hundred.

Show your work.

12 On Saturday, the stadium snack bar sold 286 small drinks, 341 medium drinks, and 277 large drinks. About how many drinks were sold?

_____

13 Last week, Mrs. Larson drove 191 miles on Monday, 225 miles on Wednesday, and 107 miles on Friday. About how many miles did she drive altogether?

_____

14 Of the 832 people at the hockey game, 292 sat on the visiting team side. The rest sat on the home team side. About how many people sat on the home team side?

Reasonable Answers

Use rounding to decide if the answer is reasonable. Write your estimate. Then write *yes* or *no* for the reasonableness of the answer.

15 $604 - 180 = 586$

_____

17 $268 - 57 = 107$

_____

16 $377 + 191 = 568$

_____

18 $41 + 395 = 300$

_____

✓ **Check Understanding**

Explain how to round a number with a 7 in the tens place to the nearest hundred.

Round 2-Digit Numbers to the Nearest Ten

Round each number to the nearest ten.

1. 63 _____

2. 34 _____

3. 78 _____

4. 25 _____

5. 57 _____

6. 89 _____

7. 42 _____

8. 92 _____

Round 3-Digit Numbers to the Nearest Ten

Round each number to the nearest ten.

9. 162 _____

10. 741 _____

11. 309 _____

12. 255 _____

13. 118 _____

14. 197 _____

15. 503 _____

16. 246 _____

17. **Explain Your Thinking** When you round a number to the nearest ten, how do you know whether to round up or round down?

_____

_____

_____

Estimate the Answer

Solve each problem.

18 The chart at the right shows how many smoothies were sold at the Juice Hut yesterday. By rounding each number to the nearest ten, estimate how many smoothies were sold in all.

Smoothies Sold at Juice Hut

13 raspberry-peach smoothies

38 strawberry-banana smoothies

44 guava-mango smoothies

61 peach-blueberry smoothies

19 A store has 52 necklaces, 75 bracelets, 36 rings, and 23 earrings. Round each number to the nearest ten to find *about* how many pieces of jewelry the store has.

20 Roz rented a movie that is 123 minutes long. She watched 48 minutes of it. Round each number to the nearest ten to estimate how many more minutes she has to watch.

Use the table at the right to solve Problems 21–23.

21 Estimate the total number of books the school received by rounding each number to the nearest hundred.

Jefferson Elementary School Books Received	
Math	436
Reading	352

22 Estimate the total number of books the school received by rounding each number to the nearest ten.

23 Find the total number of math and reading books. Which of your estimates is closer to the actual total?

Reasonable Answers

Use rounding to decide if the answer is reasonable.
Write your estimate. Write *yes* or *no* for the reasonableness
of the answer.

24 $93 - 29 = 64$

_____

25 $113 + 57 = 140$

_____

26 $83 + 19 = 102$

_____

27 $336 + 258 = 594$

_____

28 $468 - 158 = 280$

_____

29 $437 + 149 = 536$

_____

30 $725 - 285 = 590$

_____

31 $249 + 573 = 822$

_____

32 $542 - 167 = 475$

_____

What's the Error?

Dear Math Students,

Today my teacher asked me to estimate the answer to this problem:

Ms. Smith's class brought in 384 cans for the food drive. Mr. Alvarez's class brought in 524 cans. About how many cans did the two classes bring in?

$$
\begin{array}{r}
384 \rightarrow \quad 300 \\
+\ 524 \rightarrow \quad +\ 500 \\
\hline
800
\end{array}
$$

About 800 cans were brought in.

Is my answer correct? If not, please correct my work and tell me what I did wrong.

Your friend,
Puzzled Penguin

(33) Write an answer to Puzzled Penguin.

_____

_____

Estimate the Number of Objects

Jar D has 100 Beans. Estimate how many beans are in the other jars.

(34) Jar A _____

(35) Jar B _____

(36) Jar C _____

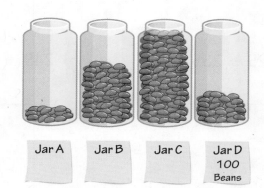

Jar A   Jar B   Jar C   Jar D 100 Beans

✔ **Check Understanding**

Round each number to the nearest ten.

83 _____   98 _____   245 _____   362 _____

Round to the Nearest Ten

Name _____   Date _____

Write the correct answer.

1 Round to the nearest hundred.

678

_____

2 Round to the nearest ten.

524

_____

3 Write the number shown by the place value drawing.

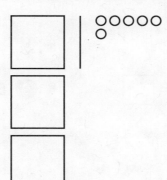

_____

4 Round to the nearest ten.

567

_____

5 Gerard has 365 baseball cards. He puts as many of them as he can into piles of 100. How many piles of 100 does he make?

_____

Name _____   Date _____

PATH to
FLUENCY

Multiply.

1 1 × 3 = ☐

2 3 × 2 = ☐

3 4 × 3 = ☐

4 4 × 1 = ☐

5 2 × 5 = ☐

6 6 × 1 = ☐

7 6 × 6 = ☐

8 8 × 4 = ☐

9 5 × 7 = ☐

10 9 × 3 = ☐

11 8 × 8 = ☐

12 6 × 9 = ☐

13 7 × 10 = ☐

14 10 × 10 = ☐

15 8 × 9 = ☐

Solve and Discuss

Solve each problem. Label your answer. Use your MathBoard or a separate sheet of paper.

1 Elena made necklaces for her friends. She used 586 green beads and 349 red beads. How many beads did Elena use in all?

_____

2 Fabrice has a collection of 485 basketball cards and 217 baseball cards. How many sports cards does Fabrice have in all?

_____

PATH to FLUENCY **Introduce Addition Methods**

Tonya and Mark collect seashells. Tonya has 249 shells and Mark has 386 shells. How many shells do they have in all?

Here are three ways to find the answer:

Show All Totals Method	**New Groups Below Method**	**New Groups Above Method**
249 + 386 ─── 500 120 + 15 ─── 635	249 + 386 _{1 1} ─── 635	^{1 1} 249 + 386 ─── 635

Proof Drawing:

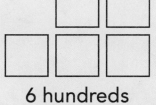

6 hundreds
(5 hundreds
+ 1 new hundred)

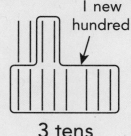

I new hundred

3 tens
(2 tens + 1 new ten)

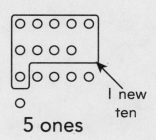

5 ones

I new ten

PATH to FLUENCY Practice Addition Methods

Solve each problem. Make proof drawings to show that your answers are correct.

3 Ryan has two stamp albums. One album has 554 stamps, and the other has 428 stamps. How many stamps does Ryan have in all?

_____

4 Ali has 128 photos of her pets and 255 photos of her family. How many photos does Ali have altogether?

_____

5 One week Ashley read 269 pages. The next week she read 236 pages. What is the total number of pages she read in the two weeks?

_____

6 The online store has 445 comedy movies and 515 drama movies. How many comedy and drama movies does the store have altogether?

_____

✔ **Check Understanding**

Tell which addition method you prefer and why.

Explore Multidigit Addition

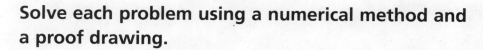

Name _____

Solve and Discuss

Solve each problem using a numerical method and a proof drawing.

1 There are 359 cars and 245 trucks in the parking garage. How many vehicles are in the garage?

_____

2 The Creepy Crawler exhibit at the science museum has 693 spiders and 292 centipedes. How many spiders and centipedes are there in all?

_____

3 On Saturday, 590 people went to the art museum. On Sunday, 355 went to the museum. How many people went to the museum altogether?

_____

4 There were 120 people on the ferry yesterday. Today the ferry had 767 people. How many people in all were on the ferry during the past two days?

_____

What's the Error?

Dear Math Students,

Today I found the answer to 168 + 78, but I don't know if I added correctly. Please look at my work. Is my answer right? If not, please correct my work and tell what I did wrong.

$$\begin{array}{r} 168 \\ + 78 \\ \hline 948 \end{array}$$

Your friend,
Puzzled Penguin

5 Write an answer to Puzzled Penguin.

_____

_____

PATH to FLUENCY Line Up the Places to Add

Write each addition vertically. Line up the places correctly. Then add and make a proof drawing.

6 179 + 38 = _____

7 650 + 345 = _____

8 407 + 577 = _____

✓ Check Understanding

Explain why it is important to line up place values before adding.

Discuss Addition Methods

Decide When to Group

**Decide which new groups you will make.
Then add to see if you were correct.**

1   123
      + 247

2   358
      + 434

3   732
      + 189

4   416
      + 396

Add.

5   647
      + 178

6   132
      + 763

7   554
      + 257

8   168
      + 692

9   384
      + 586

10   631
       + 189

11   464
       + 446

12   313
       + 649

13 576 + 265 = _____

14 568 + 219 = _____

15 389 + 511 = _____

16 137 + 284 = _____

Write an equation and solve the problem.

17 The first animated film at the movie theatre
lasted 129 minutes. The second film lasted
104 minutes. How many minutes in all did
the two movies last?

_____

Solve and Discuss

Write an equation and solve the problem.   *Show your work.*

18 Jacob has 347 basketball cards in his collection. He has 256 baseball cards. How many cards does he have altogether?

_____

19 Jasmine's family drove for two days to visit her grandparents. They drove 418 miles on the first day and 486 miles on the second day. How many miles did they drive in all?

_____

20 The florist ordered 398 roses and 562 tulips. How many flowers did the florist order in all?

_____

21 The suitcase that Emilio packed weighed 80 pounds. His wife packed three suitcases. Each of her suitcases weighed 30 pounds. How many pounds in all did their suitcases weigh?

_____

22 Write and solve an addition word problem where 287 and 614 are addends.

_____

_____

_____

✓ **Check Understanding**

Explain how you know when you need to group when adding two 3-digit numbers.

The Grouping Concept in Addition

Name _____

Add Three-Digit Numbers

School Carnival Rides	
Rides	Tickets Sold
Twister	298
Monster Mix	229
Crazy Coaster	193
Mega Wheel	295
Bumper Cars	301

Write an equation and solve the problem.

Show your work.

1 How many people went on the two most popular rides?

_____

2 The total tickets sold for which two rides was 494?

_____

3 Tickets for the Monster Mix and Crazy Coaster sold for $2. How much money did the school earn on the ticket sales for these two rides?

_____

4 About how many tickets were sold for Twister, Monster Mix, and Mega Wheel altogether?

_____

5 The total tickets sold for which three rides equals about 900?

_____

CC SS Content Standards **3.OA.D.8, 3.NBT.A.1, 3.NBT.A.2**
Mathematical Practices **MP1, MP4, MP6**

Use Addition to Solve Problems

Student Collections	
Type of Collection	**Number of Objects**
rocks	403
stamps	371
shells	198
buttons	562
miniature cars	245

Write an equation and solve the problem.   *Show your work.*

6 How many objects are in the two smallest collections?

_____

7 The total number of objects in two collections is 760. What are the collections?

_____

8 Are the combined collections of shells and buttons greater than or less than the combined collections of rocks and stamps?

_____

9 Is the estimated sum of stamps, shells, and miniature cars closer to 700 or to 800?

_____

10 Yuji has a number of sports cards that is 154 greater than the number of rocks. How many cards does Yuji have?

_____

✔ **Check Understanding**

Suppose your classmate got a sum of 343 for Problem 6. Describe the error. _____

Practice Addition

Write the correct answer.

Show your work.

1 The bookstore sold 273 books in the morning and 385 books in the afternoon before it closed. How many books did it sell that day?

_____

2 What new groups will need to be made to add 345 and 276?

_____

_____

3 Holly's farm has 143 goats and 287 sheep. How many animals does the farm have in all? Write an equation and solve the problem.

_____

Add.

4 $227 + 98 =$ _____

5 $47 + 26 =$ _____

PATH to FLUENCY

Divide.

1 $3 \div 3 = \boxed{}$

2 $8 \div 2 = \boxed{}$

3 $9 \div 3 = \boxed{}$

4 $16 \div 2 = \boxed{}$

5 $25 \div 5 = \boxed{}$

6 $28 \div 4 = \boxed{}$

7 $32 \div 8 = \boxed{}$

8 $40 \div 4 = \boxed{}$

9 $48 \div 6 = \boxed{}$

10 $56 \div 7 = \boxed{}$

11 $63 \div 9 = \boxed{}$

12 $54 \div 6 = \boxed{}$

13 $64 \div 8 = \boxed{}$

14 $72 \div 8 = \boxed{}$

15 $90 \div 9 = \boxed{}$

Discuss Subtraction Methods

Solve this word problem.

> Mr. Kim had 134 kites in his hobby store. He sold 58 of them. How many kites does he have now?

1 Write a subtraction that you could do to answer this question.

_____

2 Make a place value drawing for 134. Take away 58. How many are left?

3 Write a numerical solution method for what you did in the drawing.

4 Describe how you ungrouped to subtract.

_____

_____

_____

_____

What's the Error?

Dear Math Students,

Today I found the answer to 134 – 58, but I don't know if I did it correctly. Please look at my work. Is my answer right? If not, please correct my work and tell what I did wrong.

```
  134
–  58
 ────
  124
```

Your friend,
Puzzled Penguin

5 Write an answer to Puzzled Penguin.

_____

_____

 Subtraction Detective

To avoid making subtraction mistakes, look at the top number closely. Do all the ungrouping *before* you subtract. The magnifying glass around the top number helps you remember to be a "subtraction detective."

Subtract. Show your ungroupings numerically and with proof drawings.

6 (371)
– 86

7 (163)
– 47

8 (459)
–175

 Check Understanding

Complete. Always subtract the _____

number from the _____ number.

Ungroup to Subtract

PATH to FLUENCY Ungroup to Subtract

Solve each problem. Show your work numerically and with proof drawings.

1 Lakesha bought a box of 500 paper clips. So far, she has used 138 of them. How many are left?

_____

2 A movie theater has 400 seats. At the noon show, 329 seats were filled. How many seats were empty?

_____

3 At the start of the school year, Ms. Endo had a new box of 300 crayons for her class. Now 79 crayons are broken. How many unbroken crayons are there?

_____

PATH to FLUENCY Subtract Across Zeros

Solve each problem. Show your work numerically and with proof drawings.

4 The students at Freedom Elementary School have a goal of reading 900 books. They have read 342 books. How many books do the students have left to read?

_____

5 There are 500 fiction books in the Lee School Library. There are 179 fewer non-fiction books than fiction books. How many books are non-fiction?

_____

6 The students at Olympia Elementary School collected 1,000 bottles for recycling. The students at Sterling Elementary collected 768 bottles. How many more bottles did the students at Olympia collect?

_____

(PATH to FLUENCY) Practice Subtracting Across Zeros

Subtract. Make proof drawings for Exercises 7–10.

7
```
  800
- 391
```

8
```
  500
- 333
```

9
```
  400
- 217
```

10
```
  900
- 818
```

11
```
  600
- 575
```

12
```
  700
- 248
```

13
```
  200
- 109
```

14
```
  800
- 519
```

15 **Math Journal** Write a word problem that is solved by subtracting a 2-digit number from a 3-digit number that has a zero in both the ones and tens places. Then solve the problem.

(PATH to FLUENCY) Practice Deciding When to Ungroup

Subtract. Make proof drawings if you need to on MathBoards or on a separate sheet of paper.

16 912 − 265

17 323 − 147

18 280 − 136

19 489 − 263

20
$$
\begin{array}{r}
754 \\
-\ 389 \\
\hline
\end{array}
$$

21
$$
\begin{array}{r}
912 \\
-\ 437 \\
\hline
\end{array}
$$

22
$$
\begin{array}{r}
341 \\
-\ 178 \\
\hline
\end{array}
$$

23
$$
\begin{array}{r}
603 \\
-\ 464 \\
\hline
\end{array}
$$

✓ Check Understanding

Subtract. 300 − 156. Make a proof drawing to show that your answer is correct.

Subtract Across Zeros

Name _____

PATH to FLUENCY **Ungroup from Left or Right**

Tony and Maria each solved this problem:

On Tuesday morning, a bookstore had 463 copies of a new bestseller. By the end of the day, 275 copies were sold. How many copies were left?

Tony	Maria
Tony started ungrouping from the left.	Maria started ungrouping from the right.

Tony

Tony started ungrouping from the left.

1. He has enough hundreds.

2. He does not have enough tens. He ungroups 1 hundred to make 10 more tens.

3. He does not have enough ones. He ungroups 1 ten to make 10 more ones.

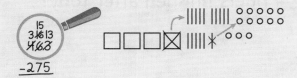

4. Complete the subtraction.

Maria

Maria started ungrouping from the right.

1. She does not have enough ones. She ungroups 1 ten to make 10 more ones.

2. She does not have enough tens. She ungroups 1 hundred to get 10 more tens.

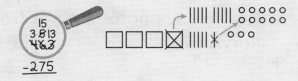

3. She has enough hundreds.

4. Complete the subtraction.

PATH to FLUENCY Choose a Method to Subtract

Subtract.

1 686
    − 387

2 340
    − 167

3 765
    − 498

4 841
    − 253

5 912
    − 575

6 853
    − 194

7 705
    − 429

8 998
    − 299

9 513
    − 156

10 627 − 348

11 544 − 169

12 810 − 261

Solve.

13 Rory is putting 302 digital photos in an album. Of these, 194 are from her trip to Florida. How many photos are not from Rory's trip?

14 There were 645 bike riders in a race. Toby finished eighty-seventh. How many riders finished after Toby?

✓ **Check Understanding**

Explain two subtraction methods—ungrouping from the left and ungrouping from the right.

Discuss Methods of Subtracting

PATH to FLUENCY Relate Addition and Subtraction

**Solve each problem. Make a proof drawing
if you need to.**

1 There were 138 students in the gym for the
assembly. Then 86 more students came in. How
many students were in the gym altogether?

_____

2 There were 224 students in the gym for the
assembly. Then 86 students left. How many
students were still in the gym?

_____

3 Look at your addition, subtraction, and proof
drawings from Problems 1 and 2. How are
addition and subtraction related?

_____

_____

_____

Solve and Discuss

Solve. Label your answers.

4 Marly had 275 baseball cards. Her brother gave her a collection of 448 baseball cards. How many baseball cards does Marly have now?

_____

5 Write a subtraction word problem related to the addition word problem in Problem 4. Then find the answer without doing any calculations.

_____

_____

_____

6 Bill drove 375 miles on the first day of his cross-country trip. The next day he drove an additional 528 miles. How many miles did Bill drive on the first two days of his trip?

_____

7 Write a subtraction problem related to the addition word problem in Problem 6. Then find the answer without doing any calculations.

_____

_____

_____

✓ Check Understanding

Draw a Math Mountain to show the relationship between the numbers in Problems 6 and 7.

Relate Addition and Subtraction

Subtract and Check

Show your work.

Solve each problem.

1 Ken collects photographs as a hobby. He has 375 photographs in his collection at home. If Ken brought 225 of his photographs to share with his classmates, how many photographs did he leave at home?

_____

2 Of the 212 third- and fourth-grade students, 165 attended the school festival. How many students did not attend the festival?

_____

3 Becky has 653 marbles in her collection. Riley has 438 marbles in her collection. How many more marbles does Becky have than Riley?

_____

4 Andrea and John need 750 tickets to get a board game. They have 559 tickets. How many more tickets do they need?

_____

PATH to FLUENCY Practice Deciding When to Ungroup

Answer each question.

Adair subtracted 595 from 834.

5 Did she have to ungroup to make more tens? Explain.

_____

_____

_____

6 Did she have to ungroup to make more ones? Explain.

_____

_____

_____

Beatrice subtracted 441 from 950.

7 Did she have to ungroup to make more tens? Explain.

_____

_____

_____

8 Did she have to ungroup to make more ones? Explain.

_____

_____

_____

Wan subtracted 236 from 546.

9 Did he have to ungroup to make more tens? Explain.

_____

_____

_____

10 Did he have to ungroup to make more ones? Explain.

_____

_____

_____

✓**Check Understanding**

Explain how to decide when to ungroup in a subtraction problem.

Subtraction Practice

Name _____

PATH to FLUENCY Practice Addition and Subtraction

Add or subtract.

① 112
+ 459

② 572
− 357

③ 253
+ 328

④ 710
− 464

⑤ 461
− 182

⑥ 540
+ 175

⑦ 921
− 653

⑧ 398
− 99

⑨ 712
+ 189

⑩ 600
− 223

⑪ 809
− 576

⑫ 634
+ 287

Solve.

⑬ The height of Angeline Falls in Washington is 450 feet. Snoqualmie Falls in Washington is 182 feet lower than Angeline Falls. What is the height of Snoqualmie Falls?

⑭ Jill scored 534 points at the arcade on Friday night. She scored 396 points on Saturday night. How many points did she score altogether?

_____

_____

Solve Real World Problems

The students at Liberty Elementary collected pennies for a fundraiser.

Pennies Collected					
Grade	1	2	3	4	5
Number of Pennies	225	436	517	609	342

Write an equation and solve the problem.   *Show your work.*

15 How many pennies did Grades 2 and 5 collect?

_____

16 How many more pennies did Grades 1 and 3 together collect than Grade 4?

_____

17 Is the total number of pennies collected by Grades 1 and 4 greater than or less than the total number collected by Grades 3 and 5?

_____

18 The total number of pennies collected by which three grades equals about 900?

_____

19 The Kindergarten students collected 198 fewer pennies than the Grade 3 students. How many pennies did the Kindergarteners collect?

_____

✓ **Check Understanding**

Describe a real world situation in which you would need to add or subtract.

Addition and Subtraction Practice

Solve Multistep Word Problems

Solve each problem. Label your answers.   *Show your work.*

1   Isabel bought 36 pieces of fruit for her soccer team. There are 16 apples, 12 bananas, and the rest are pears. How many pieces of fruit are pears?

_____

2   Toby has a collection of sports cards. He had 13 baseball cards, 16 basketball cards, and 14 football cards. Toby sold 15 cards and he bought 17 hockey cards. What is the total number of cards in Toby's collection now?

_____

3   There are 15 more boys than girls in the school band. There are 27 girls. How many students are in the school band?

_____

4   Finn delivered 13 pizzas. Then he delivered 8 more pizzas. Altogether, he delivered 6 fewer pizzas than Liz. How many pizzas did Liz deliver?

_____

5   Majeed built 7 car models and 14 airplane models. Jasmine built 9 more car models than Majeed and 6 fewer airplane models. How many models did Jasmine build in all?

_____

Reasonable Answers

Use rounding to decide if the last number is reasonable. Write
yes **or** *no*. **Then add or subtract to see if you were correct.**

6 Nathan counted 28 large dogs and 37 small dogs
at the dog park. He said he saw 55 dogs in all.

_____

7 There are 122 third- and fourth-grade students at
Cedar Creek Elementary School. There are 67 students
in third grade, so there are 55 students in fourth grade.

_____

8 The pet supermarket sold 245 bags of dog food and
167 bags of cat food. The supermarket sold 312 bags
of pet food in all.

_____

9 There were 432 people at the basketball game.
257 people sat on the home team side, so 175 people
sat on the visiting team side.

_____

10 The Pecos River is 234 miles longer than the
Yellowstone River. The Yellowstone River is
692 miles long. The Pecos River is 826 miles long.

_____

✔ **Check Understanding**
Describe a strategy you used to solve Problem 8.

Solve Word Problems

Name _____

Math and Maps

The Pony Express was a mail service from St. Joseph, Missouri, to Sacramento, California. The Pony Express service carried mail by horseback riders in relays.

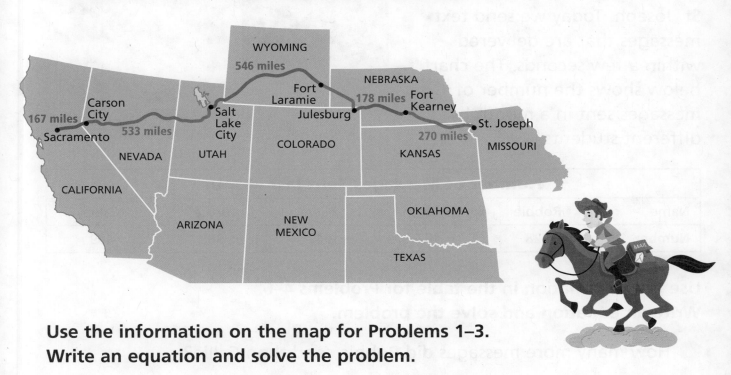

**Use the information on the map for Problems 1–3.
Write an equation and solve the problem.**

1 How many miles did the Pony Express riders travel on a trip from Sacramento to Salt Lake City?

_____

2 The total distance from St. Joseph to Fort Laramie is 616 miles. How many miles is it from Julesburg to Fort Laramie?

_____

3 Write and solve a problem that can be answered using the map.

_____

_____

Use a Table

It took the Pony Express 10 days to deliver letters between Sacramento and St. Joseph. Today we send text messages that are delivered within a few seconds. The chart below shows the number of messages sent in a month by different students.

Number of Messages Sent last Month					
Name	Robbie	Samantha	Ellen	Bryce	Callie
Number	528	462	942	388	489

Use the information in the table for Problems 4–6.
Write an equation and solve the problem.

4 How many more messages did Robbie send than Callie?

_____

5 How many more messages did Ellen send than Bryce and Samantha combined?

_____

6 Tamara said that Robbie and Bryce together sent 806 messages. Is that number reasonable? Explain. Then find the actual number to see if you are correct.

_____

_____

_____

Focus on Mathematical Practices

Subtract.

1 $765 - 56 = $ _____

2 $72 - 35 = $ _____

Solve.

3 524 people watch the town parade. 178 of them are children. How many people watching the parade are adults?

_____

4 Roberto has a collection of 243 CDs. He scratched 152 of them. How many of his CDs are not scratched?

_____

5 Amaya has 476 pennies. Then she finds 359 more pennies. How many pennies does she have now?

_____

PATH to FLUENCY

Multiply or divide.

1 $1 \div 1 = \boxed{}$

2 $3 \times 5 = \boxed{}$

3 $6 \div 2 = \boxed{}$

4 $4 \times 3 = \boxed{}$

5 $9 \div 3 = \boxed{}$

6 $8 \times 2 = \boxed{}$

7 $12 \div 3 = \boxed{}$

8 $7 \times 6 = \boxed{}$

9 $8 \div 1 = \boxed{}$

10 $7 \times 3 = \boxed{}$

11 $20 \div 4 = \boxed{}$

12 $5 \times 7 = \boxed{}$

13 $36 \div 9 = \boxed{}$

14 $9 \times 2 = \boxed{}$

15 $54 \div 9 = \boxed{}$

1 Select the way that shows three hundred fifty-seven. Mark all that apply.

Ⓐ 357

Ⓑ 3 hundreds + 57 tens

Ⓒ 3 hundreds + 5 tens + 7 ones

Ⓓ

Ⓔ 300 + 5 + 7

2 Make a place value drawing for the number.

691

3 A shop sells 564 posters. It sells 836 calendars. Round each number to the nearest ten to estimate about how many more calendars the shop sells than posters.

about _____ more calendars

4 Write the number in the box that shows how it should be rounded to the nearest hundred.

479   440   655   405   643

400	500	600	700

5 For numbers 5a–5e, use rounding to decide whether the answer is reasonable. Choose Yes or No.

5a. $187 - 43 = 144$ ○ Yes   ○ No

5b. $328 + 87 = 385$ ○ Yes   ○ No

5c. $652 + 189 = 841$ ○ Yes   ○ No

5d. $1,293 - 126 = 367$ ○ Yes   ○ No

5e. $2,946 - 488 = 2,458$ ○ Yes   ○ No

6 Choose the difference that completes the number sentence.

$$425 - 346 = \boxed{\begin{array}{c} 79 \\ 89 \\ 121 \\ 771 \end{array}}$$

7 Subtract.

$$700 - 255 =$$

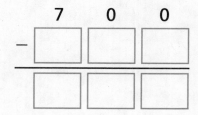

```
    7   0   0
-  [ ] [ ] [ ]
   _____
  [ ] [ ] [ ]
```

8 Add.

```
   521
 + 129
```

(A) 640   (C) 650

(B) 641   (D) 651

For numbers 9 and 10, add or subtract. Make a proof drawing to show that your answer is correct.

9
```
   497
 + 326
```
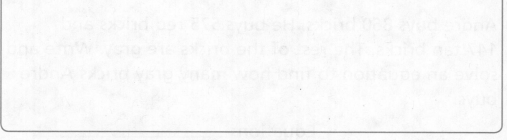

10
```
   690
 - 493
```
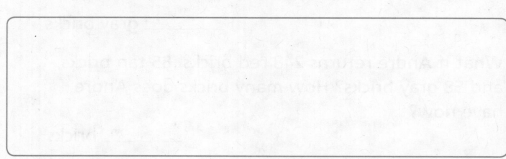

For numbers 11 and 12, add or subtract.   *Show your work.*

11   437
     + 273

Which method did you use to add?

I used the | New Groups Above
New Groups Below
Show All Totals | Method.

12   617
     − 549

Did you ungroup to subtract? Explain why or why not.

13 Andre buys 860 bricks. He buys 575 red bricks and
147 tan bricks. The rest of the bricks are gray. Write and
solve an equation to find how many gray bricks Andre
buys.

Equation: _____

_____ gray bricks

What if Andre returns 248 red bricks, 85 tan bricks,
and 58 gray bricks? How many bricks does Andre
have now?

_____ bricks

© Houghton Mifflin Harcourt Publishing Company

14 Pia collects 245 acorns in a jar. For numbers 14a–14d, select True or False for each statement.

14a. Pia collects 193 more acorns.
She now has 338 acorns.   ○ True   ○ False

14b. Pia gives 160 acorns to Ana.
She now has 85 acorns.   ○ True   ○ False

14c. Pia collects 286 more acorns.
She uses 143 to decorate a tray.
She now has 388 acorns.   ○ True   ○ False

14d. Pia gives her two sisters 85 acorns
each. She now has 160 acorns.   ○ True   ○ False

15 Li earns 321 points in the first round of a math contest. He earns another 278 points in the second round and 315 points in the third round. Li says he has 804 points.

Is Li's answer reasonable? Explain.

Find the actual answer to check if you are correct.

16 Darian sells 293 bags of popcorn and 321 bags of peanuts.

Part A

How many bags of popcorn and peanuts does Darian sell?

_____ bags

Part B

Write a subtraction word problem related to how many bags of popcorn and peanuts Darian sells. Then find the answer without doing any calculations.

17 A zoo has 209 reptiles. There are 93 lizards and 52 turtles. The rest are snakes. How many snakes are at the zoo?

_____ snakes

Raise Money

The students at Kevin's school are collecting
pennies for a service project. They plan to
use the money to buy flowers to plant at
a local park. They need 1,000 pennies to
buy each flat of flowers.

1 Kevin has collected 873 pennies.
Round 873 to the nearest 100. Is the
rounded number less than 1,000? Explain.

2 What would you have to add to 873 to get 1,000?
How do you know your answer is reasonable?

3 Write an addition word problem related to
Problem 2. Explain how the problems are related.

4 June, Ella, and Joshua also are collecting pennies
for the service project. June collected 324 pennies,
Ella collected 442 pennies, and Joshua collected
248 pennies.

Part A

Estimate to decide whether these three students
collected enough pennies to buy a flat of flowers.

Part B

Find the actual answer to check if you are correct.
Explain your strategy.

Part C

How many more pennies do the students need
to collect to buy a second flat of flowers? Show
your work.

Part D

Write an addition word problem related to
Part C. Explain how the problems are related.

Halves and Fourths in Measurement

Fractions in Measurement	
Halves	**Quarters**

Length

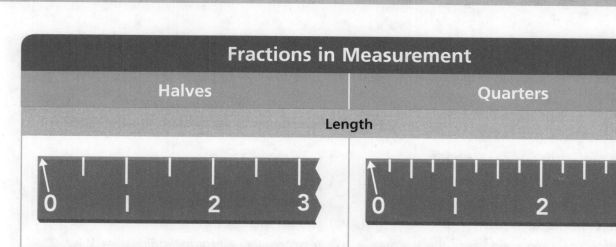

Money

Half-Dollar   Half-Dollar

4 Quarters

Time

30 minutes + 30 minutes
= 60 minutes
= 1 hour

15 minutes + 15 minutes +
15 minutes + 15 minutes
= 60 minutes
= 1 hour

Liquid Capacity

Measures and Units of Time

Table of Measures

Metric	Customary

Length/Area

Metric	Customary
1 meter (m) = 10 decimeters (dm) 1 meter (m) = 100 centimeters (cm) 1 decimeter (dm) = 10 centimeters (cm) 1 square centimeter = 1 cm² A metric unit for measuring area. It is the area of a square that is one centimeter on each side.	1 foot (ft) = 12 inches (in.) 1 yard = 3 feet (ft) 1 mile (mi) = 5,280 feet (ft) 1 square inch = 1 in² A customary unit for measuring area. It is the area of a square that is one inch on each side.

Liquid Volume

Metric	Customary
1 liter (L) = 1,000 milliliters (mL)	1 tablespoon (tbsp) = $\frac{1}{2}$ fluid ounce (fl oz) 1 cup (c) = 8 fluid ounces (fl oz) 1 pint (pt) = 2 cups (c) 1 quart (qt) = 2 pints (pt) 1 gallon (gal) = 4 quarts (qt)

Table of Units of Time

Time

1 minute (min) = 60 seconds (sec) 1 hour (hr) = 60 minutes 1 day = 24 hours 1 week (wk) = 7 days 1 month, about 30 days 1 year (yr) = 12 months (mo) or about 52 weeks	1 year = 365 days 1 leap year = 366 days

Properties of Operations

Associative Property of Addition

$(a + b) + c = a + (b + c)$	$(2 + 5) + 3 = 2 + (5 + 3)$

Commutative Property of Addition

$a + b = b + a$	$4 + 6 = 6 + 4$

Identity Property of Addition

$a + 0 = 0 + a = a$	$3 + 0 = 0 + 3 = 3$

Associative Property of Multiplication

$(a \cdot b) \cdot c = a \cdot (b \cdot c)$	$(3 \cdot 5) \cdot 7 = 3 \cdot (5 \cdot 7)$

Commutative Property of Multiplication

$a \cdot b = b \cdot a$	$6 \cdot 3 = 3 \cdot 6$

Identity Property of Multiplication

$a \cdot 1 = 1 \cdot a = a$	$8 \cdot 1 = 1 \cdot 8 = 8$

Zero Property of Multiplication

$a \cdot 0 = 0 \cdot a = 0$	$5 \cdot 0 = 0 \cdot 5 = 0$

Distributive Property of Multiplication over Addition

$a \cdot (b + c) = (a \cdot b) + (a \cdot c)$	$2 \cdot (4 + 3) = (2 \cdot 4) + (2 \cdot 3)$

Problem Types

Addition and Subtraction Problem Types

	Result Unknown	Change Unknown	Start Unknown
Add to	Aisha had 274 stamps in her collection. Then her grandfather gave her 65 stamps. How many stamps does she have now? *Situation and solution equation:*[1] $274 + 65 = s$	Aisha had 274 stamps in her collection. Then her grandfather gave her some stamps. Now she has 339 stamps. How many stamps did her grandfather give her? *Situation equation:* $274 + s = 339$ *Solution equation:* $s = 339 - 274$	Aisha had some stamps in her collection. Then her grandfather gave her 65 stamps. Now she has 339 stamps. How many stamps did she have to start? *Situation equation* $s + 65 = 339$ *Solution equation:* $s = 339 - 65$
Take from	A store had 750 bottles of water at the start of the day. During the day, the store sold 490 bottles. How many bottles did they have at the end of the day? *Situation and solution equation:* $750 - 490 = b$	A store had 750 bottles of water at the start of the day. The store had 260 bottles left at the end of the day. How many bottles did the store sell? *Situation equation:* $750 - b = 260$ *Solution equation:* $b = 750 - 260$	A store had a number of bottles of water at the start of the day. The store sold 490 bottles of water. At the end of the day 260 bottles were left. How many bottles did the store have to start with? *Situation equation:* $b - 490 = 260$ *Solution equation:* $b = 260 + 490$

[1]A situation equation represents the structure (action) in the problem situation. A solution equation shows the operation used to find the answer.

Addition and Subtraction Problem Types (continued)

	Total Unknown	Addend Unknown	Other Addends Unknown
Put Together/ Take Apart	A clothing store has 375 shirts with short sleeves and 148 shirts with long sleeves. How many shirts does the store have in all?	Of the 523 shirts in a clothing store, 375 have short sleeves. The rest have long sleeves. How many shirts have long sleeves?	A clothing store has 523 shirts. Some have short sleeves and 148 have long sleeves. How many of the shirts have short sleeves?

Total Unknown

Math drawing:[1]

$$
\begin{array}{c}
s \\
\diagdown \diagup \\
375 \quad 148
\end{array}
$$

Situation and solution equation:
$375 + 148 = s$

Addend Unknown

Math drawing:

$$
\begin{array}{c}
523 \\
\diagdown \diagup \\
375 \quad s
\end{array}
$$

Situation equation:
$523 = 375 + s$

Solution equation:
$s = 523 - 375$

Other Addends Unknown

Math drawing:

$$
\begin{array}{c}
523 \\
\diagdown \diagup \\
s \quad 148
\end{array}
$$

Situation equation
$523 = s + 148$

Solution equation:
$s = 523 - 148$

Both Addends Unknown is a productive extension of this basic situation, especially for small numbers less than or equal to 10. Such take apart situations can be used to show all the decompositions of a given number. The associated equations, which have a total on the left of the equal sign, help children understand that the = sign does not always mean *makes* or *results* in but always does mean *is the same number as*.

Both Addends Unknown

A clothing store has 523 shirts. Some have short sleeves and some have long sleeves. Write out a few situation equations for how many short sleeve and long sleeve shirts the store could have. Then describe the pattern you see.

Math Drawing:

$$
\begin{array}{c}
523 \\
\diagdown \diagup \\
s \quad 148 \\
\square \quad \square
\end{array}
$$

Situation Equation:
$523 = s + l$

[1]These math drawings are called math mountains in Grades 1–3 and break apart drawings in Grades 4 and 5.

Problem Types

Addition and Subtraction Problem Types (continued)

	Difference Unknown	Greater Unknown	Smaller Unknown
Compare	At a zoo, the female black bear weighs 175 pounds. The male black bear weighs 260 pounds. How much more does the male black bear weigh than the female black bear? At a zoo, the female black bear weighs 175 pounds. The male black bear weighs 260 pounds. How much less does the female black bear weigh than the male black bear? *Math drawing:* 260 175 d *Situation equation:* 175 + d = 260 or d = 260 − 175 *Solution equation:* d = 260 − 175	**Leading Language** At a zoo, the female black bear weighs 175 pounds. The male black bear weighs 85 pounds more than the female black bear. How much does the male black bear weigh? **Misleading Language** At a zoo, the female black bear weighs 175 pounds. The female black bear weighs 85 pounds less than the male black bear. How much does the male black bear weigh? *Math drawing:* m 175 85 *Situation and solution equation:* 175 + 85 = m	**Leading Language** At a zoo, the male black bear weighs 260 pounds. The female black bear weighs 85 pounds less than the male black bear. How much does the female black bear weigh? **Misleading Language** At a zoo, the male black bear weighs 260 pounds. The male black bear weighs 85 pounds more than the female black bear. How much does the female black bear weigh? *Math drawing:* 260 f 85 *Situation equation* f + 85 = 260 or f = 260 − 85 *Solution equation:* f = 260 − 85

A comparison sentence can always be said in two ways. One way uses *more*, and the other uses *fewer* or *less*. Misleading language suggests the wrong operation. For example, it says *the female black bear weighs 85 pounds less than the male*, but you have to add 85 pounds to the female's weight to get the male's weight.

Multiplication and Division Problem Types

	Product Unknown	Group Size Unknown	Number of Groups Unknown
Equal Groups	A teacher bought 5 boxes of markers. There are 8 markers in each box. How many markers did the teacher buy? *Math drawing:* *Situation and solution equation:* $n = 5 \cdot 8$	A teacher bought 5 boxes of markers. She bought 40 markers in all. How many markers are in each box? *Math drawing:* *Situation equation:* $5 \cdot n = 40$ *Solution equation:* $n = 40 \div 5$	A teacher bought boxes of 8 markers. She bought 40 markers in all. How many boxes of markers did she buy? *Math drawing:* *Situation equation* $n \cdot 8 = 40$ *Solution equation:* $n = 40 \div 8$

Problem Types

Multiplication and Division Problem Types (continued)

	Product Unknown	Factor Unknown	Factor Unknown
Arrays	For the yearbook photo, the drama club stood in 3 rows of 7 students. How many students were in the photo in all? Math drawing: $$3 \begin{matrix} 7 \\ \circ\circ\circ\circ\circ\circ\circ \\ \circ\circ\circ\circ\circ\circ\circ \\ \circ\circ\circ\circ\circ\circ\circ \end{matrix}$$ Situation and solution equation: $n = 3 \cdot 7$	For the yearbook photo, the 21 students in drama club stood in 3 equal rows. How many students were in each row? Math drawing: n n — Total: 21 n Situation equation: $3 \cdot n = 21$ Solution equation: $n = 21 \div 3$	For the yearbook photo, the 21 students in drama club stood in rows of 7 students. How many rows were there? Math drawing: 7 7 — Total: 21 7 Situation equation $n \cdot 7 = 21$ Solution equation: $n = 21 \div 7$
Area	The floor of the kitchen is 2 meters by 5 meters. What is the area of the floor? Math drawing: 5 2 ▭ A Situation and solution equation: $A = 5 \cdot 2$	The floor of the kitchen is 5 meters long. The area of the floor is 10 square meters. What is the width of the floor? Math drawing: 5 w ▭ 10 Situation equation: $5 \cdot w = 10$ Solution equation: $w = 10 \div 5$	The floor of the kitchen is 2 meters wide. The area of the floor is 10 square meters. What is the length of the floor? Math drawing: l 2 ▭ 10 Situation equation $l \cdot 2 = 10$ Solution equation: $l = 10 \div 2$

MathWord **Power**

Word Review

Work with a partner. Choose a word from a current unit or a review word from a previous unit. Use the word to complete one of the activities listed on the right. Then ask your partner if they have any edits to your work or questions about what you described. Repeat, having your partner choose a word.

Activities

- Give the meaning in words or gestures.
- Use the word in a sentence.
- Give another word that is related to the word in some way and explain the relationship.

Crossword Puzzle

Create a crossword puzzle similar to the example below. Use vocabulary words from the unit. You can add other related words, too. Challenge your partner to solve the puzzle.

	¹s	u	m	
²a		u		
d		b		
³a	d	d	i	t	i	o	⁴n
e		r		u
n		a		m
⁵a	d	d		b
		c		e
		t		r
		i		
⁶r	e	g	r	o	u	p
		n		

Across

1. The answer to an addition problem
3. _____ and subtraction are operations that undo each other.
5. To put amounts together
6. When you trade 10 ones for 1 ten, you _____.

Down

1. The operation that you can use to find out how much more one number is than another
2. In 24 + 65 = 89, 24 is an _____.
4. A combination of the digits 0, 1, 2, 3, 4, 5, 6, 7, 8, and 9

Vocabulary Activities

Word Wall

With your teacher's permission, start a word wall in your classroom. As you work through each lesson, put the math vocabulary words on index cards and place them on the word wall. You can work with a partner or a small group choosing a word and giving the definition.

Word Web

Make a word web for a word or words you do not understand in a unit. Fill in the web with words or phrases that are related to the vocabulary word.

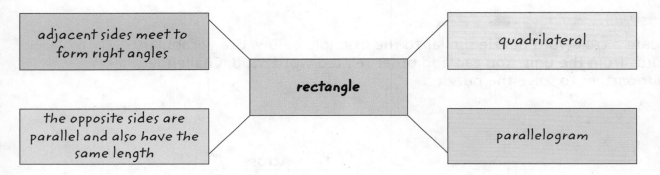

adjacent sides meet to form right angles		quadrilateral
	rectangle	
the opposite sides are parallel and also have the same length		parallelogram

Alphabet Challenge

Take an alphabet challenge. Choose three letters from the alphabet. Think of three vocabulary words for each letter. Then write the definition or draw an example for each word.

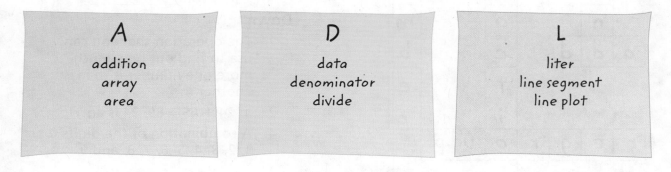

A	D	L
addition	data	liter
array	denominator	line segment
area	divide	line plot

Concentration

Write the vocabulary words and related words from a unit on index cards. Write the definitions on a different set of index cards. Choose 3 to 6 pairs of vocabulary words and definitions. Mix up the set of pairs. Then place the cards facedown on a table. Take turns turning over two cards. If one card is a word and one card is a definition that matches the word, take the pair. Continue until each word has been matched with its definition.

area

The total number of square units that cover a figure.

Math Journal

As you learn new words, write them in your Math Journal. Write the definition of the word and include a sketch or an example. As you learn new information about the word, add notes to your definition.

polygon: a closed plane figure with sides made of straight line segments.

In concave polygons, there exists a line segment with endpoints inside the polygon and a point on the line segment that is outside the polygon.

Vocabulary Activities

What's the Word?

Work together to make a poster or bulletin board display of the words in a unit. Write definitions on a set of index cards. Mix up the cards. Work with a partner, choosing a definition from the index cards. Have your partner point to the word on the poster and name the matching math vocabulary word. Switch roles and try the activity again.

the bottom number in a fraction that shows the total number of equal parts in the whole

fraction	fourths
unit fraction	eighths
denominator	halves
numerator	sixths
equivalent	
equivalent fractions	
equivalence chain	
thirds	

A

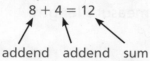

addend
One of two or more numbers to be added together to find a sum.

Example:

$$8 + 4 = 12$$

addend   addend   sum

addition
A mathematical operation that combines two or more numbers.

Example:

$$23 + 52 = 75$$

addend   addend   sum

adjacent sides
Two sides of a figure that meet at a point.

Example:

Sides a and b are adjacent.

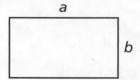

A.M.
The time period between midnight and noon.

analog clock
A clock with a face and hands.

angle
A figure formed by two rays or two line segments that meet at an endpoint.

area
The total number of square units that cover a figure.

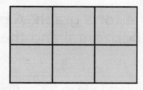

Example:
The area of the rectangle is 6 square units.

array
An arrangement of objects, pictures, or numbers in columns and rows.

Associative Property of Addition (Grouping Property of Addition)
The property stating that changing the way in which addends are grouped does not change the sum.

Example:
$$(2 + 3) + 1 = 2 + (3 + 1)$$
$$5 + 1 = 2 + 4$$
$$6 = 6$$

Glossary

Associative Property of Multiplication (Grouping Property of Multiplication)

The property stating that changing the way in which factors are grouped does not change the product.

Example:
$(2 \times 3) \times 4 = 2 \times (3 \times 4)$
$6 \times 4 = 2 \times 12$
$24 = 24$

axis (plural: axes)

A reference line for a graph. A graph has 2 axes; one is horizontal and the other is vertical.

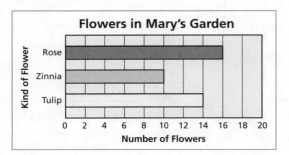

Flowers in Mary's Garden

B

bar graph

A graph that uses bars to show data. The bars may be horizontal, as in the graph above, or vertical, as in the graph below.

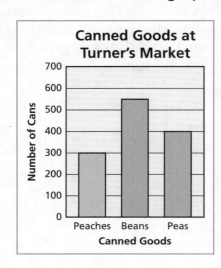

Canned Goods at Turner's Market

C

capacity

The amount a container can hold.

centimeter (cm)

A metric unit used to measure length.

100 centimeters = 1 meter

column

A part of a table or array that contains items arranged vertically.

● ● ● ●
● ● ● ●
● ● ● ●
● ● ● ●

Commutative Property of Addition (Order Property of Addition)

The property stating that changing the order of addends does not change the sum.

Example:
$3 + 7 = 7 + 3$
$10 = 10$

Commutative Property of Multiplication (Order Property of Multiplication)

The property stating that changing the order of factors does not change the product.

Example:
$5 \times 4 = 4 \times 5$
$20 = 20$

comparison bars*

Bars that represent the greater amount, lesser amount, and difference in a comparison problem.

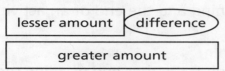

concave

A polygon for which you can connect two points inside the polygon with a segment that passes outside the polygon.

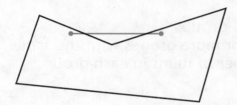

convex

A polygon is convex if all of its diagonals are inside it.

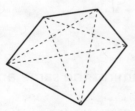

cup (c)

A customary unit of measure used to measure capacity.

1 cup = 8 fluid ounces

2 cups = 1 pint

4 cups = 1 quart

16 cups = 1 gallon

D

data

A collection of information about people or things.

decagon

A polygon with 10 sides.

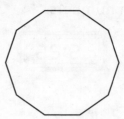

decimeter (dm)

A metric unit used to measure length.

1 decimeter = 10 centimeters

decompose

To separate or break apart (a geometric figure or a number) into smaller parts.

denominator

The bottom number in a fraction, which shows the total number of equal parts in the whole.

Example:

$\frac{1}{3}$ ◄——— denominator

diagonal

A line segment that connects two corners of a figure and is not a side of the figure.

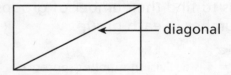

difference

The result of subtraction or of comparing.

digit

Any of the symbols 0, 1, 2, 3, 4, 5, 6, 7, 8, 9.

*A classroom research-based term developed for *Math Expressions*

Glossary

digital clock
A clock that displays the hour and minutes with numbers.

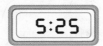

Distributive Property
You can multiply a sum by a number, or multiply each addend by the number and add the products; the result is the same.

Example:
$3 \times (2 + 4) = (3 \times 2) + (3 \times 4)$

$3 \times 6 \quad = \quad 6 \quad + \quad 12$

$18 \quad = \quad 18$

dividend
The number that is divided in division.

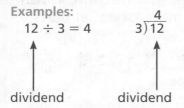

Examples:
$12 \div 3 = 4$ $3\overline{)12}^{\,4}$

dividend   dividend

division
The mathematical operation that separates an amount into smaller equal groups to find the number of groups or the number in each group.

Example:
$12 \div 3 = 4$ is a division number sentence.

divisor
The number that you divide by in division.

Example:
$12 \div 3 = 4$ $3\overline{)12}^{\,4}$

divisor   divisor

E

elapsed time
The time that passes between the beginning and the end of an activity.

endpoint
The point at either end of a line segment or the beginning point of a ray.

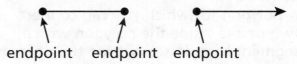

endpoint   endpoint   endpoint

equal groups
Two or more groups with the same number of items in each group.

equation
A mathematical sentence with an equal sign.

Examples:
$11 + 22 = 33$
$75 - 25 = 50$

equivalent
Equal, or naming the same amount.

equivalent fractions
Fractions that name the same amount.

Example:

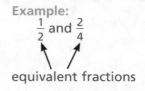

$\frac{1}{2}$ and $\frac{2}{4}$

equivalent fractions

estimate
A reasonable guess about how many or about how much.

even number
A whole number that is a multiple of 2. The ones digit in an even number is 0, 2, 4, 6, or 8.

expanded form

A number written to show the value of each of its digits.

Examples:
347 = 300 + 40 + 7
347 = 3 hundreds + 4 tens + 7 ones

expression

A combination of numbers, variables, and/or operation signs. An expression does not have an equal sign.

Examples:
4 + 7   a − 3

F

factor

Any of the numbers that are multiplied to give a product.

Example:
4 × 5 = 20

factor factor product

fluid ounce (fl oz)

A unit of liquid volume in the customary system that equals $\frac{1}{8}$ cup or 2 tablespoons.

foot (ft)

A customary unit used to measure length.

1 foot = 12 inches

fraction

A number that names part of a whole or part of a set.

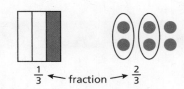

$\frac{1}{3}$ ← fraction → $\frac{2}{3}$

frequency table

A table that shows how many times each event, item, or category occurs.

Frequency Table	
Age	**Number of Players**
7	1
8	3
9	5
10	4
11	2

function table

A table of ordered pairs that shows a function.

For every input number, there is only one possible output number.

Rule: add 2	
Input	**Output**
1	3
2	4
3	5
4	6

G

gallon (gal)

A customary unit used to measure capacity.

1 gallon = 4 quarts = 8 pints = 16 cups

gram (g)

A metric unit of mass. One paper clip has a mass of about 1 gram.

1,000 grams = 1 kilogram

Glossary

group
To combine numbers to form new tens, hundreds, thousands, and so on.

height
A vertical distance, or how tall something is.

hexagon
A polygon with six sides.

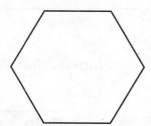

horizontal
Extending in two directions, left and right.

horizontal bar graph
A bar graph with horizontal bars.

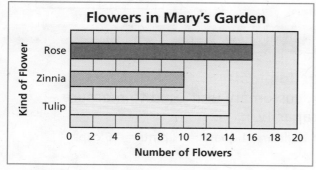

hundreds

3 hundreds

347 has 3 hundreds.

hundreds

Identity Property of Addition
If 0 is added to a number, the sum equals that number.

Example:
3 + 0 = 3

Identity Property of Multiplication
The product of 1 and any number equals that number.

Example:
$10 \times 1 = 10$

improper fraction
A fraction in which the numerator is equal to or is greater than the denominator. Improper fractions are equal to or greater than 1.
$\frac{5}{5}$ and $\frac{8}{3}$ are improper fractions.

inch (in.)
A customary unit used to measure length.

12 inches = 1 foot

is greater than (>)
A symbol used to compare two numbers.

Example:
6 > 5

6 is greater than 5.

is less than (<)
A symbol used to compare two numbers.

Example:
5 < 6

5 is less than 6.

key
A part of a map, graph, or chart that explains what symbols mean.

kilogram (kg)
A metric unit of mass.

1 kilogram = 1,000 grams

kilometer (km)
A metric unit of length.

1 kilometer = 1,000 meters

L

line
A straight path that goes on forever in opposite directions.

line plot
A diagram that shows frequency of data on a number line. Also called a *dot plot*.

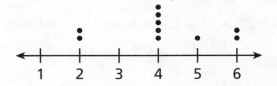

line segment
A part of a line. A line segment has two endpoints.

liquid volume
A measure of how much a container can hold. Also called *capacity*.

liter (L)
A metric unit used to measure capacity.

1 liter = 1,000 milliliters

M

mass
The amount of matter in an object.

mental math
A way to solve problems without using pencil and paper or a calculator.

meter (m)
A metric unit used to measure length.

1 meter = 100 centimeters

method
A procedure, or way, of doing something.

mile (mi)
A customary unit of length.

1 mile = 5,280 feet

milliliter (mL)
A metric unit used to measure capacity.

1,000 milliliters = 1 liter

mixed number
A whole number and a fraction.

$1\frac{3}{4}$ is a mixed number.

multiple
A number that is the product of the given number and any whole number.

multiplication
A mathematical operation that combines equal groups.

Example:

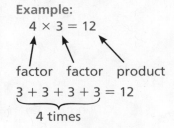

$4 \times 3 = 12$

factor   factor   product

$3 + 3 + 3 + 3 = 12$

4 times

Glossary

N

number line
A line on which numbers are assigned to lengths.

numerator
The top number in a fraction that shows the number of equal parts counted.

Example:

$\frac{1}{3}$ ←——— numerator

O

octagon
A polygon with eight sides.

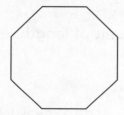

odd number
A whole number that is not a multiple of 2. The ones digit in an odd number is 1, 3, 5, 7, or 9.

ones

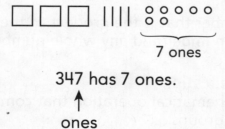

7 ones

347 has 7 ones.

ones

opposite sides
Sides of a polygon that are across from each other; they do not meet at a point.

Example:

Sides *a* and *c* are opposite.

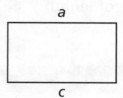

Order of Operations
A set of rules that state the order in which the operations in an expression should be done.

STEP 1: Perform operations inside parentheses first.

STEP 2: Multiply and divide from left to right.

STEP 3: Add and subtract from left to right.

ounce (oz)
A customary unit used to measure weight.

16 ounces = 1 pound

P

parallel lines
Two lines that are the same distance apart.

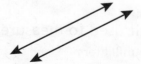

parallelogram
A quadrilateral with both pairs of opposite sides parallel.

pentagon
A polygon with five sides.

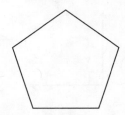

perimeter
The distance around a figure.

Example:
Perimeter = 3 cm + 5 cm + 3 cm + 5 cm = 16 cm

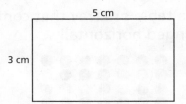

5 cm

3 cm

pictograph
A graph that uses pictures or symbols to represent data.

Favorite Ice Cream Flavors

Peanut Butter Crunch	🍦 🍦
Cherry Vanilla	🍦 🍦 🍦
Chocolate	🍦 🍦 🍦 🍦 🍦

Each 🍦 stands for 4 votes.

pint (pt)
A customary unit used to measure capacity.

1 pint = 2 cups

place value
The value assigned to the place that a digit occupies in a number.

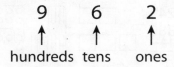

9   6   2

hundreds tens ones

place value drawing
A drawing that represents a number. Hundreds are represented by boxes, tens by vertical lines, and ones by small circles.

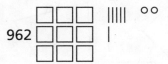

962

P.M.
The time period between noon and midnight.

polygon
A closed plane figure with sides made up of straight line segments.

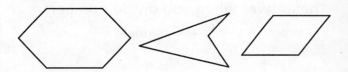

pound (lb)
A customary unit used to measure weight.

1 pound = 16 ounces

product
The answer when you multiply numbers.

Example:

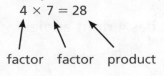

4 × 7 = 28

factor factor product

*A classroom research-based term developed for *Math Expressions*

© Houghton Mifflin Harcourt Publishing Company

proof drawing*
A drawing used to show that an answer is correct.

$$\begin{array}{r} 249 \\ + 386 \\ \hline 11 \\ 635 \end{array}$$
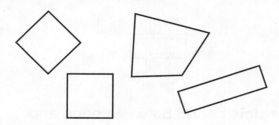

Q

quadrilateral
A polygon with four sides.

quart (qt)
A customary unit used to measure capacity.

1 quart = 4 cups

quotient
The answer when you divide numbers.

Examples:
$35 \div 7 = 5$ $7)\overline{35}$ ← quotient

quotient

R

ray
A part of a line that has one endpoint and goes on forever in one direction.

rectangle
A parallelogram that has 4 right angles.

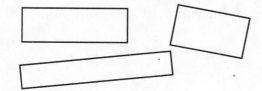

rhombus
A parallelogram with equal sides.

right angle
An angle that measures 90°.

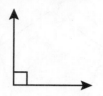

round
To find about how many or how much by expressing a number to the nearest ten, hundred, thousand, and so on.

row
A part of a table or array that contains items arranged horizontally.

S

scale
An arrangement of numbers in order with equal intervals.

side (of a figure)
One of the line segments that make up a polygon.

side

simplify

To write an equivalent fraction with a smaller numerator and denominator.

situation equation*

An equation that shows the action or the relationship in a problem.

Example:
$35 + n = 40$

solution equation*

An equation that shows the operation to perform in order to solve the problem.

Example:
$n = 40 - 35$

square

A rectangle with four sides of the same length.

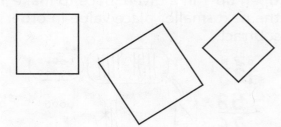

square number

The product of a whole number and itself.

Example:
$4 \times 4 = 16$

↑
square number

square unit

A unit of area equal to the area of a square with one-unit sides.

standard form

The name of a number written using digits.

Example:
1,829

subtract

To find the difference of two numbers.

Example:
$18 - 11 = 7$

subtraction

A mathematical operation on two numbers that gives the difference.

Example:
$43 - 40 = 3$

sum

The answer when adding two or more addends.

Example:
$37 + 52 = 89$

addend   addend   sum

T

table

An easy-to-read arrangement of data, usually in rows and columns.

Favorite Team Sport	
Sport	**Number of Students**
Baseball	35
Soccer	60
Basketball	40

*A classroom research-based term developed for *Math Expressions*

Glossary

tally chart

A chart used to record and organize data with tally marks.

Tally Chart	
Age	Tally
7	I
8	III
9	IIII̶

tally marks

Short line segments drawn in groups of 5. Each mark, including the slanted mark, stands for 1 unit.

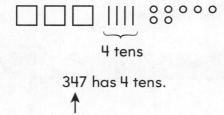

means 13
5   5   3

tens

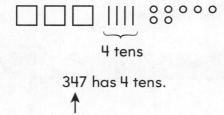

4 tens

347 has 4 tens.
↑
tens

thousands

Thousands	Hundreds	Tens	Ones
6	7	8	2

There are 6 thousands in 6,782.

total

The answer when adding two or more addends. The sum of two or more numbers.

Example:

672 + 228 = 900

addend   *addend*   total *sum*

trapezoid

A quadrilateral with exactly one pair of parallel sides.

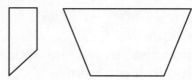

triangle

A polygon with three sides.

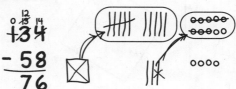

U

ungroup*

To open up 1 in a given place to make 10 of the next smaller place value in order to subtract.

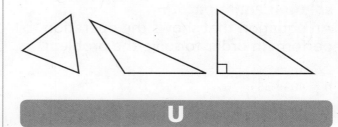

unit fraction

A fraction whose numerator is 1. It shows one equal part of a whole.

Example:

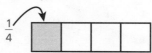

$\frac{1}{4}$

unit square

A square whose area is 1 square unit.

A classroom research-based term developed for Math Expressions

V

variable

A letter or symbol used to represent an unknown number in an algebraic expression or equation.

Example:
2 + n
n is a variable.

Venn diagram

A diagram that uses circles to show the relationship among sets of objects.

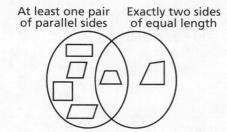

At least one pair of parallel sides · Exactly two sides of equal length

vertex

A point where sides, rays, or edges meet.

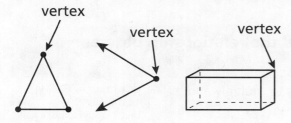

vertex · vertex · vertex

vertical

Extending in two directions, up and down.

vertical bar graph

A bar graph with vertical bars.

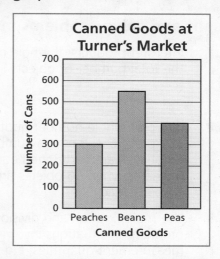

Canned Goods at Turner's Market

Number of Cans / Canned Goods: Peaches, Beans, Peas

W

weight

The measure of how heavy something is.

word form

A name of a number written using words instead of digits.

Example:
Nine hundred eighty-four

Y

yard (yd)

A customary unit used to measure length.

1 yard = 3 feet = 36 inches

Z

Zero Property of Multiplication

If 0 is multiplied by a number, the product is 0.

Example:
$3 \times 0 = 0$

3.OA Operations and Algebraic Thinking

Represent and solve problems involving multiplication and division.

3.OA.A.1	Interpret products of whole numbers, e.g., interpret 5 × 7 as the total number of objects in 5 groups of 7 objects each.	Unit 1 Lessons 1, 2, 3, 4, 5, 6, 7, 8, 9, 10, 12, 13, 14, 16, 18, 19; Unit 2 Lessons 2, 4, 7, 9, 10, 11, 13, 15
3.OA.A.2	Interpret whole-number quotients of whole numbers, e.g., interpret 56 ÷ 8 as the number of objects in each share when 56 objects are partitioned equally into 8 shares, or as a number of shares when 56 objects are partitioned into equal shares of 8 objects each.	Unit 1 Lessons 4, 5, 6, 7, 9, 10, 12, 13, 14, 15, 16, 17, 18, 19; Unit 2 Lessons 2, 4, 7, 9, 10, 11, 13, 15
3.OA.A.3	Use multiplication and division within 100 to solve word problems in situations involving equal groups, arrays, and measurement quantities, e.g., by using drawings and equations with a symbol for the unknown number to represent the problem.	Unit 1 Lessons 2, 3, 4, 5, 6, 7, 9, 10, 13, 14, 16, 17, 18, 19; Unit 2 Lessons 2, 4, 7, 9, 10, 11, 13, 15; Unit 6 Lessons 2, 3, 8, 9, 11; Unit 7 Lessons 1, 2, 3, 4
3.OA.A.4	Determine the unknown whole number in a multiplication or division equation relating three whole numbers.	Unit 1 Lessons 1, 4, 5, 6, 7, 8, 9, 10, 12, 13, 14, 16, 18, 19; Unit 2 Lessons 1, 2, 3, 4, 5, 6, 7, 8, 9, 10, 11, 13, 14, 15; Unit 6 Lessons 2, 3

Understand properties of multiplication and the relationship between multiplication and division.

3.OA.B.5	Apply properties of operations as strategies to multiply and divide.	Unit 1 Lessons 3, 6, 11, 12, 14, 15, 19; Unit 2 Lessons 1, 8, 12, 15
3.OA.B.6	Understand division as an unknown-factor problem.	Unit 1 Lessons 4, 5, 6, 7, 8, 9, 10, 11, 12, 13, 14, 15, 16, 17, 18; Unit 2 Lessons 1, 2, 3, 4, 5, 6, 7, 8, 9, 10, 11, 12, 13, 14

Multiply and divide within 100.

3.OA.C.7	Fluently multiply and divide within 100, using strategies such as the relationship between multiplication and division (e.g., knowing that 8 × 5 = 40, one knows 40 ÷ 5 = 8) or properties of operations. By the end of Grade 3, know from memory all products of two one-digit numbers.	Unit 1 Lessons 1, 2, 3, 4, 5, 6, 7, 8, 9, 10, 11, 12, 13, 14, 15, 16, 17, 18, 19; Unit 2 Lessons 1, 2, 3, 4, 5, 6, 7, 8, 9, 10, 11, 12, 13, 14, 15

© Houghton Mifflin Harcourt Publishing Company

 Major   **Supporting** ■ **Additional**

Solve problems involving the four operations, and identify and explain patterns in arithmetic.

3.OA.D.8	Solve two-step word problems using the four operations. Represent these problems using equations with a letter standing for the unknown quantity. Assess the reasonableness of answers using mental computation and estimation strategies including rounding.	Unit 2 Lessons 9, 10, 11, 13; Unit 3 Lesson 17; Unit 6 Lessons 7, 8, 9, 10, 11
3.OA.D.9	Identify arithmetic patterns (including patterns in the addition table or multiplication table), and explain them using properties of operations.	Unit 1 Lessons 1, 5, 6, 7, 8, 10, 12, 15, 19; Unit 2 Lessons 1, 3, 5, 6, 8, 14, 15; Unit 3 Lesson 17

3.NBT Number and Operations in Base Ten

Use place value understanding and properties of operations to perform multi-digit arithmetic.

3.NBT.A.1	Use place value understanding to round whole numbers to the nearest 10 or 100.	Unit 3 Lessons 1, 2, 3, 4, 5, 6, 10, 17, 18; Unit 6 Lessons 4, 8
3.NBT.A.2	Fluently add and subtract within 1000 using strategies and algorithms based on place value, properties of operations, and/or the relationship between addition and subtraction.	Unit 3 Lessons 1, 2, 3, 4, 5, 6, 7, 8, 9, 10, 11, 12, 13, 14, 15, 16, 17, 18; Unit 4 Lessons 12, 13; Unit 6 Lessons 1, 2, 3, 4, 5, 6, 7, 8, 9, 10, 11
3.NBT.A.3	Multiply one-digit whole numbers by multiples of 10 in the range 10–90 (e.g., 9×80, 5×60) using strategies based on place value and properties of operations.	Unit 2 Lesson 12

3.NF Number and Operations–Fractions

Develop understanding of fractions as numbers.

3.NF.A.1	Understand a fraction $\frac{1}{b}$ as the quantity formed by 1 part when a whole is partitioned into b equal parts; understand a fraction $\frac{a}{b}$ as the quantity formed by a parts of size $\frac{1}{b}$.	Unit 4 Lessons 1, 2, 4, 5; Unit 5 Lessons 9, 10
3.NF.A.2	Understand a fraction as a number on the number line; represent fractions on a number line diagram.	Unit 4 Lessons 2, 3, 4
3.NF.A.2.a	Represent a fraction $\frac{1}{b}$ on a number line diagram by defining the interval from 0 to 1 as the whole and partitioning it into b equal parts. Recognize that each part has size $\frac{1}{b}$ and that the endpoint of the part based at 0 locates the number $\frac{1}{b}$ on the number line.	Unit 4 Lessons 2, 3; Unit 5 Lesson 8

3.NF.A.2.b	Represent a fraction $\frac{a}{b}$ on a number line diagram by marking off a lengths $\frac{1}{b}$ from 0. Recognize that the resulting interval has size $\frac{a}{b}$ and that its endpoint locates the number $\frac{1}{b}$ on the number line.	Unit 4 Lessons 2, 3
3.NF.A.3	Explain equivalence of fractions in special cases, and compare fractions by reasoning about their size.	Unit 4 Lessons 2, 3, 4, 5; Unit 5 Lessons 7, 10
3.NF.A.3.a	Understand two fractions as equivalent (equal) if they are the same size, or the same point on a number line.	Unit 5 Lessons 8, 9
3.NF.A.3.b	Recognize and generate simple equivalent fractions, e.g., $\frac{1}{2} = \frac{2}{4}$, $\frac{4}{6} = \frac{2}{3}$. Explain why the fractions are equivalent, e.g., by using a visual fraction model.	Unit 5 Lessons 7, 8, 10
3.NF.A.3.c	Express whole numbers as fractions, and recognize fractions that are equivalent to whole numbers.	Unit 4 Lessons 2, 3; Unit 5 Lesson 8
3.NF.A.3.d	Compare two fractions with the same numerator or the same denominator by reasoning about their size. Recognize that comparisons are valid only when the two fractions refer to the same whole. Record the results of comparisons with the symbols >, =, or <, and justify the conclusions, e.g., by using a visual fraction model.	Unit 3 Lessons 4, 5; Unit 4 Lessons 4, 5; Unit 5 Lesson 9

3.MD Measurement and Data

Solve problems involving measurement and estimation of intervals of time, liquid volumes, and masses of objects.

3.MD.A.1	Tell and write time to the nearest minute and measure time intervals in minutes. Solve word problems involving addition and subtraction of time intervals in minutes, e.g., by representing the problem on a number line diagram.	Unit 4 Lessons 7, 8, 9, 10, 11
3.MD.A.2	Measure and estimate liquid volumes and masses of objects using standard units of grams (g), kilograms (kg), and liters (l). Add, subtract, multiply, or divide to solve one-step word problems involving masses or volumes that are given in the same units, e.g., by using drawings (such as a beaker with a measurement scale) to represent the problem.	Unit 7 Lessons 1, 2, 3, 4

■ **Major**　■ **Supporting**　■ **Additional**

© Houghton Mifflin Harcourt Publishing Company

Represent and interpret data.

3.MD.B.3	Draw a scaled picture graph and a scaled bar graph to represent a data set with several categories. Solve one- and two-step "how many more" and "how many less" problems using information presented in scaled bar graphs.	Unit 1 Lesson 19; Unit 4 Lessons 12, 13, 15
3.MD.B.4	Generate measurement data by measuring lengths using rulers marked with halves and fourths of an inch. Show the data by making a line plot, where the horizontal scale is marked off in appropriate units—whole numbers, halves, or quarters.	Unit 4 Lessons 6, 14, 15, 16

Geometric measurement: understand concepts of area and relate area to multiplication and to addition.

3.MD.C.5	Recognize area as an attribute of plane figures and understand concepts of area measurement.	Unit 1 Lesson 11; Unit 2 Lesson 2; Unit 4 Lesson 6; Unit 5 Lessons 1, 3, 5, 6
3.MD.C.5.a	A square with side length 1 unit, called "a unit square," is said to have "one square unit" of area, and can be used to measure area.	Unit 1 Lesson 11; Unit 2 Lesson 2; Unit 5 Lessons 1, 3
3.MD.C.5.b	A plane figure that can be covered without gaps or overlaps by n unit squares is said to have an area of n square units.	Unit 1 Lesson 11; Unit 2 Lesson 2; Unit 5 Lessons 1, 3, 6
3.MD.C.6	Measure areas by counting unit squares (square cm, square m, square in, square ft, and improvised units).	Unit 2 Lessons 2, 3; Unit 5 Lessons 1, 2, 4, 6
3.MD.C.7	Relate area to the operations of multiplication and addition.	Unit 1 Lessons 11, 12, 14; Unit 2 Lessons 1, 6, 8; Unit 5 Lessons 2, 5; Unit 7 Lesson 9
3.MD.C.7.a	Find the area of a rectangle with whole-number side lengths by tiling it, and show that the area is the same as would be found by multiplying the side lengths.	Unit 1 Lesson 11; Unit 2 Lesson 2; Unit 5 Lessons 1, 2
3.MD.C.7.b	Multiply side lengths to find areas of rectangles with whole number side lengths in the context of solving real world and mathematical problems, and represent whole-number products as rectangular areas in mathematical reasoning.	Unit 1 Lessons 11, 14; Unit 2 Lessons 2, 6; Unit 5 Lessons 1, 2, 3, 4, 5; Unit 7 Lesson 9
3.MD.C.7.c	Use tiling to show in a concrete case that the area of a rectangle with whole-number side lengths a and $b + c$ is the sum of $a \times b$ and $a \times c$. Use area models to represent the distributive property in mathematical reasoning.	Unit 1 Lessons 11, 12, 14; Unit 2 Lesson 1 Unit 5 Lesson 2
3.MD.C.7.d	Recognize area as additive. Find areas of rectilinear figures by decomposing them into non-overlapping rectangles and adding the areas of the non-overlapping parts, applying this technique to solve real world problems.	Unit 1 Lessons 11, 12; Unit 5 Lessons 2, 4, 5, 6

Geometric measurement: recognize perimeter as an attribute of plane figures and distinguish between linear and area measures.

3.MD.D.8	Solve real world and mathematical problems involving perimeters of polygons, including finding the perimeter given the side lengths, finding an unknown side length, and exhibiting rectangles with the same perimeter and different areas or with the same area and different perimeters.	Unit 5 Lessons 1, 2, 3, 5; Unit 7 Lesson 9

3.G Geometry

Reason with shapes and their attributes.

3.G.A.1	Understand that shapes in different categories (e.g., rhombuses, rectangles, and others) may share attributes (e.g., having four sides), and that the shared attributes can define a larger category (e.g., quadrilaterals). Recognize rhombuses, rectangles, and squares as examples of quadrilaterals, and draw examples of quadrilaterals that do not belong to any of these subcategories.	Unit 7 Lessons 5, 6, 7, 8, 9
3.G.A.2	Partition shapes into parts with equal areas. Express the area of each part as a unit fraction of the whole.	Unit 4 Lessons 1, 2, 4, 5; Unit 5 Lesson 10

■ **Major**   ■ **Supporting**   ■ **Additional**

Common Core State Standards for Mathematical Practice

MP1 Make sense of problems and persevere in solving them.

Mathematically proficient students start by explaining to themselves the meaning of a problem and looking for entry points to its solution. They analyze givens, constraints, relationships, and goals. They make conjectures about the form and meaning of the solution and plan a solution pathway rather than simply jumping into a solution attempt. They consider analogous problems, and try special cases and simpler forms of the original problem in order to gain insight into its solution. They monitor and evaluate their progress and change course if necessary. Older students might, depending on the context of the problem, transform algebraic expressions or change the viewing window on their graphing calculator to get the information they need. Mathematically proficient students can explain correspondences between equations, verbal descriptions, tables, and graphs or draw diagrams of important features and relationships, graph data, and search for regularity or trends. Younger students might rely on using concrete objects or pictures to help conceptualize and solve a problem. Mathematically proficient students check their answers to problems using a different method, and they continually ask themselves, "Does this make sense?" They can understand the approaches of others to solving complex problems and identify correspondences between different approaches.

Unit 1 Lessons 3, 4, 5, 6, 7, 9, 10, 12, 14, 16, 18, 19
Unit 2 Lessons 1, 2, 4, 7, 9, 10, 13, 15
Unit 3 Lessons 3, 4, 5, 6, 7, 8, 9, 10, 11, 12, 13, 14, 15, 16, 17, 18
Unit 4 Lessons 9, 10, 11, 12, 13, 14, 15, 16
Unit 5 Lessons 2, 5, 9, 10
Unit 6 Lessons 1, 2, 3, 4, 5, 6, 7, 8, 9, 10, 11
Unit 7 Lessons 2, 3, 9

MP2 Reason abstractly and quantitatively.

Mathematically proficient students make sense of quantities and their relationships in problem situations. They bring two complementary abilities to bear on problems involving quantitative relationships: the ability to decontextualize—to abstract a given situation and represent it symbolically and manipulate the representing symbols as if they have a life of their own, without necessarily attending to their referents—and the ability to contextualize, to pause as needed during the manipulation process in order to probe into the referents for the symbols involved. Quantitative reasoning entails habits of creating a coherent representation of the problem at hand; considering the units involved; attending to the meaning of quantities, not just how to compute them; and knowing and flexibly using different properties of operations and objects.

Unit 1 Lessons 1, 3, 5, 7, 8, 10, 11, 12, 19
Unit 2 Lessons 1, 2, 3, 5, 6, 8, 13, 15
Unit 3 Lessons 1, 2, 5, 6, 8, 9, 11, 12, 13, 14, 15, 16, 17, 18
Unit 4 Lessons 1, 2, 3, 4, 5, 6, 9, 12, 14, 16
Unit 5 Lessons 1, 2, 3, 4, 5, 7, 8, 9, 10
Unit 6 Lessons 1, 2, 3, 4, 8, 11
Unit 7 Lessons 1, 2, 3, 5, 9

Common Core State Standards for Mathematical Practice

MP3 Construct viable arguments and critique the reasoning of others.

Mathematically proficient students understand and use stated assumptions, definitions, and previously established results in constructing arguments. They make conjectures and build a logical progression of statements to explore the truth of their conjectures. They are able to analyze situations by breaking them into cases, and can recognize and use counterexamples. They justify their conclusions, communicate them to others, and respond to the arguments of others. They reason inductively about data, making plausible arguments that take into account the context from which the data arose. Mathematically proficient students are also able to compare the effectiveness of two plausible arguments, distinguish correct logic or reasoning from that which is flawed, and—if there is a flaw in an argument—explain what it is. Elementary students can construct arguments using concrete referents such as objects, drawings, diagrams, and actions. Such arguments can make sense and be correct, even though they are not generalized or made formal until later grades. Later, students learn to determine domains to which an argument applies. Students at all grades can listen or read the arguments of others, decide whether they make sense, and ask useful questions to clarify or improve the arguments.

Unit 1 Lessons 1, 2, 3, 4, 5, 6, 7, 8, 9, 10, 11, 12, 13, 14, 15, 16, 18, 19
Unit 2 Lessons 1, 2, 3, 4, 5, 6, 8, 9, 10, 11, 12, 13, 14, 15
Unit 3 Lessons 1, 2, 3, 4, 5, 6, 7, 8, 9, 10, 12, 13, 14, 15, 16, 17, 18
Unit 4 Lessons 1, 2, 3, 4, 5, 6, 7, 8, 9, 10, 11, 12, 13, 14, 15, 16
Unit 5 Lessons 1, 2, 3, 4, 5, 6, 7, 8, 9, 10
Unit 6 Lessons 1, 2, 3, 4, 5, 6, 7, 8, 9, 10, 11
Unit 7 Lessons 1, 2, 3, 4, 5, 6, 8, 9

MP4 Model with mathematics.

Mathematically proficient students can apply the mathematics they know to solve problems arising in everyday life, society, and the workplace. In early grades, this might be as simple as writing an addition equation to describe a situation. In middle grades, a student might apply proportional reasoning to plan a school event or analyze a problem in the community. By high school, a student might use geometry to solve a design problem or use a function to describe how one quantity of interest depends on another. Mathematically proficient students who can apply what they know are comfortable making assumptions and approximations to simplify a complicated situation, realizing that these may need revision later. They are able to identify important quantities in a practical situation and map their relationships using such tools as diagrams, two-way tables, graphs, flowcharts and formulas. They can analyze those relationships mathematically to draw conclusions. They routinely interpret their mathematical results in the context of the situation and reflect on whether the results make sense, possibly improving the model if it has not served its purpose.

Unit 1 Lessons 2, 3, 4, 5, 6, 7, 9, 10, 13, 14, 16, 17, 18, 19
Unit 2 Lessons 2, 4, 7, 9, 11, 13, 15
Unit 3 Lessons 3, 4, 8, 9, 10, 11, 12, 14, 16, 17, 18
Unit 4 Lessons 9, 10, 11, 12, 13, 14, 16
Unit 5 Lessons 2, 5, 9, 10
Unit 6 Lessons 1, 2, 3, 4, 8, 9, 10, 11
Unit 7 Lessons 1, 2, 3, 4, 9

MP5 Use appropriate tools strategically.

Mathematically proficient students consider the available tools when solving a mathematical problem. These tools might include pencil and paper, concrete models, a ruler, a protractor, a calculator, a spreadsheet, a computer algebra system, a statistical package, or dynamic geometry software. Proficient students are sufficiently familiar with tools appropriate for their grade or course to make sound decisions about when each of these tools might be helpful, recognizing both the insight to be gained and their limitations. For example, mathematically proficient high school students analyze graphs of functions and solutions generated using a graphing calculator. They detect possible errors by strategically using estimation and other mathematical knowledge. When making mathematical models, they know that technology can enable them to visualize the results of varying assumptions, explore consequences, and compare predictions with data. Mathematically proficient students at various grade levels are able to identify relevant external mathematical resources, such as digital content located on a website, and use them to pose or solve problems. They are able to use technological tools to explore and deepen their understanding of concepts.

Unit 1 Lessons 1, 4, 5, 6, 7, 8, 9, 10, 11, 12, 13, 14, 15, 16, 17, 18, 19
Unit 2 Lessons 1, 2, 3, 4, 5, 6, 7, 8, 9, 10, 11, 12, 13, 14, 15
Unit 3 Lessons 1, 2, 3, 4, 5, 6, 7, 8, 13, 17, 18
Unit 4 Lessons 1, 2, 3, 5, 6, 7, 8, 9, 10, 11, 14, 16
Unit 5 Lessons 1, 2, 6, 7, 8, 10
Unit 6 Lessons 4, 11
Unit 7 Lessons 2, 3, 5, 7, 8, 9

MP6 Attend to precision.

Mathematically proficient students try to communicate precisely to others. They try to use clear definitions in discussion with others and in their own reasoning. They state the meaning of the symbols they choose, including using the equal sign consistently and appropriately. They are careful about specifying units of measure, and labeling axes to clarify the correspondence with quantities in a problem. They calculate accurately and efficiently, express numerical answers with a degree of precision appropriate for the problem context. In the elementary grades, students give carefully formulated explanations to each other. By the time they reach high school they have learned to examine claims and make explicit use of definitions.

Unit 1 Lessons 1, 2, 3, 4, 5, 6, 7, 8, 9, 10, 11, 12, 13, 14, 15, 16, 18, 19
Unit 2 Lessons 1, 2, 3, 4, 5, 6, 7, 8, 9, 10, 11, 12, 13, 14, 15
Unit 3 Lessons 1, 2, 3, 4, 5, 6, 7, 8, 9, 10, 11, 12, 13, 14, 15, 16, 17, 18
Unit 4 Lessons 1, 2, 3, 4, 5, 6, 7, 8, 9, 10, 11, 12, 13, 14, 15, 16
Unit 5 Lessons 1, 2, 3, 4, 5, 6, 7, 8, 9, 10
Unit 6 Lessons 1, 2, 3, 4, 5, 6, 7, 8, 9, 10, 11
Unit 7 Lessons 1, 2, 3, 4, 5, 6, 7, 8, 9

MP7 Look for and make use of structure.

Mathematically proficient students look closely to discern a pattern or structure. Young students, for example, might notice that three and seven more is the same amount as seven and three more, or they may sort a collection of shapes according to how many sides the shapes have. Later, students will see 7×8 equals the well remembered $7 \times 5 + 7 \times 3$, in preparation for learning about the distributive property. In the expression $x^2 + 9x + 14$, older students can see the 14 as 2×7 and the 9 as $2 + 7$. They recognize the significance of an existing line in a geometric figure and can use the strategy of drawing an auxiliary line for solving problems. They also can step back for an overview and shift perspective. They can see complicated things, such as some algebraic expressions, as single objects or as being composed of several objects. For example, they can see $5 - 3(x - y)^2$ as 5 minus a positive number times a square and use that to realize that its value cannot be more than 5 for any real numbers x and y.

Unit 1 Lessons 1, 2, 4, 5, 6, 7, 8, 10, 11, 12, 13, 15, 17, 19
Unit 2 Lessons 1, 3, 5, 6, 14, 15
Unit 3 Lessons 1, 2, 3, 4, 11, 14, 16, 17, 18
Unit 4 Lessons 1, 2, 3, 13, 16
Unit 5 Lessons 1, 4, 6, 7, 10
Unit 6 Lessons 1, 2, 3, 5, 8, 11
Unit 7 Lessons 1, 5, 6, 7, 8, 9

MP8 Look for and express regularity in repeated reasoning.

Mathematically proficient students notice if calculations are repeated, and look both for general methods and for shortcuts. Upper elementary students might notice when dividing 25 by 11 that they are repeating the same calculations over and over again, and conclude they have a repeating decimal. By paying attention to the calculation of slope as they repeatedly check whether points are on the line through (1, 2) with slope 3, middle school students might abstract the equation $(y - 2)/(x - 1) = 3$. Noticing the regularity in the way terms cancel when expanding $(x - 1)(x + 1)$, $(x - 1)(x^2 + x + 1)$, and $(x - 1)(x^3 + x^2 + x + 1)$ might lead them to the general formula for the sum of a geometric series. As they work to solve a problem, mathematically proficient students maintain oversight of the process, while attending to the details. They continually evaluate the reasonableness of their intermediate results.

Unit 1 Lessons 1, 3, 5, 7, 8, 10, 13, 15, 19
Unit 2 Lessons 1, 3, 5, 6, 10, 12, 14, 15
Unit 3 Lessons 5, 6, 14, 17, 18
Unit 4 Lessons 1, 2, 3, 4, 5, 6, 15, 16
Unit 5 Lessons 3, 6, 7, 8, 10
Unit 6 Lessons 1, 4, 11
Unit 7 Lessons 8, 9

Index

find by decomposing and adding, 55, 56, 60, 313–314, 319–322, 439

find with Tangrams, 329–332

of a rectangle, 309–314

rectangles with same and different perimeter, 317

relate multiplication and addition, 55, 60, 67, 313–314

of a square, 311A–311B

square units, 112, 309–311

use tiling to show Distributive Property, 112–114, 312

using multiplication, 56

Arrays, 19–22

columns and rows, 19, 21–22

fast arrays, 16, 46, 124

Assessment *See also* **Check Sheets.**

Dashes, 85–90, 137–142, 157–162

Diagnostic Checkup, 167, 168

On-Going Assessment. *See also* Check Sheets.

Fluency Check, 96, 174, 202, 212, 232, 298, 344, 377, 392, 418, 441

Quick Quiz, 33, 47, 69, 95, 143, 173, 201, 211, 231, 261, 277, 297, 333, 343, 377, 391, 417, 441

Strategy Check, 34, 48, 70, 144, 262, 334

Performance Assessment

Unit Performance Task, 103–104, 181–182, 239–240, 305–306, 351–352, 399–400, 455–456

Summative Assessment

Unit Review/Test, 97–102, 175–180, 233–238, 299–304, 345–350, 393–398, 449–454

Associative Property of Addition, 73

Associative Property of Multiplication, 72–73

B

Bar graphs, 288

horizontal, 283, 286–287, 289, 293

making, 284, 289

reading and interpreting, 283–284, 286–288

scale, 283, 289–290

using to solve problems, 286–288, 290, 293

vertical, 283, 288, 289

Basic Facts Fluency. *See* **Addition; Division; Multiplication; Subtraction.**

C

Check Sheets

0s-10s, 130

1s and 0s, 77–78

2s, 5s, 9s, and 10s, 43–44

3s, 4s, 0s, 1s, 78

3s and 4s, 57–58

5s and 2s, 29–30

6s, 7s, and 8s, 129

6s and 8s, 115–116

7s and squares, 125–126

10s and 9s, 39–40

Circle

compare fractions on, 255

Clock. *See* **Manipulatives; Time.**

Commutative Property

of Addition, 73

of Multiplication, 22, 73, 155

Comparison bars, 370

Comparison problems, 368–370

comparison drawing, 20, 368

misleading language, 371

unknown amount, 369–371

use comparison bars, 370

using data in a bar graph, 286–288

using data in a pictograph, 285

without the words *more* or *fewer*, 372

Count-bys

0s and 1s, 53

2s, 17

3s, 53

4s, 53

5s, 17

6s, 109

7s, 109

Index

Equal Shares drawings, 8–9, 21–22, 24, 61

Equal sign (=), 358

Equation, 6, 365–366, 383–384
for area of rectangle, 313–314
expressing relationships, 358
relationship to Math Mountains, 355
situation equation and solution equations, 365–366
solving addition and subtraction equations, 207–210, 358, 359, 364
solving equations by using inverse operations, 23–26
solving multiplication and division equations, 52, 74, 75, 79–80, 121–122, 135–142, 362–363
using a symbol to represent an unknown, 23–26, 37, 121–122
using a variable to represent an unknown, 37, 360, 365–366
writing, 37, 45, 74, 75, 121–122, 146, 171, 358, 360, 365–366, 383–388
writing related equations, 24–26, 36, 52

Equivalent fractions, 335–338. *See also* **Fractions.**

Estimate, 195
capacity, 404
to check answers, 196, 198, 383–384
differences, 196
to find reasonable answers, 196–199, 383–384
length, 258
liquid volume, 404
to the nearest hundred, 195–196, 198, 199
to the nearest ten, 197–198
number of objects, 200
quantities, 200
sums, 196, 198, 209–210, 383–384
using rounding, 195–200, 383–384
weight and mass, 411, 414

Even number, 28

Expanded form, 189, 193

Expression, 358

F

Factor, 6, 361–362, 365–366. *See also* **Multiplication.**

Family Letter, 1–4, 11–14, 105–106, 183–186, 241–242, 263–264, 279–280, 307–308, 354–355, 401–402, 419–420

Fast array drawings, 46, 118, 124

Fluency Check. *See* **Assessment.**

Fraction bars, 245, 247, 253, 254

Fraction circles, 255, 255A

Fraction rectangles, 243A

Fractions, 245
compare, 253–256
denominator, 245
equivalence chains, 338
equivalent fractions, 335–338
halves, fourths, and eighths, 335
improper, 250
length measurement, 257–258
line plot with, 259–260, 292
mixed numbers, 250
on a number line, 248–254, 337–338
numerator, 245
paper folding, 341–342
part of a whole, 243–244, 255–255B
thirds and sixths, 336
unit, 243–247, 253–254
whole numbers expressed as, 250–251

Fractions in Measurement, S1

Fraction Strips, 355A

Frequency tables, 284, 289, 291, 292, 296

Functions
finding and writing the rule, 10
function table, 10
using a rule, 10

G

Geometry. *See also* **Area; Perimeter.**
adjacent sides, 432
angle, 421, 422
right angle, 421, 422–423

Index

Math Mountain

relate addition and subtraction, 355, 359–360, 364

relationship to equations, 355, 364

total, 364

unknown number, 359–360

Math Tools. *See also* **Area; Equation; Math Mountain.**

drawings and equations, 24

fast-array drawings, 46

Quick 9s multiplication and division, 41–42

represent word problems, 357

Measurement. *See also* **Estimate; Time.**

area

on a dot array, 309–310

of a rectangle, 112–114, 309–314, 439

square units, 112, 309–311, 439

centimeter, 309–310

choosing appropriate unit, 409, 411

generate data for line plots, 259, 292, 296

inch, 257–258, 259

length

customary units, 256–257

estimate, 258

liquid volume (capacity), 415

customary units, 403–406

estimate, 404

measure, 403–408

metric units, 407–408

using drawings, 405–406

mass, 416

estimate, 414

perimeter

on a dot array, 309–310

problem solving, 275, 407–408

of a rectangle or square, 309–310, 315–316, 439

time

add and subtract on number line, 273–274

before and after the hour, 265, 266, 269–270

analog clock, 265, 266, 267, 269–270

digital clock, 265, 266, 267

elapsed time, 271–272

to five minutes, 269

A.M. and P.M., 266, 271, 272, 275

to the minute, 269–270

using a clock to find, 265, 266, 267, 269–270

using a number line to add, 273–274

weight

customary units, 409–410

estimate, 414

using drawings to solve problems, 409–410

Mental math, 383–384

multiplication, 156

Mixed numbers, 250

Multiplication. *See also* **Check Sheets.**

by 0, 71–74

by 1, 71–74

by 2, 27–32

by 3, 49–51

by 4, 59–61

by 5, 5–10, 17–23, 29–32

by 6, 107–111

by 7, 123–126

by 8, 115–117

by 9, 39

by 10, 35–40

Dashes, 85–90, 137–142, 157–162

Diagnostic Multiplication Checkup, 167

equations, 6, 7–9, 19, 21–22, 24, 32, 36, 37, 45, 75–76, 121–122, 135–142, 147

models, 42, 112–114

arrays, 19–22

drawings, 21–22, 113–114, 127

equal groups, 7–10

equal shares drawings, 8–9, 61

fast-array drawings, 46, 114, 118, 124

Product Cards, 167A, 167C, 167E, 167G, 167I

Properties

Associative Property, 72–73, 155

Commutative Property, 22, 73

Identity Property, 73

Zero Property, 72–73

© Houghton Mifflin Harcourt Publishing Company

N

O

P

Q

Index

Z

Number Tables

Multiplication Table and Scrambled Tables (Volume 1)

A

×	1	2	3	4	5	6	7	8	9	10
1	1	2	3	4	5	6	7	8	9	10
2	2	4	6	8	10	12	14	16	18	20
3	3	6	9	12	15	18	21	24	27	30
4	4	8	12	16	20	24	28	32	36	40
5	5	10	15	20	25	30	35	40	45	50
6	6	12	18	24	30	36	42	48	54	60
7	7	14	21	28	35	42	49	56	63	70
8	8	16	24	32	40	48	56	64	72	80
9	9	18	27	36	45	54	63	72	81	90
10	10	20	30	40	50	60	70	80	90	100

B

×	2	4	3	1	5	10	6	8	7	9
5	10	20	15	5	25	50	30	40	35	45
3	6	12	9	3	15	30	18	24	21	27
1	2	4	3	1	5	10	6	8	7	9
4	8	16	12	4	20	40	24	32	28	36
2	4	8	6	2	10	20	12	16	14	18
7	14	28	21	7	35	70	42	56	49	63
9	18	36	27	9	45	90	54	72	63	81
10	20	40	30	10	50	100	60	80	70	90
8	16	32	24	8	40	80	48	64	56	72
6	12	24	18	6	30	60	36	48	42	54

C

×	8	6	4	9	7	9	6	7	4	8
5	40	30	20	45	35	45	30	35	20	40
3	24	18	12	27	21	27	18	21	12	24
2	16	12	8	18	14	18	12	14	8	16
3	24	18	12	27	21	27	18	21	12	24
5	40	30	20	45	35	45	30	35	20	40
9	72	54	36	81	63	81	54	63	36	72
4	32	24	16	36	28	36	24	28	16	32
7	56	42	28	63	49	63	42	49	28	56
6	48	36	24	54	42	54	36	42	24	48
8	64	48	32	72	56	72	48	56	32	64

D

×	6	7	8	7	8	6	7	8	6	8
2	12	14	16	14	16	12	14	16	12	16
3	18	21	24	21	24	18	21	24	18	24
4	24	28	32	28	32	24	28	32	24	32
5	30	35	40	35	40	30	35	40	30	40
7	42	49	56	49	56	42	49	56	42	56
8	48	56	64	56	64	48	56	64	48	64
6	36	42	48	42	48	36	42	48	36	48
9	54	63	72	63	72	54	63	72	54	72
8	48	56	64	56	64	48	56	64	48	64
6	36	42	48	42	48	36	42	48	36	48

Illustrator: Josh Brill

Did you ever try to use shapes to draw animals like the moose on the cover?

Over the last 10 years Josh has been using geometric shapes to design his animals. His aim is to keep the animal drawings simple and use color to make them appealing.

Add some color to the moose Josh drew. Then try drawing a cat or dog or some other animal using the shapes below.

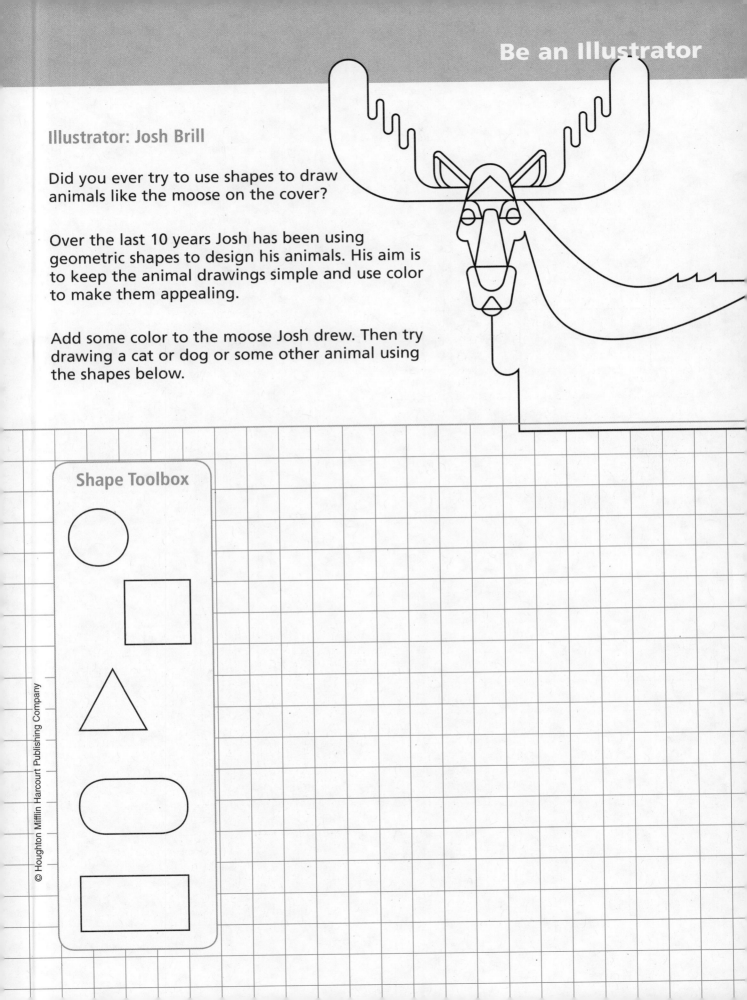

Shape Toolbox